6754077

PRACTICAL CORPORATE PLANNING

Practical
Corporate Planning

JOHN ARGENTI

London
GEORGE ALLEN & UNWIN
Boston   Sydney

First published in 1980

GEORGE ALLEN & UNWIN LTD
40 Museum Street, London WC1A 1LU

658.4
A691p

British Library Cataloguing in Publication Data

Argenti, John
    Practical corporate planning.
    1. Corporate planning
    I. Title
    658.4′01   HD30.28   79–41737

    ISBN 0–04–658230–4
    ISBN 0–04–658231–2 Pbk

Typeset in 10 on 11 point Times by Northampton Phototypesetters Ltd
and printed in Great Britain
by Billing & Sons Ltd, Guildford, London and Worcester

Contents

9 Action Plans, Budgets and Monitoring

Targets for subsidiaries, 179. Targets for cost centres, 183. Budgets, 185. Monitoring confidence, 188. Revising the corporate plan, 191. Summary, 194.

To my wife

Introduction

Who this book is for

This book is written for chief executives, very senior executives and non-executive directors of companies who have not yet adopted corporate planning and are thinking of doing so. I particularly have in mind small to medium-sized companies employing, say, between 50 and 5,000 people.

It is a practical guide – no jargon, no mathematics, no 'sophisticated' planning techniques. After an introductory chapter the book takes the reader straight through the corporate planning process, starting at the beginning and going on till it reaches the end, pointing out the snags and pitfalls on the way.

I venture to suggest that chief executives and others in large and very large companies, and management academics and students also, may find the book of interest. Some of these have, I believe, led themselves into considerable confusion by persuading themselves that corporate planning is a very advanced concept that requires the setting up of a specialist department complete with economists, computer specialists and a whole string of assorted acolytes.

I hold the view that even in a very large company, certainly in small and medium-sized ones, corporate planning is essentially extremely simple (although this does not mean that it is easy) and that it can best be done by ordinary executives rather than by high-powered specialists. A decade ago in my introduction to my book *Corporate Planning. A Practical Guide* I wrote: 'corporate planning can now be lifted out of the hands of its few high priests and placed in those of the average senior executive'. That was a decade ago; the world has admittedly become more hostile and difficult, but managers today are far better trained and informed than they were then.

So, I feel totally confident in handing this tool over to the top echelons of even quite small companies. The system of corporate planning described in this book is specially designed as a do-it-yourself kit – a sort of painting by numbers. I am totally confident that a great many companies will successfully adopt this new and somewhat more simple and streamlined version of my system, just as large numbers of companies all over the world have used the original version described in *Corporate Planning. A Practical Guide*.

How to use this book

I suggest that you read it straight through before taking any positive action to launch corporate planning in your company. You may find that, simple though the process is, it is too formal, too slow or too expensive in management time or that your company is too small; there are many good reasons why you may reject my thesis. Happily, there are many why you should accept it, in which case I suggest that after reading it yourself you hand the book over to your colleagues or inform them in some other way what all this is about.

Then start. Keep the book handy, so that any problems that emerge can be looked up. If you are not sure what the next step is or where the next pitfall may be met, refer to the book again. In other words use it just as a housewife uses a cookbook; if she is wise, she reads straight through a recipe before starting, to make sure that she has all the ingredients, equipment and skill. She refers back to the recipe during the preparation and cooking processes.

One other comment: in *Corporate Planning. A Practical Guide* I found it necessary to explain a number of management terms and techniques in some detail in case the reader was not familiar with them. I shall not do this here; this book is devoted solely to explaining how to do *corporate planning*. My experience in recent years has shown me, for example, that the modern finance director knows very well what 'leverage' means, that 'brainstorming' is known to almost everyone (and used by few!), that marketing managers know what a product life cycle is, and so on. I am not sure that they did a decade ago, but they certainly do now.

Acknowledgements

I am enormously indebted to four very experienced people in the field of corporate planning who read this book while it was in draft form and who each made a number of extremely valuable comments, as a result of which I made a number of major improvements in the text. My profound thanks are ·due, then, to Hazel Davies, Tony Hall, Robert Perrin·and Bernard Taylor.

Conventions and abbreviations

I shall use the following conventions and abbreviations throughout the book:

Inflation.   Except where specifically stated to the contrary all the figures in the text will be in real terms, that is, without inflation. So, when I say, for example, 'and they hoped to achieve £20m. in five years' time', this will mean £20m. in real terms, that is, in the base year's values.

Money.   The pound sterling (£) will be used in all examples and illustrations. I could just as well use dollars, marks or yen – in no case would it matter – but I shall use the English currency because the book is written in English.

Years.   I shall often have to refer to past years, the current year and several years into the future, especially when illustrating examples of forecasts and so forth. The notation 'year 0' will be used to mean the current financial year (or the year that in the example is used as the base year) and 'year 1, year 2, . . . year 10' to mean future years. The notation 'year −1, year −2 . . . year −10' will be used to indicate last year, the year before, and so on back to ten years ago.

Cases.   Throughout the book real life examples will be used to illustrate various points and principles. However, in the interests of brevity some distortion of the actual situation will be unavoidable, so pseudonyms rather than companies' real names will be used throughout. As added protection against identification a company's real product, location or whatever will, where necessary, be changed.

CHAPTER 1

What Is Corporate Planning?

Corporate planning has been widely used for at least two decades all over the world, but there are still a number of very damaging misconceptions about it. In the early days, for example, its exponents liked to pretend that all that had to be done was to apply corporate planning to a company, rather like sprinkling a magic fertiliser over it, and behold: its business would bloom, and its profits would blossom. Another and rather contrary view was that corporate planning was just a fancy name for five-year budgeting – a belief that is still a very common one.

Another school of thought still holds that it is necessary to be very clever indeed to do corporate planning and to have degrees from several universities.

So unhelpful are all these fantasies that I am going to take the whole of the first two sections of this chapter to say what corporate planning is and what it is not. It really is absolutely vital to get the central idea of corporate planning clear; otherwise, the whole exercise from start to finish will be an utter waste of time.

What it is not

As its name suggests, corporate planning involves planning the company as a whole – as a *corporate* whole. So, corporate planning is absolutely not the same as product planning, market planning, production planning, financial planning or manpower planning. All these types of planning are planning for parts or sections of a company. Most companies, even quite small ones, already employ product managers, marketing directors, production planners and finance directors to look after these areas of planning.

As soon as a corporate plan starts to spell out product plans, manpower plans and financial plans, it is in grave danger of over-reaching itself and becoming a busybody.

I emphasise this because some corporate planners still believe that corporate planning means planning for the whole company, and they prepare enormous plans in which every aspect of the company is determined for years ahead in solemn detail.

What a ridiculous thing to try to do! It is possible to plan in great detail for a short time ahead (this is what such operational planners as production schedulers and stock controllers do) and to plan in broad outline over a very long period (this is what sensible corporate planners do), but it is *not* possible to plan in meticulous detail over a long time horizon. No wonder it used to be thought that corporate planners had to have high intellectual qualities; no wonder they spent so much of their time using computers; no wonder they produced huge planning documents full of bewildering complexities! Believe it or not, many companies, including some quite big ones that ought to know better, still try to plan like this.

So, that is one misconception out of the way; corporate planning is planning for the company as a whole, not planning the whole company! Another misconception is the idea that corporate planning is a technique that, if applied, suddenly causes the company's profits to soar. This misconception arose in the 1960s when, due to a long period of economic expansion in the developed nations, many companies that were just starting to use corporate planning experienced a period of vigorous growth of profits. Naturally, they claimed that their success was due to corporate planning, thus carefully ignoring the fact that countless other companies were also doing very nicely in spite of never having heard of it.

At that time too, many expanding companies diversified and made numerous acquisitions, and many companies that diversified and made acquisitions expanded. So, corporate planning also became confused with expansion, mergers and diversification to such an extent that it began to be thought that, if a company was not diversifying or merging, it could not be doing corporate planning. If it was doing corporate planning, it was presumably about to diversify or make an acquisition. So, let me put this misconception right; corporate planning is planning the long term future of a company. This may involve an acquisition, a merger or a diversification, but it may not. It may on the contrary involve a divestment, a splitting off or a closing down.

Yet another misconception involves confusion over the distinction between marketing and corporate planning. This arises because in most corporate plans one of the crucially important strategies involves products or markets or both. It is difficult to imagine a corporate plan that does not include a product–market strategy, but this does not mean that they are the same thing. Whereas marketing is solely or mainly concerned with products, markets, customers, promotion, distribution, and so on, corporate planning includes everything: production, research, people, finance, tax and anything else, so long as it is sufficiently important to the future of the company to warrant attention in the plan.

Another completely erroneous idea is that corporate planning is enormously sophisticated and advanced. Big-company corporate planners certainly like to use such techniques as computer models, risk analysis, cross-impact analysis and directional policy matrices. My strong belief is that none of these are much use; but that is not really relevant, for I go further than this and hold the view that, if you have to use advanced techniques, you are completely off course! If you are faced with a situation that is so complex that you have to use advanced techniques, you are simply not standing far enough away from your company. Get further away from it, and only then will you be able to see the half-dozen things about the company that really matter. Advanced techniques are not needed to handle half a dozen large chunks of data. If you have to use such techniques, you are not doing corporate planning; you are far too involved with detail.

Some people believe that corporate planning and long range planning are synonymous. Not quite. It is possible to make a long range plan for anything. It takes several years to build a ship or sink a new mine, and these could be the subject of long range plans, but they would not be corporate plans. So, not all long range plans are corporate. On the other hand a corporate plan is concerned with changes in the overall shape of a company, and it usually takes years to make such changes (decades for very large companies). So, all corporate plans are necessarily long range.

Although corporate planning and strategic planning are closely linked, they are not synonymous either. Corporate planning can (crudely) be divided into two parts: deciding corporate objectives and then determining corporate strategies. So, strategic planning is the second part of corporate planning.

Now consider the distinction between a budget and a corporate plan. Many years ago, when companies first started to draw up budgets, they did so only for the following year. The idea was to ask everyone in the company what his department or section was hoping to do the following year and, having agreed this with him and made sure that it fitted in with what everyone else was going to do, to use it as a control. Each month the actual performance of each manager's section, department or subsidiary company would be compared with his budget. As well as the most successful and valuable management tool ever invented, budgetary control must have been the first example of really participative management; anyone who is anyone in a company is invited to contribute to his firm's budget discussions.

As I say, this idea came into use decades ago, but gradually companies found that they had to plan further ahead – not just one year but two, three or five. I have even seen a twelve-year budget! Suddenly, the nature of the budget was changed. It was, I believe, a bad day when this marvellous short term tool was thus stretched into a long term one. Just consider the differences between one-year budgets and five-year ones:

*In spite of the fact that it is not possible to make long term forecasts in the same way as short term ones – none of the techniques that work quite well for short term forecasts, such as exponential smoothing, work for long term forecasts – companies prepare five-year budgets in almost exactly the same way as one-year budgets. They even use the same forms. Apparently, it is believed that asking a manager to project five years ahead is exactly like asking him to do it for one year but for four extra years. However, whereas projecting from the past *one* year into the future is not idiotic, projecting five years is.

Also, can you see how the whole meaning of the questions is different? Ask a sales manager, for example, about next year, and he will tell you what he *expects* to see. Ask him about five years ahead, and he will tell you what he *wants* to see. In the short term there is not much that he can do to impose his will on the world, so he can only say what will probably happen; in the longer term he has time to bring about the changes that *he* wants. So, there is this subtle change from asking what he expects to asking what he wants – *not* the same question at all!

*The errors in long term forecasts are usually enormous, but in most budgetary-control documents there is no column for a statement of errors. Why not? Because in short term forecasts the errors are usually relatively small, and, of course, the forms were designed for short term forecasts. Does this matter? Yes, very much. In long range planning *the* central problem is that forecasts are liable to enormous errors. A long range planner who forgets this is guilty of the most appalling negligence. Yet, here we have five-year forecasts where there is not even a space on the forms for the most important piece of data of all: the size of the errors!

*Take inflation. In a one-year budget it is sensible to ensure that all figures include inflation. It would be extremely difficult to make the monthly variance reports if inflation were not included, quite apart from the nonsense that this would make of the plans, especially the cash flow plans, in the budget. However, in five-year plans it is very much simpler to work in real terms – to exclude inflation, although admittedly it does have to be included for some purposes. So, here again, this time on a purely practical plane, the one-year exercise is different from the five-year.

*There is another distinction. The one-year budget is a planning *and* control document, whereas the five-year budget is only a planning exercise. So, there is no reason at all why they should look alike, share the same forms or be prepared at the same time by the same people. This does not mean that they must be different; it only means that they can be. In fact I think that they should be; the one-year budget is always prepared under great pressure and right at the end of the current year – not exactly the best atmosphere for long term contemplation, although it is probably ideal for hard down-to-earth short-term decision-making.

*Finally consider this. The budget is an exercise in which the executives show how they hope to exploit the company's *existing* resources. Long range plans are not concerned with this at all but rather with what resources there will be. It is a totally different question. I am in no way convinced that the same people should attempt to answer both questions – certainly not at the same time, under the year-end pressures and on the same forms!

Long range budgets, then, are wholly different from short range budgets. Yet, in most companies they are prepared at the same time, by the same people and in the same mad rush!

What I am saying is quite simple. I am suggesting that, although the budgeting process is a magnificent short range planning procedure, it is wholly inappropriate, as the list above suggests, for long range planning. If I had to indicate one reason above all why it is so inappropriate, this would be the point made above: that the budget is a procedure for planning how to get the best out of the company's existing resources next year and concentrates everyone's mind on this question with remorseless efficiency. Thus, everything about it, right down to the headings on the forms, is designed to exclude wide-ranging discussions on topics of such apparently remote philosophical interest as 'Should we be in this business at all?' Yet, this is exactly the sort of question that corporate planning sets out to ask!

Instead of adapting a short-term planning tool, let us design a long-range planning tool specially for the job. So, while leaving the one-year budgeting process alone, I am suggesting that we abandon long range budgets altogether and use the process known as corporate planning instead. As a matter of fact, right at the end of the corporate planning process a mass of figures emerges that looks exactly like a normal five-year budget. All that changes – and it is a fundamental change, of course – is the method by which they are produced. Instead of projecting from the company's past and present to where we expect it to be in, say, five years' time, let us take an imaginative leap to where we *want* it to be in five years. Then, we can look back and work out how to get there from where we are now. Thus, the corporate planning process is *diametrically opposite* the budgeting process.

There is another thing that corporate planning is not. It is not 'co-ordinating'. Some companies take the plans of their departments or subsidiaries as the building blocks of their corporate plan. The plan is thus the sum of all the plans of the parts. This is an absurd empty shadow of a corporate plan, however, for, although it is entirely right and sensible to take into account the aims and ambitions of the senior second-level executives, a corporate plan that is merely the co-ordination of partial plans will lead to a company that is merely what these second-level managers want it to become – not necessarily the right answer, not by any means. At worst it can reflect any aversion to change that they may have; at the other extreme it may call for such changes as to jeopardise the future of the company.

Another misconception: it is most unfortunate that the word 'plan' appears in the corporate planning title at all. In most people's minds the word 'plan' implies a schedule drawn up in the most rigorous detail. A good plan is one that is totally comprehensive and all embracing, leaving nothing to chance. A poor plan is one that is sketchy and ill defined, with great gaping blanks in it showing where the incompetent planner has failed to make precise decisions. However, this is a *good* corporate plan! A corporate plan drawn up in meticulous detail is the plan of an idiot. It should have great gaps; it should be sketchy; at least, large parts of it should.

One other thing corporate planning is not. It is not forecasting. Most people understand this now. Forecasting is used in planning, but the two are certainly not synonymous. For a company, forecasting is trying to predict what is going to happen in the future whether it wants it to or not; planning is deciding how to bring about a situation that it wants to happen. This is why it is necessary to decide objectives before starting to plan; it is not necessary to decide objectives before making a forecast.

What it is

In one sense corporate planning is just like all other types of long range planning; it is an attempt to decide how best to respond to, or anticipate, change. Thus, the factory manager will have a long range plan that shows how his factory will look in a few years' time, knowing what he knows about possible changes in technology. The marketing director will be planning his product range for some years ahead, knowing what he knows about product life cycles and changes in the market place.

So it is with corporate planning. There is nothing mysterious or special about it except that it is concerned with plans one step up the hierarchy, that is, not plans for parts of a company but plans for the company as a whole – the forest, not the trees.

However, at this level there are, I believe, only a very few questions that need concern the corporate planner in any company. The long term destiny of any company depends, I believe, on two, three or four absolutely huge decisions. Get these wrong, and no amount of brilliant marketing, research or effort will turn the company into a star performer. Get them right . . .

I believe that corporate planning consists largely of identifying what these few questions are for a given company and answering them. Most of the questions are non-numerical; and as will be seen, my system of planning does not involve a large number of calculations until right at the end, when the 'five-year budgets' emerge.

This is why I do not think that it is necessary to be a genius to do corporate planning. Corporate plans are simple, not complex; but they are also difficult, not easy. Part of the difficulty is that the future is uncertain; part is that many of these decisions are judgements, sometimes moral ones. Not only is this the wrong field for geniuses, but it is a rather barren area for computers and advanced management techniques too. It is, however, just the area of decision-making where experienced senior line managers are in their element. There is no doubt in my mind who the best corporate planners are for any company; they are its own top executives.

A corporate plan, then, is a plan consisting of a very few simple but momentous statements about the long term future of the company as a whole. Let me give an example. Imagine a company manufacturing farm chemicals in Britain. It is extremely successful in this business, and its market share is moving up towards 25 per cent. However, let us imagine, the political climate is hostile to monopolies (defined as companies whose market share is more than 25 per cent), and several large companies in several industries have recently been rudely shaken by the Monopolies Commission. This company therefore decides to use its strongly positive cash flow to acquire companies in the field of fertilisers, pharmaceuticals and foodstuffs. This is its corporate plan. It can be restated in four exceedingly brief sentences as below; and once it is committed to action, and once these various companies have been acquired, its destiny will be sealed for decades. It will be extremely difficult to turn back once it has set out on this radical new course. Consider these brief sentences:

(1) Our company may soon have a 25 per cent market share.

(2) Monopolies are being powerfully constrained by our government.
(3) Therefore, we shall diversify, using our cash flow.
(4) We shall move into foodstuffs, fertilisers and pharmaceuticals.

Now it may be objected that this corporate plan is really far too brief. Surely, it may be argued, there should be further levels of decisions – sentences (5), (6), and so on, consisting of a very large mass of detailed descriptions concerning all manner of aspects of all these new business areas? Perhaps there should be, but I believe that, before this company gets down to detail, it should spend a vast amount of time examining statements (3) and (4). Indeed, I believe that these statements *are* the corporate plan and that all further detail that may be needed is at least an order of magnitude less important. Are these statements valid? I believe not. Statement (3) does not follow from (1) and (2), for example. The mere fact that the company may face some hostility from the Monopolies Commission does not mean that it *must* diversify. It could consider a number of alternatives, including not diversifying and meeting the problem head on. Even if diversification is indicated, why three areas? Why not two or four? Why those three? Why not farm drainage systems or veterinary products? Also, why adopt the structure of a diversified British company? Why not become a world farm-chemical company by purchasing foreign competitors in the field that it understands? Why not go into farming?

The point that I am making here is absolutely fundamental to this book. I believe that most companies take these big decisions without any discussion at all. These decisions are so big that the executives simply do not know how to tackle decisions of that magnitude, so they slide over or round these big ones and tackle the details. Most executives are completely at home with detail. They can be measured, planned and controlled; it is not possible to measure broad concepts like diversify.

This is why so many corporate planning systems start off with 'deciding the mission of the company'. These systems do not say how to decide it; a company just decides it and then does its corporate planning. So, is 'mission' an input to the corporate planning process? I believe this to be quite idiotic; the big decision receives far less discussion than the details. No. Let us have a system where the mission is the *output*.

Let me give some other brief examples that raise questions that are so fundamental to the company concerned that they should be the subject of a corporate plan:

*Consider a company that is the smallest of the three firms remaining in a declining industry. It knows that it is almost certain to receive a bid from one (or even both) of the others within the next few years. Should it wait and accept this bid, or should it try to diversify out of this industry?

(Let me make a comment. It is quite clear that this is not a production department problem, nor a marketing one nor a finance one. It concerns the entire corporate destiny. The answer, whichever way the company goes, can be given in a few words – one very simple sentence, but one of momentous consequence for the whole company.)

*Take a British company manufacturing one advanced product. Its sole use is in coal-mining, and the company's only customer is the nationalised Coal Board. Should it strive to extricate itself from this one-product one-customer situation or not?

*Take a huge company such as IBM. It has 70 per cent of world markets. How does it see itself in ten or twenty years' time? With 80 per cent? With more products in the same field – computers, data-handling, and so on – or with different products as well? Will it be even bigger, or split into a dozen independent offspring, or what?

*A small head office staff controls a group of fourteen engineering companies. No doubt each subsidiary has its own corporate plan, but some of the questions that a group plan should answer are these: Do we want to have fourteen subsidiaries in, say, ten years' time, or twenty-four, or thirty-four, or four? What size should the smallest and the largest be? Should they all be raising the technological content of their (very different) products, or should only a few of them be doing this? Only two are exporting to developing nations; how do we see this in ten years' time?

A comment: in this last example I have posed four questions, but it would not take much imagination to think of several dozen more. Now, surely that conflicts with my view that corporate planning is concerned with only a tiny number of such questions in any given company? In fact, although the corporate planners in this company should ask a great many such questions, some will turn out on examination not to be important; others will be important but should be postponed (there is no merit whatever in answering a question that needs no answer nor in planning something that need not be planned); others will be both urgent and important but can be given flexible tactical answers. Only comparatively few will need to be tackled now in a corporate plan. It is unquestionably part of the planning team's task to identify what needs to be planned and what does not. It will be found, in my experience, that most corporate plans boil down to just a very few, very large decisions. Alas, all too many corporate plans are vast detailed extravaganzas, due, I believe, to an attempt to be 'comprehensive' and 'meticulous'.

Many corporate plans will contain decisions on products and markets. The example quoted above of a single-product single-customer company is one such; clearly, the company can only escape by entering a new market or by launching a new product in a new market, since the whole of its present market is monopolised by one customer. Because product–market decisions are so important, it is sometimes not easy to identify the dividing line between corporate planning and marketing, but the dividing line between corporate planning and, say, purchasing is equally hazy. Take a company distributing bananas in markets of the Western world. Its outstanding problem has nothing to do with products or markets. It is the increasing political instability of the banana-growing nations; the very phrase 'banana republic' epitomises the problem. Is this a sourcing problem or one demanding attention in a corporate plan? I believe that it is the latter, since any fundamental solution or mitigation of this problem is almost certain to involve alterations to the whole structure of the company's activities. At least it will include major alterations to parts of the company other than the purchasing function. To put it another way, the problem is so embedded in the very nature of the company's business that a lasting solution will probably not be found at the level of purchasing or sourcing strategies, and it will have to be tackled one step higher in the hierarchy, that is, at the level of *corporate* strategy.

Corporate planning decisions, then, are decisions that affect the whole structure of the company many years or decades into the future – huge decisions taken in conditions of extreme uncertainty about the future. It is the size of these decisions, the fact that there are so few of them and the enormous errors in the forecasts on which they always have to be based that characterise corporate planning decisions.

How should decisions of this sort be taken? Most of the rest of this book will be devoted to answering this question. All that I need to say now is that these decisions are taken by examining the company's strategic situation *in its totality*. Since this is a lengthy exercise, it is tackled systematically. The planners work systematically through a checklist of factors affecting the company strategically, and at the end of this long difficult process a set of answers to the strategic questions comes out. These are then subjected to a number of tests or evaluations; and if they pass, they are adopted and put into action – and carefully monitored, of course. However, I do not wish to expand here on *how* these questions can best be answered, as an outline is given in a section below. I must turn to another vital question: *who* should answer these questions? Who should do the corporate planning in any given company?

Who should do it?

One of the most remarkable trends over the past few decades has been the decline of the entrepreneur and the autocrat. These people used to play a far larger part in society than they do in the developed nations today. In those days most companies were still quite small, the world was relatively stable, pressure groups had not yet begun to question the morality of every move a company made, and governments were neutral or even helpful towards companies.

Gradually, as companies grew in size and the business environment became more complex and more hostile, the autocrat began to make mistakes. His problem was that he could not sufficiently grasp *all* the aspects of his business – not just the changing technology of production methods and new materials, not just new legislation, not just new attitudes among his workforce, not just the significance of a new competitor in, say, Japan. All these and dozens of other ever-changing factors were bursting and exploding all round him. Very few individuals can grasp all of this at once; it takes a whole team of people.

In the 1950s, as the entrepreneur was moving to the side of the stage, the corporate planner made his debut. Some autocrats recruited corporate planners rather as drowning men clutch at straws. Many appointed planners who were academically brilliant. This had two consequences. First, the planners, not being experienced practical people, did not understand the real world, so their plans were impractical. Secondly, the other executives, who were already resentful at seeing this interloper planning the future of their company (including their departments, of course) without consulting them, were less than enthusiastic about the plans handed down to them. For these reasons the appointment of a highly qualified specialist planner reporting to the chief executive, as shown in Exhibit 1.1 (a), is not recommended. I have to add that many companies still do this. Two other similar mistakes, as I believe them to be, can be made.

Some companies, believing corporate planning to have something to do with budgeting, place the corporate planner under the finance director. Apart from the fact that corporate planning is diametrically opposite budgeting, if you do this, any plan that emerges from this arrangement will be more financial than corporate; to put it mildly, it will not be as strong in its treatment of technology, management style or engineering aspects as it will be in its treatment of financial aspects. In my opinion it is therefore dangerous to place the corporate planner in the position shown in Exhibit 1.1 (b). Note that this is true for all departments: place the corporate planner in the research department, and the plan will be weak on finance and human relations; place him under the managing director of subsidiary A, and it will be weak on subsidiaries B and C; and so on. In any case this position places the corporate planner in such a lowly position in the management hierarchy that he cannot be expected to make a very significant contribution.

Exhibit 1.1   Where to put the corporate planner in the organisation chart

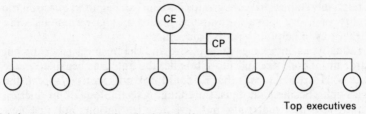

(a) As an assistant to the chief executive

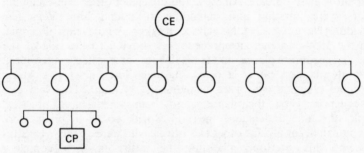

(b) Reporting to one of the top executives

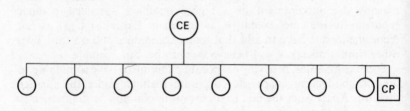

(c) As one of the top executives themselves

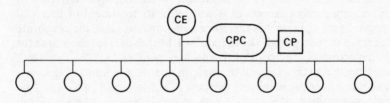

(d) As secretary of a corporate planning team or committee

The other mistake, which seems to me much less severe than the two mentioned above, is to place the corporate planner in the position shown in Exhibit 1.1 (c). Here, he is equal to the other executive directors, thus avoiding the problems of the two cases above, but now there is nothing to stop him from doing all the planning himself. (Let us not forget that his colleagues on the board are all extremely busy people running their own departments or subsidiary companies.) If he does this, we are simply back where we started with the problem that no one man can today understand all the complexities of the modern world. The plans will almost certainly be defective. Even if they were perfect, the other executives would feel little enthusiasm for them.

The plain fact is that with rare exceptions no single individual can produce a balanced corporate plan. The problem has a direct parallel in executive management, where most large companies and a growing number of small ones have found that they have had to make a radical alteration to their management style. If one man cannot manage the company, several men must do it together – in other words a team. Gone is the dictatorial autocratic boss who, all-knowing and all-seeing, makes all the decisions and issues orders to his subordinates, none of whom dare to question him even on their own specialism. Nowadays, the boss is *primus inter pares* – the leader of a team whose 'decision' is often little more than a statement that a consensus exists in his team. 'OK, most of us seem to agree that . . .' is the nearest the boss gets to making a 'decision' in most circumstances today.

This style has two enormous advantages. First, it overcomes the problem that defeats so many autocrats, namely, that the business world is today so multifaceted that no one man can comprehend the implications of everything happening around him. Secondly, it is participative. Not only do more people have a chance to make a contribution to the running of their company, but also, when the plan is agreed, it is their plan; they have agreed it and will work hard to bring it to a satisfactory conclusion.

However, it also has two enormous disadvantages. Attempts are often made to deny these disadvantages by planning enthusiasts, but we should be well advised to note them. The first is that it takes longer to reach a decision or make a plan with six people, or sixty, than with just one. A corporate plan prepared by a team will take a year; if one man prepared it, he could have it ready in weeks. Of course, as I have emphasised, his would almost certainly be unworkable, but that does not alter the fact, which should be recognised, that a team will take much longer.

The other major disadvantage of team work is that a team's decisions, compared with an entrepreneur's decisions, are said to be dull, unimaginative and unexciting. I believe this to be quite true, but let us remember this: as a company grows in size not only does it become more *difficult* to run entrepreneurially, but in addition society actually *demands* that it be run less entrepreneurially. Society is not alarmed when a very small company fails in an attempt to exploit an imaginative entrepreneurial hunch, but it is much less amused when a large or well-established company does this. I am afraid, then, that corporate planning does produce less exciting strategies than would an entrepreneur. I think that it is probably right that this is so.

There may be a third disadvantage of the team method of management, which can be summarised in one word, namely, 'compromise'. It is not difficult to imagine a company in which one faction of the top management team may be inspired by one particular strategy while another faction is devoted to another concept of the company, which in its eyes is even more attractive. It is also easy to imagine such a company's adopting a weak-kneed woolly compromise, having none of the vigour of either of these ideas and earning the wholehearted commitment of no one, as a result of 'team discussions'.

In spite of these admittedly serious potential dangers my own answer to the question 'Who should do the corporate planning?' can now be given: *not* the corporate planner! It should be done by a team *assisted* by a corporate planner, perhaps even guided or cajoled by him, but it must be the team's plan that emerges, not his.

The planning team

Who should be members of the team? Since corporate planning is concerned with the long term future of the company as a whole, it is inconceivable for the team not to include the chief executive. If he is not included, the entire exercise will be worthless, in my view. He should really be the team leader, and I should fear for the validity of any plan emanating from any team not led by the chief executive. The view from the chief executive's chair is quite unlike the view that anyone else in a company gets. He may be only *primus inter pares* these days, but he is still *primus* – the central pillar in the colonnade.

Who else? The problem is usually not whom to include but whom to exclude. In most companies the reins of power end in the hands of only a very few men in addition to the chief executive: the chairman, the finance-director and one or two others. Furthermore, everyone in the company knows that these three, four or perhaps five men are the ones running the show. There is therefore seldom any question about who will form the team. The only question is whom else to bring in, bearing in mind that whoever is excluded will naturally be offended, affronted and deeply anxious for the future of his part of the company, which, he may feel, he will not be allowed to decide.

Some companies exclude all executives who are responsible for profit centres, divisions or any part of the company at all. One reason for including only executives with corporate responsibilities is that each executive with responsibility for a part of the company will be fighting for his part, not for the corporate whole. Furthermore, such companies argue, a strong research director, for example, will bend and distort the corporate plan towards greater use of his department; a strong managing director of subsidiary A will twist the balance of the plan away from subsidiaries B and C. It certainly does happen; one school of thought says that it should happen. For example, if you have a research director whose views carry great weight, it is right for the strategies to be research biased. This school of thought goes further and says to let everyone who can contribute to a corporate plan do so. What is a chairman for, if he is not to act as conductor to a great orchestra of differing views?

However, in the case of groups the position may be different. Here there are often a number of executives on the group board who have corporate responsibilities but no responsibilities at all for any operating companies, divisions, profit centres or functions. Their duties are solely corporate, and in this case it seems sensible to limit the group planning team to these people. If this is done, however, very great care is usually taken to ensure that close links are maintained between the group planning team and the subsidiary company planning teams. Either a group member sits on all subsidiary teams, or a delegate (normally the managing director) from each subsidiary sits on the group team, or the company employs a full-time corporate planner who acts as secretary and link man to all the teams.

It is necessary to recognise that, because corporate planning is concerned with the long term future of the company, anyone who sits on the team will be in a position of great power; anyone who does not will not. Corporate planning is politically charged.

The very first practical step to take when introducing corporate planning, then, is to select the corporate planning team. Be careful to include in it those who really hold the reins of power. Let us note in passing, however, that we are now talking about a team of very busy and very highly paid people. It is just as well that a corporate plan is concerned with only a very few top questions, for, if it were otherwise, these people would never agree to serve in the team.

What is this team going to do? I suggest in the next section that the members of the team meet approximately once every two or three weeks for several hours, half a day perhaps, and that they work systematically through a sequence of questions designed to bring out the salient features of the company's strategic situation. At every stage they should reach a consensus. In all probability they will agree upon a strategy after approximately – very approximately – a dozen meetings. Then, a further few meetings will be needed to draw up action plans and budgets. That will end their work except for a brief monitoring meeting every three months. They will not be called upon again until a major revision of the plan is required, which may not be for three, four or even ten years.

Clearly, the workload is most uneven. Two consequences need to be stressed. The first is that the members of the planning team are going to have to find time for this extra task over and above their normal duties. This they will not be willing to do if the company is in serious difficulties. Indeed, in my view they *should* not be willing to do so. If the company is in trouble, that is no time to turn away from short term problems in order to study the long term future. There may not be a long term future!

The second implication is that the team will need a great deal of assistance for approximately one year but after that very little. In medium-sized and small companies, therefore, it is not appropriate to recruit a corporate planner unless there is a clear posting for him at the end of the planning period. It seems sensible to appoint him from within the company; someone on his way up, or even on his way to retirement, would be ideal. In many cases this one man may not be sufficient on his own to service the needs of the planning team during this very active year. Normally, no other formal appointments need be made, but some of the management services departments will be called on for extra work.

The position recommended for the corporate planner is as secretary to the planning team, shown diagrammatically in Exhibit 1.1(d). His duties will depend upon his seniority. It would be possible to appoint a quite junior person to this post, but he would only be expected to keep the minutes of meetings, make agenda, ensure reports were ready for each meeting, and so forth. At one step up the corporate planning assistant could be a junior manager, who would be expected to use his initiative, look up facts and figures in libraries, and so on.

Up the scale again the corporate planner could be a planning specialist or management scientist, who in addition to the above duties could advise the team on such difficult matters as how to plan using forecasts that were subject to huge errors. Also, as will be seen, there are a number of calculations to make, some of them fairly advanced, which a planner on this level could tackle. He could certainly build the financial model that is so useful in the later stages. In my view a corporate planner appointed at any level much below this one leaves too much work to the team members and may leave them without advice on several quite tricky technical planning problems.

We can imagine an even more exalted corporate planner in this position. He could be a very senior executive of equal status to those in the team, who in addition to all the secretarial and technical duties described above would be expected to make a major contribution to the team's deliberations. He would virtually be a member of the team. However, beware! If we move much further in this direction, we shall be in danger of making this man so important that the plans will be his, not the team's. The situation is dangerous enough, for the corporate planner, at whatever level he is appointed, will be working full time on the planning exercise whereas the team will be working only part time. I make no apology for repeating that it must be the team's plan that emerges, not the planner's.

Let me suggest the following rule, then. The person appointed as secretary to the planning committee – whatever his title, qualifications or status – has really only one vital function, namely, to act as the clockwork for the committee. It is he who should pull all the data together and place it before the team; it is he who should gather the team together every alternate Thursday or whenever; it is he who should pass on the team's needs and requirements for data, reports, and so on to the appropriate departments in the company. All the other aspects of this appointment should be made in the light of the nature of the company. For example, if it is short of management science skills, perhaps it should recruit a management scientist; if it is short of middle managers, perhaps it should recruit a middle manager and treat his spell as corporate planning assistant as part of his training on his way to a management post.

I must make two further major points. The first concerns the possibility of widening the team to include more people in the interests of greater participation. These additional people can be executives at one or two levels below the top three or four people in the company, or they can be trade unionists, non-executive directors, and so on. Recognise that I am now discussing the possibility of widening the team not in the interests of increasing its sum of knowledge or ability – I have dealt with that above – but in the interests of increasing participation in management decision-making. I know of one major company in Britain whose team includes many trade unionists among its twenty-five members. In Europe most large companies enjoy the two-tier board system, and some aspects of corporate planning are normally discussed at the top one, namely, the often numerous supervisory board. So, very large committees are possible.

In my view the best results are obtained if at each meeting these big teams split up into syndicates of four or five members each to discuss the particular topic on the agenda (long term targets perhaps, or market opportunities). Having each come to their own conclusions the syndicates report back to their colleagues in plenary session, and a remarkable core of agreement and overlapping opinion often emerges.

Some corporate planners believe that it is possible to involve operating management in this exercise. Certainly, the more people who can be brought into these discussions the better; the resultant plans will be more practical and commitment to them greater. However, other companies find that in real life there are only a relatively few people, even at quite senior levels, who can usefully contribute, and they believe that the disadvantages of this 'organisation development' method outweigh the advantages. As will be seen (page 183), a cascade of corporate plans may prove a more practical method of involving several levels of management in the corporate planning exercise. Also, it should not be forgotten that some parts of some company's plans may be best kept secret, nor should the problems associated with insider trading be forgotten. Some companies are composed of very highly educated employees – a scientific research company, a computer software company, and so on – none of whom would have the slightest difficulty in handling the information needed to form a balanced imaginative strategic plan. However, if the same thing were tried in a less developed nation, disaster would be certain.

The second major point is this: however well the top few people in a company know each other, and however many years they have worked together, there will almost certainly be no consensus among them on *any* of the relatively simple and supremely important questions before the planning exercise starts. In most cases they will not even have discussed the questions. This is not as amazing as it may seem. When executives discuss their company's affairs, what they are usually discussing are such problems as production schedules for next week, the product range for next year or the research programme for the next five years – all short term questions or questions relating to only one part of the company for longer periods. Almost never do they discuss the whole company for distant horizons.

How to do it

In this section I shall describe the corporate planning process, or to be more accurate the Argenti system, from start to finish. I shall be brief, because most of the rest of this book will be devoted to describing each step in the sequence in great detail. Let us recall what this process is. It is a sequence of questions that the members of the planning team should ask themselves in order to reach a consensus view of the total strategic situation of their company: sales, production, finance, competitors, technology, economics – everything, seen as a whole. A totality. Then, a strategy emerges. In other words the logic of their strategic situation points to certain actions as being the ones most likely to improve their position over the next five or ten years. Finally, an action plan and a five-year budget emerge. So, the sequence of steps is as follows:

Step 1 is, as described above, to form a planning team. I suggest a small one consisting of only the chief executive, the finance director and one to three others as appropriate.

Step 2 is, as described above, to appoint a secretary to the planning team. I suggest that he be not a mere clerk and not equal in status to the team members but somewhere in between. Many companies call him corporate planning assistant or planning manager.

Step 3 is to hold a one- or two-day seminar. The purpose of this is to explain to the team members and to all their immediate subordinates what the corporate planning exercise is all about. I strongly recommend that this seminar be held well away from the company's premises. The planning manager explains what corporate planning is, what effects it is supposed to have and how it is done. I suggest that he take 2 or 3 hours. (Of course, between his appointment and this seminar he must have attended a course on corporate planning at a university or business school and studied at least some of the literature; see bibliography.)

The participants are then broken up into three or four syndicates with between two and six people in each. (In addition to, say, four members of the planning team there may well be a dozen second-line managers present. Three syndicates of five people are excellent.) Each syndicate is given 45 minutes to discuss what it thinks the company's targets should be for year 5. Then follows 45 minutes' discussion in full session of each syndicate's views.

A similar exercise is carried out on the company's strengths and weaknesses, on its threats and opportunities and on possible strategies. Thus, the programme may look like this for a one-day seminar:

0900–1100	Corporate planner explains what it is, what it does and how to do it.
1100–1230	Syndicates discuss corporate targets. Reports to full seminar and discussion.
1330–1500	Syndicates discuss strengths and weaknesses. Reports to full seminar and discussion.
1500–1630	Syndicates discuss threats and opportunities facing the company. Reports to full seminar and discussion.
1630–1800	Syndicates discuss possible strategies for the company. Reports, discussion and conclusion.

I must make it clear, and it must be made clear at the start of the seminar, that the conclusions reached will be interesting but almost certainly not the right ones. This seminar is not intended to obtain answers; it is merely to show everyone what the questions look like. Everyone at the seminar will be making a substantial contribution to the corporate plan over the coming months, and it is appropriate that they should know what it is all about.

This seminar, in addition to identifying at least some of the salient facts about the company's strategic situation, also has a vital human-relations purpose, namely, to involve those senior executives who, not being members of the planning team itself, may very well feel profound hostility to the whole exercise if they are not drawn into it at its inception.

The door should be left wide open to these people. The planning team may like to consider making fairly frequent reports on progress to meetings of those executives who attend the seminar. Certainly, their views will have to be obtained frequently throughout the exercise; otherwise, the plans developed may be entirely impractical.

Step 4 is to hold the planning team's first meeting. This will have two main items on the agenda: discussion of the seminar and the team's own timetable. A useful start will be made if the planning manager, having recorded the seminar discussions or taken notes, makes a report to the team highlighting the main conclusions reached by the syndicates and the full sessions. Some of these will provide useful pointers to the second item, that is, the team's timetable. I suggest that the team fix the dates of its next few meetings; from the seminar discussions it will have a feel now for the time to allow itself for targets, for strengths and weaknesses, and so forth.

Step 5 is to go through the sequence of meetings, probably about twenty-five in all, at which the topics listed below are discussed in the sequence shown. Naturally, at each meeting the secretary will also present the results of any inquiries that the team has called for earlier, and the team will call for further reports to be presented to later meetings. New information concerning previous discussions may have arrived, and so forth. These are the topics:

> Discuss corporate objectives and ethos.
> Discuss targets.
> Discuss forecasts and gap.
> Discuss strengths and weaknesses.
> Discuss threats and opportunities.
> Discuss alternative strategies.
> Select the strategy.
> Evaluate the selected strategy.
> Draw up action plans and budgets.
> Monitor.

A very detailed diagram of this process appears in Exhibit 1.2 and a slightly different sequence for groups or holding companies in Exhibit 1.3.

Exhibit 1.2   The corporate planning process

A.   Starting the corporate planning process (takes up to 3 months)
(1) Form the planning team. This may include the chairman, the finance-director, one or two other top executives or non-executive directors, and the chief executive as team-leader.
(2) Appoint and then train a corporate planner to act as executive secretary to the team and as technical adviser on planning techniques.
(3) Hold a company seminar. Its main aims are (a) to describe what corporate planning is to the second (and third) level of executives and (b) to sound out their views on the company's strategic situation.
(4) Arrange the team's first meeting. The aims of this are (a) to discuss the findings of the company seminar and (b) to plan the work programme of the team and the corporate planner. Commission any reports that may have a long lead time.

B.   Setting objectives (takes up to 3 months)
(1) Determine the corporate objectives, ethos and corporate targets. Pay special attention to stating which indicators are to be used and where the company is now (year 0) and to setting both Tsat and Tmin. (Takes 1–2 meetings.)
(2) Draw up the Fo forecasts. Be careful to show the optimistic and pessimistic limits of confidence, that is, Fo.max and Fo.min. Calculate the gaps. (Takes 2–3 meetings.) The corporate planner should start building the model.

C.   Drawing up the strategic factors (takes up to 6 months)
(1) Identify all the strategic strengths and weaknesses. Then examine them carefully, writing a report on each. Then distil them to a single page. Then rank them by importance. (Takes 2–3 meetings.)
(2) Identify all strategic threats and opportunities. Then examine them carefully, writing a report on each. Then distil them to a single page or two. Then rank them by impact and probability. (Takes 5–10 meetings.)
(3) Hold a second company seminar. The aims of this are (a) to report the team's findings to the original participants, (b) to hear their views on these findings and (c) to hear their suggested alternative strategies.
(4) List alternative strategies. Eliminate, say, 90 per cent, leaving a short list of those which are most likely to be relevant to the company's total strategic situation. (Takes 1 meeting.)

D.   Selection and evaluation (takes up to 3 months)
(1) Select the best set of strategies. (Takes 1–3 meetings.)
(2) Evaluate this set of strategies by making a number of Fp forecasts, by using the strategic scorecard and by extensive research, discussion and calculation using the model. (Takes 2–4 meetings.)
(3) Prepare the corporate plan (see Exhibits 8.2–8.13) for formal approval by board.

E.   Action plans and budgets (takes a few weeks)

(1) Draw up action plans for profit centres or major cost centres. These must include one or two numerical targets plus a description of the role of each part in the corporate whole. (Takes 2–3 meetings.)

(2) Decide how the monitoring process is to be tackled: what is to be monitored, how often, and by whom. Start monitoring. (Takes 1 meeting.)

F.   Monitoring (continuous)

(1) Monitor continuously to determine the team's confidence in the current corporate plan. (Takes 1 meeting every 3 months.)

Exhibit 1.3   The corporate planning process in a group of companies

---

The detailed steps are very similar to those shown in Exhibit 1.2, but the sequence is not so simple. For a group it will follow the pattern described below:

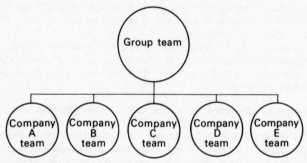

A.   Starting the process

(1) Form a group corporate planning team.

(2) Appoint and train a corporate planner.

(3) Hold a company seminar, making sure that everyone who may become a member of a subsidiary company team is invited.

(4) Form planning teams in each subsidiary. Unless these subsidiaries are very large, no corporate planner may be needed.

(5) Group team and all the subsidiary teams have their first meetings.

B.   Group objectives, ethos and targets

(1) Determine *group* objectives, ethos and targets. Subsidiaries omit this step.

(2) Subsidiaries prepare and submit to group their Fo forecasts. These may, if suitable, simply be the five-year budgets that most subsidiaries will already have prepared.

(3) Group team totals up these forecasts to derive group Fo.

(4) Calculate the gaps for the group.

C. *Drawing up the strategic factors*
(1) Group and subsidiary teams identify strengths and weaknesses.
(2) Group and subsidiary teams identify threats and opportunities. In both of these exercises, of course, the group team searches only for group factors, the subsidiary A team searches only for factors that are relevant to subsidiary A, and so on.
(3) Hold the second company seminar just as before, but this has two main aims: (a) to exchange views on all the main conclusions so far reached by all the teams; and (b) to discuss alternative strategies for all the teams. (May take 2 days.)
(4) Group team lists alternatives for the group. Subsidiary teams each list alternatives for the respective subsidiaries.

D. *and E. Selection, evaluation, and target-setting for subsidiaries*
(1) Group selects overall group strategy in which targets and role of each subsidiary is a vital part.
(2) Group evaluates this strategy in close liaison with all the subsidiaries.
(3) Group prepares its corporate plan for formal approval.
(4) Group draws up action plans and budgets to show targets for each subsidiary together with a description of the subsidiaries' role in the whole.

D. *and E. Selection, evaluation, action plans and budgets for subsidiaries*
(1) Subsidiaries now know their targets. They have already made their forecasts (B2 above), so they can now calculate their gaps.
(2) Subsidiaries have already examined all the other strategic factors, so they can now select and evaluate their strategies.
(3) Subsidiaries prepare their corporate plans for formal approval by the group.
(4) Subsidiaries draw up action plans and five-year budgets to show each department what is expected of it as part of the whole.
(5) All teams consider how to monitor.

F. *Monitoring*
(1) All teams monitor.

This exercise really falls into four main stages. The first is mainly concerned with identifying the size of the task facing the company. This stage includes the objectives, target and gap and usually takes four or five meetings. The second major stage consists of collecting together all the data needed to make a strategic decision and includes strengths and weaknesses, threats and opportunities and alternative strategies. Until all these are collected together, it is most unwise to select a strategy. The right strategy can only be seen, I believe, if the entire strategic situation of the company can be seen at once. This data collection can take as many as fifteen meetings. The actual strategic decision may come quite quickly in one meeting, or it may take several. Finally, there are a number of consequential decisions and actions to work out over, say, three or four meetings. The total is, say, twenty-five meetings, taking about a year.

Although I show the process as a straight-through one, it is really a series of spirals, back-tracking and reconsidering previous decisions. Also, of course, although I imply that it has an end, once it has started, it should continue indefinitely. However, all this is described in more detail in the relevant chapters.

I am sometimes asked 'What about all the forms needed?' There are none! Corporate planning is not like budgeting. The volume of data required is tiny compared with the masses required in most short term planning exercises. The nearest thing to a form is shown in an exhibit in Chapter 8.

This exercise is a very crude and very coarse-grained one. It requires down-to-earth common sense and a very wide knowledge of the company and its environment. This is why I believe so strongly that it should be a team of the company's own top executives rather than some brilliant specialist who does corporate planning. They need technical help at several points in the process, and, as for so many activities today, a team of executives advised by a specialist is the ideal combination.

Does it do what it is supposed to do?

This depends what it is supposed to do! If it is hoped that profits will soar after an application of corporate planning, I do not know whether it will be successful or not. Surveys show that companies using corporate planning do often display a better profit record than those which do not. I believe that corporate planning *does* improve profits. I am almost certain of it, but do not make the mistake of believing that an application of corporate planning will always have this effect. I believe that corporate planning is useless unless the company has already adopted a participative style of management. It may be the adoption of this style that causes a rise in profits not corporate planning at all! Those who design the surveys never think of asking this.

Since I do not believe that this proposition can ever be satisfactorily proved, I prefer to declare the aim of corporate planning to be 'to bring about a consensus among the top executives of a company as to their company's long term future'. Now, this I can prove. I know of many companies in which, before corporate planning was introduced, the executives had not even discussed the long term future.

I once asked the five directors of a small company what level of profits they would like to see in real terms in five years' time – in other words, 'How ambitious are you for your company?' These five men had worked together for many years on the board. They had lunched together, travelled the world together and discussed every possible aspect of their company together, but they had never discussed this. Their answers were:

> Current profits of our company   £1·5m.
> Profits that I should like to see in five years:
>> Chairman   £3m.
>> Chief executive   £3m.
>> Finance director   £4m.
>> Works director   £5m.
>> Marketing director   £5m.

I find it remarkable how widely these views are spread. To someone aiming at £3m. an aim of £5m. would surely appear to be ambitious beyond all reason; to the £5m. men an aim of £3m. would appear to be hardly worth reaching for. Also, what cautious, faint-hearted, almost cowardly strategies those middle-aged £3m. men would put forward in the view of those daring young £5m. men! (Their ages were actually, in the sequence above, 56, 54, 42, 37 and 35.) Once they got down to discussing this, they quite quickly agreed a set of targets for year 5 *and* a strategy for getting there.

I find it a constant source of fascination to watch these small groups of top executives forming into teams, discussing, arguing and agreeing their way through to a clear view of where their company stands today and what must be done to place it into a favourable position for tomorrow.

After it is all over, the top executives, having become accustomed to thinking and talking in strategic terms with horizons of several years, seem to move into a new mental gear in which they naturally see their company as an outsider may see it but with the knowledge of an insider. They see it as a corporate whole.

It seems to me that there are two ways to run a company. One is the way of the entrepreneur who, by some inspirational process that no one understands and that cannot be trained or inculcated into people not born with it, gives his company a destination – a dynamic, a trajectory. The other is to place the company into the hands of a team of professional managers. The former produces a company that may provide society with a new and exciting product, or it may go bust. The latter produces a steady worthy company that will probably not go bust but may not thrill the world with new delights either. The former can only exist if one man is running it on his own in his own way, which seldom includes planning in any form. The latter can best be run by a team, and it must be formally planned. The two methods just do not seem to mix – one man and unplanned flair, or a team that plans.

In attempting to answer the question 'Does it work?' I am suggesting that no, it cannot compete with the entrepreneur, and I should never expect it to. However, I am suggesting that it should at least protect a managed company from failure. Let me expand this a little (and see my book *Corporate Collapse*). It seems that there are three routes to failure – or to be more accurate, there are three different types of company, which each follow their own distinct route to failure.

Type I companies are very small ones that are founded and fail within a few years without ever getting off the ground. Nothing can save them, for they should really never have been launched. So, these are not relevant to our discussion.

Type II companies are launched by an entrepreneur, flourish explosively and then collapse dramatically. The cause here lies in the nature of the entrepreneur who, flushed with early success and disdaining all advice, launches into ever more ambitious schemes, one of which inevitably eventually fails, bringing down the whole company. There is nothing that a corporate planner or anyone else can do here to help either.

When we turn to Type III, things are different. Type IIIs are mature companies almost always controlled by one man who loses touch with the world in some important respect. Since he is running the company, if he loses touch, the company loses touch. A company cannot do that for long in this rapidly changing highly competitive world, so it collapses (often in two stages over a period of several years). Now, my version of corporate planning lays great stress on two elements that are relevant here: the need for a team to reach a consensus and the need to keep the company up to date – modern in every respect. Just as a factory director continually modernises his equipment and methods, so the company as a whole needs to be modernised continually. So, at the very least corporate planning should prevent failure by (1) introducing teamwork and consensus instead of autocracy and (2) modernising the company continuously.

Now, to say that corporate planning should 'at least prevent failure' is not a very impressive or voluminous claim to make for it, certainly not compared with some of the claims made on its behalf. So, although I personally think that preventing failure is a sufficient justification for doing anything in this difficult and hostile world, I should also list some of its other beneficial consequences.

The fact that a consensus emerges among the top executives over the future of their company is a major benefit. Anyone who has worked for a company where the top levels are in total accord with one another knows how invigorating and even exhilarating this is. The company comes alive; everyone feels invited to give his best endeavours to the chosen aims and goals – aims and goals that he himself has helped to choose. We all know that motivation – that knack of inspiring employees to stretch themselves not only for the company but also for their own satisfaction – is one of the great social and personal requirements of our time. Pay does not achieve it; working conditions do not; legislation certainly cannot. Whatever the secret to it is, I doubt that it would be effective in a company that did not itself know where it was going.

Most managers are so busy making and selling their products that they have no time to stand back and look at themselves as an outsider may do, or they have no time to look beyond the next year or two. To be made to do these things as a team can only be salutary. To be forced to recognise their present situation as it really exists is an object lesson in itself. Some companies fail to recognise their real situation; others recognise it but do not face up to it; others believe it to be far worse than it really is – a misapprehension that I have seen on several occasions, particularly in relation to a supposed technological threat (what a relief when it is seen in its true light!).

Corporate planning not only causes companies to face the future squarely and to give adequate consideration to problems not yet at boiling point; it also forces executives to redesign the management structure of their company, so that it is more responsive in future. We must be careful of this claim for corporate planning, however. Many people urge that the *plans* be flexible. This may be possible in some circumstances – where it is possible it should be done – but most decisions are not flexible. The decision to launch a new product, say, or to build a nitric acid plant in Brazil tends to be extremely unflexible, yet such decisions do have to be taken. No, I mean that corporate planning causes the executives to make the *company* more responsive to change. They redesign its management system, style and structure to enhance its flexibility (for an example, see Exhibit 7.1); and even if no concrete decisions come out of the planning exercise, this is justification enough.

I really cannot say whether corporate planning improves profits. I believe that it does, and I am quite sure that its other consequences are far more immediate and more verifiable – and possibly more important.

If corporate planning has such beneficial results, why, it may be asked, do not more companies adopt it? Why is it so difficult to persuade top managers to adopt it and participate in it? Part of the answer lies in the general scepticism of executives towards all planning, all advanced techniques and all experts. I share this scepticism, and this is one reason why I believe that most companies would do well to avoid recruiting a specialist to do the planning for them. Part of the answer, perhaps most of it, is that the top executives are so busy running their departments. However, I have to ask this: What sort of people are these executives who cannot devote 4 hours per fortnight to discussing their company's long term health? Whose job do they think this is supposed to be?

As to those companies in which several of the top executives want to start the corporate planning process in their company but the chief executive does not, this is a common and most delicate problem. It would be most arrogant to suggest that a chief executive who did not believe in corporate planning should be fired! In fact this is not as ridiculous as it sounds, for either this is his only foible, in which case it deserves respect, of course, or it is part of a wider and more serious circle of defects, in which case a 'palace revolution' may well be indicated. One thing is sure: if the chief executive believes in corporate planning, he will usually persuade his colleagues to allow him to introduce it. Indeed, corporate planning is introduced into most companies, not because of some external event or internal development that demands the introduction of corporate planning, but because of the arrival of a new chief executive who believes in it.

Summary

Although corporate planning has been in use for many years now, it is still the subject of several misconceptions. Some companies try to plan in meticulous detail over very long time spans; others confuse corporate planning with budgeting; others, believing corporate planning to be a vast complex exercise, appoint academically brilliant specialists to do the planning for them.

Corporate planning is in fact a quite simple exercise. However, this does not mean that it is easy. The problems are: first, that the forecasts on which many of the decisions have to be based are subject to enormous errors; and secondly, that many of these decisions are judgemental. A corporate plan does not contain an enormous number of decisions, nor does it call for a vast volume of data; these are more the characteristics of short term planning. Instead, it involves a very few but very important decisions concerning the whole structure of the company for many years into the future.

The idea that the corporate planner should prepare his company's corporate plan is still prevalent today. In fact his correct role is to assist the company's top executive team to prepare the plan. They do it; he assists. The reasoning behind this rests in the belief, for which there does seem ample evidence, that one man can no longer manage a medium-sized company on his own as the old-fashioned autocrat used to do. The reason for this is that no one man can grasp the significance for his firm of all the multitudinous events taking place in the business environment today. Hence, there is a trend towards the chief executive's becoming less of a boss and more of a team leader managing by consensus.

Now, if this is the case for managing a company, it probably holds true for planning its long term destiny as well. So, a corporate plan prepared by one man will be unbalanced or otherwise defective. It needs a team. The first step to take, then, is to form the corporate planning team. It must include the chief executive. It will probably include the finance director and one or two others. Then appoint a corporate planner as team secretary; this can, of course, be a very senior appointment.

The process itself is quite simple. The team works systematically through a sequence of questions about its company. The objectives, targets, strengths, weaknesses, and so on are all examined and discussed, until a consensus emerges as to the company's overall total strategic situation. Then, a decision is made; that is, a strategy or set of strategies is selected, and action plans are drawn up. Finally, the team stands ready to monitor progress every few months.

It is useful, in order to avoid unrealistic plans and to obtain maximum co-operation in putting the plans into effect, to seek the participation of as many senior executives as possible. To do this the planning exercise should begin with a seminar, and the team should take care to consult with, and report to, a wider circle of executives.

The effect of corporate planning may be to improve profits. A number of surveys suggest this, and I believe it to be so. However, the most easily verifiable consequence is that, whereas before corporate planning no consensus exists concerning the long term future of the company, after it a consensus does exist. The whole of the top two or three levels of the company's management can be clearly seen working towards agreed long term aims by means of an agreed set of strategies.

CHAPTER 2

Corporate Objectives and Ethos

As explained in the previous chapter, a most important feature of my system of corporate planning is the sequence of meetings held by the corporate planning team. This is the backbone of the system; each meeting is a vertebra.

I have also explained that, apart from its very first meeting to discuss the timetable, the team's first working session should be devoted to deciding corporate objectives and ethos. Now, not everyone agrees with this, but setting corporate objectives and ethos is, I believe, a relatively straightforward task for most companies. I concede that for some it is not, and I shall discuss some of these awkward ones later.

Some corporate planners claim that setting corporate objectives is only an academic exercise and has no practical value. It will indeed have no practical value if we make the mistake that some well-meaning enthusiasts continue to make in companies all over the world, namely to give their companies a set of objectives of such unctuous saintliness that they are completely and embarrassingly unattainable. We must keep our feet on the ground; if we do, the practical value of this exercise will be substantial.

Some specialists recommend that the objectives not be decided until after the strategy has been selected. Those who hold this view have, in my opinion, totally failed to understand even the first principles of management.

What are corporate objectives?

An objective is an aim, goal, mission or task. It is something that someone wants to achieve. It is an end, not a means. If this is the meaning of the word 'objective', it follows that a *corporate* objective is the aim, goal, mission or task for a *corporate* body, such as a company, a charity, a club, a government or any other organisational entity.

A corporate objective is therefore the concept that validates the entire organisation and every action that it takes. Only if the objectives for a given organisation are known can it be judged whether the actions that it takes are wise or foolish, appropriate or misguided.

Only if the objectives are known can it be judged whether a given organisation is successful or failing, desirable or undesirable, laudable or contemptible. The corporate objective, then, is the criterion, the touchstone, the yardstick by which *everything* concerning the company is judged. It is the purpose, the *raison d'être*, the justification for its very existence. Some people do in fact call it the corporate purpose.

It is obvious that a corporate objective is something almost unalterable; it must be of the essence of any organisation – permanent, unchanging. If it is changed, the entire nature of the organisation itself is changed.

It would be very difficult to exaggerate the importance of such a concept as this. It is the justification for the very existence of a company, I am suggesting – not exactly a trifle, then! So, we must get it right; we must identify what it is with care and accuracy. As for leaving it until *after* we have decided the strategies, well, it would be hard to think of anything more idiotically perverse. Only in a world of madmen does an organisation tailor its ultimate purpose to fit its strategies rather than the other way round. However, there is something else that these perverts have failed to grasp.

I believe that a corporate objective is not just a very exalted departmental objective; it is different in kind, not merely in degree. Imagine a hierarchy of objectives in a company (see Exhibit 2.1) where, at the base, junior managers are given such objectives as 'improve the efficiency of the despatch department' or 'sell an extra three units next month'. Higher up the hierarchy such departmental aims as 'close down the Southtown factory by next April' or 'launch a subsidiary company in Brazil' are set. The higher up we look, the more general and more strategic the aims and tasks become, but they are all *management* tasks and objectives set by managers at one level for the managers below them.

However, right at the top of a hierarchy of objectives there must be one that is *not* managerial in nature. Why? Simply because it *is* the top one, just as in a chain all the links are identical except the ones at the ends, which, just because they are at the ends, must be different from all the others.

In other words, although managers decide all the other objectives in a hierarchy, they do not – or should not – decide the ones at the top, namely the corporate objectives.

Exhibit 2.1 A hierarchy of objectives

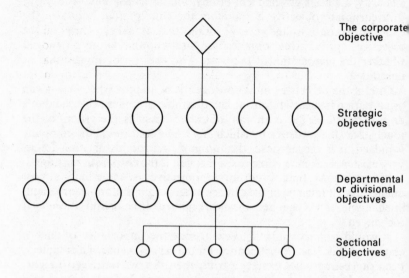

The corporate objective

Strategic objectives

Departmental or divisional objectives

Sectional objectives

Who should decide them?

If the managers ought not to decide the corporate objectives, who should? The answer must be 'the people for whose benefit the organisation exists' or, as I call them, the intended beneficiaries. Every organisation is founded to benefit a particular group or type of person; for example, schools are founded for the benefit of children, hospitals for the sick, famine relief charities for the starving, golf clubs for golfers and, in the capitalist philosophy, companies for shareholders. (If we do not accept capitalism, the intended beneficiaries are someone other than, or in addition to, shareholders, whose identity we shall consider later.)

Let us first assume for the sake of simplicity that companies are indeed founded by and for shareholders. Clearly, then, the corporate objective of any given company is to generate whatever benefit the company's shareholders want it to generate for them. If the company is owned solely and wholly by Mr Finch, the company's corporate objective – its entire *raison d'être,* its purpose – is to generate whatever satisfactions or benefits Mr Finch wants from it. This is its sole purpose. If it does not succeed in this, Mr Finch will close it down, sell it or in one way or another end it.

If on the other hand a company is quoted on a stock market and has virtually no family holdings, its *raison d'être* is quite simply to generate a return on the shares of its thousands of individual and institutional shareholders. Between the one-man band and the large public company lies every shade of size and ownership, with naturally a wide range of differing aims.

When I said above (p. 34) that for most companies it is not difficult to determine the corporate objective, I had in mind the vast majority of companies whose corporate planning team will swiftly agree that its company's top objective is to make a satisfactory return on shareholders' capital. This is, most people still believe, the pre-eminent aim of all companies, right through from the one-man band to IBM.

In theory it is incorrect for the corporate planning team, which almost always consists of managers, to decide the corporate objectives. It is always better to ask the shareholders themselves; and if they want something other than the simple traditional return on capital, it is absolutely essential for them to specify exactly what this is. It may be something as simple as 'to secure the continued independence of the company' – an aim that its managers may also wish to see – but it may be 'to provide top management jobs for Mr Finch's three sons', or 'The family's wealth is tied up in the company; the family wishes to dispose of 40 per cent of its ownership within the next few years', or 'Ten per cent of profits is to be donated to the Southtown Society for Sick Animals'.

It seems sensible, then, for the planning team to ask the shareholders exactly what they want. The team will have to know who the shareholders are, of course, and this is another question too often taken for granted. Sometimes, the answer is not straightforward at all. In some companies the employees are shareholders; but in these 'worker co-operatives' not all workers are shareholders, and not all shareholders are workers. In other companies the customers are shareholders; but the legal constitutions of, say, the co-operative societies in Britain are not identical to those of similar organisations elsewhere.

In other companies the suppliers are the shareholders – a common arrangement among farmers, wine-growers, and so on – and in others the profit-making company is owned by a non-profit-making charity. The permutations of ownership are endless.

What matters is that the corporate planning team clearly identifies who the owners are and what they want. In the capitalist system the answer is simple: the owners are the shareholders, and what they want is a return on their capital.

Who decides how much?

One of the reasons why I have suggested that it be the owners, rather than the managers, who decide corporate objectives is the possibility of the managers' perverting the company to their own purposes. That they may do so deliberately and fraudulently is not the chief threat, although it may exist. No, the danger is that they may do so by default; indeed, some people believe that this is precisely what has happened to the vast majority of companies in the Western democracies. The view that 'Companies today are run for the managers' is heard on all sides. Others hold the view that managers, again by default rather than from villainy, have allowed other pressure groups – trade unions, environmentalists, consumerists, and so on – to pervert the true purpose of many companies.

How valid this complaint is I do not know. In any case there is another similar problem to be considered. I have suggested that *the* corporate objective of the vast majority of companies is to yield a return on shareholders' capital, but I have not yet discussed the question of *how much* return. Someone has to say what return shareholders can expect, should expect or do actually expect, and someone has to say what level of return represents failure.

Now, it does not seem sensible to me to entrust the setting of the level of this criterion to the managers, since they are the very people who are responsible for achieving it. So, someone other than the managers should be invited to indicate what rate of return on capital shareholders can reasonably expect. In most companies it is entirely acceptable for the corporate planning team to be entrusted with *asking* this question – normally it would ask the shareholders themselves, bankers, stock-brokers, accountants, and so on – and with the task of collating the answers, but the answer that it eventually adopts should reflect these outside views, not those of the team.

It has to be added, however, that the views of the managers, and therefore of the corporate planning team itself, are a valid input. After all they probably know more about the company than anyone. What I wish to warn against is a level of performance selected solely or largely by the managers, who in some cases may select a very low level of achievement to make their task easy but in other cases may set a very high level out of sheer ambition and, in attempting to achieve it, place shareholders' funds at extreme risk.

Much of Chapter 3 will be devoted to the task of selecting a suitable level of performance, so all that is necessary now is to summarise the main conclusion of this chapter. A corporate objective, which must describe the *raison d'être* for the organisation as a whole, has to contain three elements: (1) the intended beneficiaries have to be identified (for most companies they are the shareholders); (2) the benefit that they expect has to be described (for most shareholders it is return on their capital); and (3) the level of performance that is acceptable to them has to be specified (for shareholders this varies, as described in the next chapter, but an example is shown in 'shorthand' in Exhibit 2.2).

Exhibit 2.2   What a shareholder may have in mind

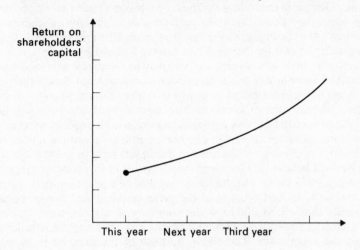

Return on shareholders' capital

This year   Next year   Third year

Fallacious corporate objectives

I shall deal with some of the more difficult types of corporate objectives in the next section. In this one I want to list some of the objectives that are still extremely popular in spite of being utter and complete nonsense.

The first candidate has to be 'survive'. One still sees companies solemnly declaring 'The prime objective of our company is to survive'. Now, it must be agreed that, if a company is currently in some trouble but has a bright longer-term future, of course it should struggle to survive, and in a sense its corporate objective can then be said to be survival. However, this is a trivial interpretation of corporate objective, which, as I have explained above, is something very fundamental indeed. It is certainly something more long term than a mere few years.

Except in this patently trivial case the survival objective is ridiculous. No one could possibly want an organisation to continue in existence unless it were capable of generating a benefit for someone. If it is generating a benefit for someone, this will be its purpose; if it is not, it will die. Quite right too. No one has ever formed an organisation for the purpose of survival, and no one ever will.

The second candidate, which is an even more popular one, is 'maximise'. Dozens of companies set themselves such corporate objectives as 'We aim to maximise long term profits', 'Our company will maximise its market capitalisation', and so on. There are three crippling defects in the use of this word in this context.

First, I doubt whether many companies really do try to maximise profits. Do companies really strain every whisker to earn more profits, even when they know that their performance is already unbelievably excellent? Do they ignore all risks, cast aside all humanity and deny all morality to extract that very last penny? I doubt it.

Secondly, how can a company tell if it has actually achieved this objective? How in five years' time does a company verify whether or not it has indeed maximised its profits over the past five years? Are we hoping to persuade an accountant to sign a certificate in which he declares 'I certify that this company maximised its profits last year'? If it is not possible to verify whether or not an objective has been achieved, I really cannot see much point in setting it in the first place.

Thirdly, I believe that the word 'maximise' is in this context literally meaningless. In the short term there may well be a profit figure that it is impossible to exceed because of the given physical and non-physical resources that are available to the company at a given time, but in the context of corporate planning we are very definitely not talking about the short term. The whole purpose of the exercise is to ask what sort of resources the company should seek to employ in five, ten or twenty years' time. I simply have no idea what the word means in an open-ended context like this. (I similarly reject the word 'optimise'.)

Finally, I come to the third major group of fallacious corporate objectives. This includes *all* management ratios, accounting ratios, operational ratios, management measures, aims, ambitions and parameters – any indicator of *management* activity whatever. These include 'increase share of the market', 'lead our industry in technology', 'become No. 1 in Europe', 'increase margin on sales', 'improve output per man', 'increase value added', 'improve return on capital employed', 'introduce several new products', and so on endlessly. All these are actions or activities and so are strategies or means. They are not aims, at least not *corporate* aims. They may be departmental aims or subsidiary company aims, but we are a *very* long way from considering what these should be (see Chapter 9).

Corporate objectives, remember, are something virtually permanent and unalterable. No company would ever decide *not* to aim to yield a return on shareholders' capital, but companies can and quite frequently do decide *not* to increase market share. Some aim to reduce it. Companies *do* aim to cut sales margins rather than to increase them. Companies *do* abandon their attempt to be the technological leader. None of these can be corporate objectives, therefore.

How does a company know when deliberately to reduce its market share? The answer is: by referring to a criterion higher up the hierarchy of objectives – in this case profits. If the managers think that profits will improve if they reduce their market share, they will reduce it; if they do not, they will not. So, profit is the corporate objective, and market share, technological status, size, and almost everything, are strategic options.

To select 'increase share of the market' as an objective at the very start of the corporate planning process is therefore ridiculous. This is precisely the sort of issue that we wish to be determined *by* the process. It is an output, not an input. Let us, therefore, at this early stage in the process rid our mind of all preconceived ideas about what is good for our particular company. The only thing that we can know at this stage is that shareholders want a return on their capital, and we know enough about how a company is put together to assume that this means that we are going to have to pay attention to profits.

We cannot even assume that growth is an objective. It is very likely that growth of profits will indeed be an objective, although not even this is certain (see page 63), but growth of anything else – such as turnover, market share, size of company, number of employees, number of nations in which the company operates – is an assumption that we dare not make at this stage. This is a strategic decision that we must not even think about until Chapter 6! It is quite amazing how many companies start their corporate planning exercise by stating what the answers are going to be.

Surely we can state as a corporate objective something like 'We are in the business of manufacturing and selling concrete mixers'? No, we cannot. It is perfectly legitimate strategy to stop making concrete mixers and only to sell them, or to stop selling them as well and to become an investment trust instead. It is unlikely, I know, but possible.

However, it will be argued, surely we can take 'increase return on capital employed' as a corporate objective at this stage? Surely we are never going to alter that one? Yes, we may! We may even aim for a *lower* return on capital employed! I agree that it is unlikely and rare, but just consider the following case. Thrush & Co. has a capital employed of £100,000 according to its balance sheet and made a profit last year of £40,000. Its factory, built and equipped in 1930, is written down to £1,200. Now, it is quite clear that one strategy that the company should consider very carefully is to re-equip its factory (it would cost £100,000 to do this, and the bank would charge £10,000 p.a. interest), so that profits before interest will rise to £60,000 p.a. Will it be a calamity if the company's return on capital employed falls to 30 per cent? No, of course it will not, because return on *shareholders'* capital will improve markedly. It is not a strategy to be rejected without thought, but this is exactly what the company would do if it selected 'improve return on capital employed' as its corporate objective.

No, there is only one corporate objective that is always valid in all conceivable circumstances for all (capitalist) companies, namely, return on *shareholders'* capital.

Some difficult cases

In most companies the task of deciding corporate objectives is, as suggested above (page 34), quite straightforward. It is a simple matter of return on shareholders' capital – or in shorthand, profits. It is certainly not maximised anything, nor survival nor any management measure or ambition.

However, when a company has two radically different groups of beneficiaries, or when the benefits being demanded by the beneficiaries cover a wide spectrum, we run into trouble.

Imagine a company owned 50 per cent by several hundred private shareholders on the one hand and 50 per cent by one man on the other. Their aims are going to be different. Even if the holdings were 51–49, 60–40 or even 70–30, the one party would still have to take some account of the wishes of the other. Reconciling such diverse requirements is not easy; but unless they are sorted out, it is difficult to make progress in the planning process. The act of raising the question, which the corporate planning team must do, can only be beneficial.

Take a company in Spain owned 51 per cent by the Spanish government's holding company ('INI') and 49 per cent by an American multinational. Clearly, one party will be keenly interested in jobs for Spanish nationals, whereas the other will be more interested in dividends. This case, where there are two different partners with two different and often conflicting aims, is quite a common one. (In my view such cases will rapidly become less common as management understanding of the problem increases.)

A typical example of a company given a set of three incompatible aims was British Leyland in 1975. The Ryder Report called not only for a return on capital from the company but also for a contribution to Britain's exports and for the maintenance of employees' jobs. There is, so far as I know, no formula linking a given return on capital with a given number of jobs or a given contribution to a nation's balance of payments. In other words no one knows – certainly no one in British Leyland knew – how to make the 'trade-offs', as they are called, between these three objectives. To put it another way, no one knew how to choose between the endless permutations between them, some of which are shown in Exhibit 2.3. Therefore, no one knew how to select one set of strategies in preference to some other set.

My own belief is that organisations having more than one objective must be the product of a fevered brain. No one in his right mind would sit down and deliberately form an organisation with two diverse

Exhibit 2.3   Some alternative objectives for British Leyland: how should the most desirable option be selected?

Option	Profits (£m.)	Contribution to UK balance of payments (£m.)	No. of employees
A	20	1,000	170,000
B	200	1,000	120,000
C	200	2,000	80,000
D	2,000	10	80,000
E	2,000	1,000	80,000
etc.			

objectives. How about a Society for the Preservation of Clog Dancing in Northern England and the Housing of the Homeless in Tasmania, for example (and these objectives are not even incompatible, merely diverse)? I cannot see why it is any more rational to allow a similar situation to develop by default or laziness. You can no more drive an organisation in two directions at once than you can a bus.

The problem of multiple benefits to multiple beneficiaries becomes particularly acute in the case of nationalised companies and in the stakeholder theory, both of which will be considered later. Even the smallest simplest company can be faced with either multiple beneficiaries or a single (or homogeneous) beneficiary who demands multiple benefits. Indeed, multiple benefits is the norm for family businesses, whose owners often require not only return on their capital but also continued independence, employment for relatives and some-times much else besides, some of which may be wildly eccentric.

This, however, should not present any real difficulties to the corporate planning team, for it only needs to go and ask these beneficiaries to clarify their demands. Normally, this is all that is necessary. Let us remember that in most companies these aims have not been given a moment's thought for years or decades, and nothing but good can flow from this exercise. Old hidden family feuds, squabbles and misunderstandings can be brought out into the open and discussed in the rational objective atmosphere of the corporate planning exercise.

However, suppose that these conflicting aims cannot be reconciled? Suppose that the more they are clarified, the more clearly everyone can see that they are irreconcilable? Then, there are at least three courses open. The first is to accept the situation and attempt to devise a strategy that meets both sets of objectives. The second, which is far preferable if the dichotomy is wide, is to split the company's ownership into two and cause one party to move out altogether with suitable compensation. The third is to appoint some form of higher authority than the existing board of directors: either a new independent chairman who can hold a reasonable balance between the factions, or a representative board on which each party is represented and at whose meetings corporate objectives can be thrashed out. A supervisory board, although clumsy, is sometimes the only solution for larger companies. In these various ways the problem of balancing the split of benefits between the contestants can be taken out of the hands of the executives, who can then get on with their management tasks.

It is true of many companies that are large and mature in age that their corporate objectives have not been subjected to scrutiny for several decades, and it is even more true of many other types of organisation. The larger and more ancient they are, the more they will have lost their sense of direction. It is a vital part of the corporate planning team's task to obtain a new or sharpened consensus on what these corporate objectives should be in the modern world.

If a consensus cannot be obtained, it is necessary to do something about this. Either recognise that it cannot, split the beneficiaries, or appoint a new independent chairman, but do *something*. Corporate objectives are too important to be swept under the carpet.

Ethos

The philosophy underlying the whole of this chapter so far has been unashamed capitalism – nineteenth-century capitalism at that, for I have repeatedly stated that *the* corporate objective of the normal company is to yield a return on shareholders' capital and have so far totally ignored the claims of employees, customers, suppliers and the state.

I am not certain that even the darkest nineteenth-century capitalists were quite as evil as we are now told that they were – and there were a considerable number whose humanity and generosity can still be a lesson to us today – but a capitalism that ignores the claims of society is plainly now unthinkable.

I use the word 'ethos' to mean 'how a company thinks it should conduct itself in society'. Every organisation has to consider this, because no organisation could continue to exist in a society that was affronted by its behaviour; and since a company is essentially a somewhat self-seeking organisation (unlike a charity, for example, which essentially exists to help the underdogs in society), companies have to be particularly careful how they behave.

The almost total coverage of television, radio and other media across the entire population of the developed world has drawn particular attention to corporate behaviour in recent decades, and this has resulted in a remarkable unanimity of view on ethos. Most companies know, from only a casual glance at the media reports, how they are expected to behave towards their employees, their customers, their competitors, their suppliers, their bankers and creditors, their governments, their local community, their foreign subsidiaries, their handicapped employees, their female employees, environmentalist lobbies, wildlife lobbies – in fact just about everyone ever likely to come into contact with them.

In most nations there is a mountain of legislation covering every aspect of the responsibilities of organisations. Indeed, there is now so much of it that some of it is beginning to look self-contradictory, if not within national boundaries then certainly across them. Some of this legislation is barely intelligible, some is unenforceable and some is merely ridiculous, but taken together as a whole it does give employers a reasonable guide to what is expected of them as a minimum.

Now, in most companies the corporate planning team will not need to spend very much time discussing ethos, because, as I say, a fairly well-structured and widely disseminated consensus, underpinned by this wealth of legislation, exists in most companies in most nations. However, it is not enough to adopt a code of behaviour for today; the company will need one for tomorrow's world as well, and this will require some discussion.

In most firms there will also be one or two areas of particular sensitivity, and it may be appropriate for the corporate planning team to draw attention to these and perhaps to reach firm conclusions. Take a large company operating in a small town, for example. Clearly, the local community will be acutely interested in any plans for the growth or the contraction of the company, and the company may well feel that it should decide what its obligations really are towards this community.

Again, a company trading in certain areas of the world may need to decide its attitude to bribery or to what level of wages to pay in very poor nations. Some companies employ materials or processes that may be injurious to health. Others may supply medical goods that can, if misused, be injurious. Others manufacture and sell alcohol, tobacco or other addictive drugs. Other firms are so large that they could almost by accident cause a small supplier to go bankrupt. In all such cases it may be desirable to determine the company's attitude. In some companies a particular code of ethics, a particular tradition or a particular religion may pervade its actions; and if this is liable to be incompatible with the consensus view of the society in which the company operates, a clear and rather detailed statement of ethos is needed. One very large English food manufacturing company, still managed by the descendants of its Quaker founders, is now selling alcoholic drinks. Some tobacco companies are careful to define their attitude to their product. Some consumer goods companies declare their scruples over the excessive use of the marketing concept. Shipping companies have to think about 'flags of convenience'. Publishers must consider pornography. Some engineering firms have to ask themselves about manufacturing arms. One company that I know is concerned that its health product, although harmless, is ineffective – a fact known to previous generations of managers but not thought to be of any concern of theirs so long as customers believed in it.

When it comes to deciding ethos, then, the task of most corporate planners is relatively simple. Either nothing at all needs to be said, or a brief statement like 'The company will behave as modern society would have it behave' is all that is necessary. Occasionally, one particular problem area may have to be examined. Occasionally, a company will decide not to conform to one or more of society's current norms. There is, however, one area that many companies like to high-light and to make statements about in greater detail than I have suggested above, namely, its attitude to its employees. I shall outline some of the factors to be considered below.

There seems to be one further golden rule: 'Find out!' If the company is not sure what its employees expect from it, what the local community wants or what the various classes of shareholders require, it should go and ask them! It is rare in Britain for companies to ask even their shareholders for their views, let alone their employees, suppliers or others who come into social or business contact with the company. Some do not even know what their customers want.

Employees' objectives

It is generally recognised today that good relations with employees are even more important than relations with customers, suppliers, the local community and other third parties. Many companies like to draw particular attention to this emphasis on their employee well-being by including a formal declaration in their statement of ethos.

Some companies like to keep it brief and rather general – for example, 'We seek to make this a pleasant and rewarding place for our employees to work in' – but others like to go into rather more detail. In this case their statements will fall naturally into four parts:

(1) A statement on remuneration. Usually, this declares the company's hope that the take-home pay of all their employees at all levels will rise in real terms at least as fast as that of employees in similar companies. (One company that I know declared that each employee's pay would rise at the same rate as shareholders' dividends. This was a splendid sentiment but a

dangerous one to make when dividends had been held back by government policy while pay had not!)

(2) A statement on security. Frequently, this includes a statement of company policy on notice of dismissal or closure of factory or department, but sometimes it also refers to security from a fall in pay due to demotion, illness or new methods, and it sometimes includes pensions policy, maternity leave and rights to return, and so forth.

(3) A statement on working conditions. This describes the company's intentions about office accommodation and factory conditions as regards noise, heat, smell, safety, equipment, and so on.

(4) Finally, a statement on job satisfaction. Here the company explains what it hopes to do for all levels of employees, management and specialist staff to make their work more satisfying. It covers career plans, training, management development, promotion prospects, job enrichment, and so on.

There is little merit in detailed statements of this sort unless the company has taken some trouble to think them out and unless there is really going to be some commitment to them. It was sugary jelly-like statements in this area that in earlier years gave such a bad reputation to corporate planning. On the other hand, if the company really means what it says, such statements can lead to a prolonged and mutually satisfying improvement in human relationships.

Objectives for nationalised companies

I have mentioned (page 42) the troublesome case of a company having two disparate owners with differing needs and the even more troublesome case of British Leyland, which was saddled with three conflicting corporate objectives and given no hint of how the conflict could be resolved.

Nationalised companies face this problem in a form that is even more acute, since their 'beneficiaries' are everyone in the nation, and the benefits include the full range of human needs and desires. Not only do the employees, suppliers, customers and local community lay claim to special benefits from these companies, as they do from all very large companies, but in addition almost any pressure group with the gall to do so can find some reason or other for staking a claim.

Left to themselves the chief executives of these nationalised companies could almost certainly handle this problem with the same blend of common sense and humanity that chief executives of IBM, General Motors, ICI, Mitsubishi and countless other very large firms have exhibited for years. However, to 'leave them to themselves' would be tantamount to stating that a nationalised company should behave in exactly the same independent way as one that had not been nationalised.

Perhaps the root problem of the nationalised company is that, in Britain in particular, its relationship with its political masters has never been properly thought out. There are three possible relationships, and successive governments swing wildly from one to the other to the endless confusion of all concerned. The three relationships are: (1) to be entirely autonomous and independent of the government; (2) to be semi- autonomous; and (3) to be totally integrated into the machinery of government. Each relationship is fairly clear and easily defined; the problems arise from the swinging from one to the other.

Take the case of the nationalised company that is independent of government. In this case the company behaves in every way like a non-nationalised company of the same type and size, and the sole difference is that any dividends go to the government. (I am not too sure what advantages this arrangement would bring the government concerned, but it is certainly a nice simple one!)

The other simple arrangement lies at the other end of the scale of autonomy. Here the company is so totally integrated into the machinery of government that it becomes a mere cog in the government's social and political policies as well as its economic ones. Here the chief executive does what he is told; if unemployment in Northtown is high, for example, this is where he will build his new factory, not in Southtown where it would be more profitable. Notice that no corporate objectives at all can be set for this organisation, because it is not a corporate body but an arm or subsidiary of a bigger organisation, namely, the government. However, the relationship is perfectly clear, and there can be few misunderstandings. The problem here is the exact opposite of the one above, however. There the profit motive will preclude many socially worthwhile projects, whereas here the company can be made to indulge in endless social projects to the endless cost of the taxpayer – a phenomenon well known in Britain for three decades.

The third relationship, namely, semi-autonomy, is not a mere compromise in the middle of these extremes. If we must have nationalis-ation, this one, although more complex, seems to me quite sensible. Here the corporate objective may begin 'to make a satisfactory return on the shareholders' (that is, the government's) capital . . .' – and in this respect the nationalised company will be just like an independent private company – but the statement will continue '. . . and to under-take specific social projects on a costed basis as directed by the government'. In other words this company is expected to make a profit *and* to undertake social projects, *but* these will be paid for. Thus, for example, if a branch line of a nationalised railway is making a loss of £10m. p.a., and the government wants that line to remain open for social reasons, the government should pay the company a specific subvention of £10m. for these specific reasons. Also, if the government wishes to use its nationalised companies to keep down prices or reduce unemployment, the cost to each undertaking of doing so can be costed out and a specific subvention given. (It would indeed be refreshing to know that the politician who makes the decision knows what it will cost.) Under this scheme, which is common enough in Europe, no general subsidies are paid; they are all specific, and the company is expected to make a profit. This middle solution lends itself to another useful concept, namely, the setting up of a management body for each nationalised company that is independent of government albeit linked to government through a suitable charter or other constitutional instrument. In this way each nationalised undertaking could be held at one remove from government, thus reducing the number and frequency of changes of policy that otherwise so curse these unhappy organisations.

Many nationalised industries define their objectives not in terms of return on shareholders' (that is, government's) capital but in terms of 'provide a service'. Thus, a nationalised airline, for example, will strive to 'provide a service for air passengers'. Some aim both to provide a service *and* to make a small profit, but which of these is the prime aim I am not sure. In any case the profit aim is made rather easy to attain by writing off government loans whenever this seems convenient.

As to 'provide a service', this is nonsense. There is no way in which its achievement can be verified. In many cases these organisations are monopolies, so the service that they give cannot be compared with others. One big-city bus company aims to 'maximise passenger-miles per pound of budget'. Not only is this unverifiable, because it uses the word 'maximise' (see page 40), and not only does it sidestep the question of what the budget should be, but in addition it is set in terms of an operational ratio (passenger-miles) and so is a departmental objective masquerading as a corporate objective (see page 35). No, this is useless as *corporate* objective.

The whole area of corporate objectives for nationalised companies is a fascinating one, which must, however, not detain us further. Suffice it to say that, if anyone is still in doubt as to the crucial importance of correctly identifying corporate objectives, I suggest to him that the failure of successive British governments to determine the corporate objectives for nationalised companies has resulted, over the past three decades, in a waste of national financial and managerial resources on a scale that can only be called catastrophic.

The stakeholder theory

As I understand the rules of modern capitalism, the shareholder is recognised as the intended beneficiary – indeed, as the sole intended beneficiary. However, contrary to popular opinion this does not place the shareholder in the position of first in the queue for his company's benefits. Quite the contrary; he is the last man in the queue. He is the 'residual legatee'. He can take anything that is left over *after* the company has met its obligations to the rest of society. Furthermore, it is society that decides what these obligations are to be. If the company has nothing left over after meeting them, the shareholder gets nothing; indeed, if the company cannot meet these obligations, it has to dip into its reserves (which are part of the 'shareholders' funds') in order to do so.

Exhibit 2.4   Diagram of the capitalist system

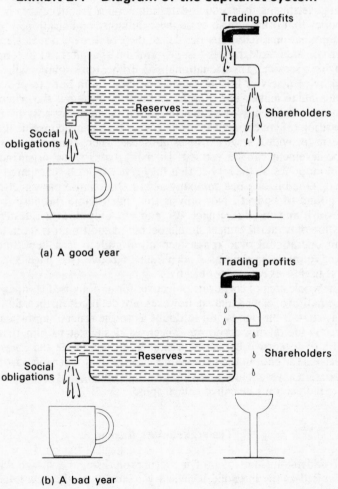

(a) A good year

(b) A bad year

Exhibit 2.4 shows this capitalist philosophy. In Exhibit 2.4 (a) the trading profits are pouring in so fast that the company can not only meet its obligations (the diameter of the 'obligations' pipe is decided by society) but also fill the shareholders' cup till it runs over. However, in Exhibit 2.4 (b) the trading profits are poor, and the flow of obligations has drawn down the level of reserves, so the shareholder gets nothing. Moreover, he not only gets no dividend but also loses some of his capital reserves.

Now, the stakeholder theory says that shareholders do not, or ought not to, enjoy this special relation. Everyone who has anything to do

Exhibit 2.5 Diagram of the stakeholder system

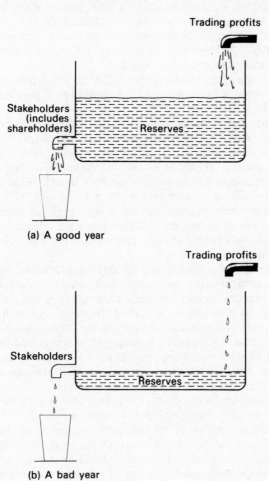

(a) A good year

(b) A bad year

with a company – shareholders, employees, the local community – should be deemed to have a stake in that company. Not only is this theory put forward to right a wrong that does not exist, namely, the belief that shareholders are first in the queue, but in addition it seems to me to make the position of stakeholders worse *vis-à-vis* the shareholder, not better. In Exhibit 2.5(a) everyone does very well indeed; but if the company has a bad year, everyone does very badly indeed (see Exhibit 2.5(b), where shareholders receive smaller dividends, employees receive smaller wages, and everyone suffers equally).

Apart from this defect there are a number of other theoretical questions to which I know no satisfactory answers. Who are these stakeholders? Clearly, they include shareholders, employees, customers, the state and the local community. Is there anyone else? What about suppliers (who are seldom mentioned by stakeholder theorists – oddly, in my view)? What about competitors, pensioned employees and the underprivileged? I have seen 'technology' listed as a stakeholder, but I do not understand what that means.

Also, assuming that we know who they all are, what do they want from the company? Can they ask for anything? If not, what can the company deny them, and on what grounds?

Also, who should decide who the stakeholders are to be, and who should decide whether they can have what they want? Suppose, for example, that we agree that shareholders and employees are the two most important stakeholders, and suppose that they are given powerful representation on their company's board. What recognition will they be willing to give to the other stakeholders' claims? The question is not an academic one, as many people all over the world would argue that these two stakeholders have already caused the legitimate claims of other groups, customers in particular, to be rudely brushed aside.

We do not have the mechanisms for making these decisions. Not even the European supervisory boards, to which such great thought has been given, yet function at all effectively, although they certainly function better than any alternatives in Britain. However, not even in Europe have they made the necessary changes in the centuries-old laws based upon Roman and Napoleonic concepts of property and the rights of ownership, not to mention the duties of directors enshrined in Companies Acts for generations. *De jure* all companies are still capitalist, even if *de facto* they are already socialist.

Also, if there are half a dozen equal but diverse stakeholders, who decides where the company should invest resources, who decides whether the company has failed and should be wound up, who decides which managers to appoint, dismiss or promote, and who decides whether the company should expand overseas, not at home?

Also, does the company have to recruit locally when unemployment is high, even though the company is already overmanned and making a loss? This may sound ridiculous, but what exactly are the criteria for deciding what each stakeholder's 'equal' stake must be? For example, does a 10 per cent cut in shareholders' dividend equal 10 per cent fewer jobs for the local community or 5 per cent fewer?

My point is this: capitalism may be outdated and inappropriate in the world of today, and the stakeholder theory may be the philosophy of the future, but it certainly needs some polishing before I should like to use it as a guide to my corporate actions!

Quite apart from these theoretical objections I believe that there is a huge practical one as well. I do not believe that anyone really knows how to manage a multipurpose organisation in practice. In my view the stakeholder theory, which finds great favour among those who manage larger organisations, is greatly responsible for the severe loss of nerve in these organisations. In attempting to be all things to all men they have simply become nothing to anyone. In attempting to play Father Christmas to the whole of society without any clear rules regulating who gets which present, their managers have lost their way in a maze that they were never trained to understand. Most managers have been instructed in the art of project appraisal, for example, using return on investment as the criterion, but, they have not been taught how to use multiple-criteria project-appraisal techniques – and that makes the generous assumption that such techniques have any validity. However, let us leave aside the practical problems, daunting though these may be. The nub of the question that I am raising here is a value judgement – a philosophical and ethical conundrum – namely: is the stakeholder theory wrong?

Another statement of corporate objective, vaguely related to the stakeholder theory, suggests that companies exist 'to provide the goods and services needed (or required) by society'. I am less than convinced by this concept. I doubt that it reflects the motives of most businessmen, although it may reflect the views of managers in large organisations. I assume that profit is used as an indicator of success or failure in providing what society requires, but this still leaves a number of questions unanswerable under the theory.

Should a company produce goods for export to another nation (that is, another society)? If a company is making a loss, what should be done about it? If it is making a good profit, should it introduce another product to make an even better profit? Should it provide any products at a loss? All these questions are given fairly clear answers under the capitalist theory but not under this one. In any case I am sure that few new companies would ever be formed if the purpose in forming them were merely to 'provide goods and services for society'. If it were to 'make a profit for the founding shareholders', this would be a different matter!

Summary

In the first of their working sessions the corporate planning team will discuss corporate objectives. A corporate objective, or purpose, is the *raison d'être* of the entire company as a corporate entity. It is determined by or for the people for whose benefit the company exists, namely, under the capitalist system, the shareholders. (In the stake-holder theory the intended beneficiaries are the people deemed to have a stake in the company. This raises the questions of who these people are and what they are entitled to ask of the company.)

For most companies in capitalist nations there will be no difficulty in agreeing that their sole purpose is to generate a return on share-holders' capital, subject to a vital constraint, namely, the manner in which the company discharges the obligations imposed upon it by society and by its own ethos. Morally, it would be quite wrong for any benefit to accrue to any shareholders (who are or should be in the position of residual legatees) unless and until all these obligations had been discharged. Many companies today take special care to define their obligations and attitudes to their employees.

Some severe misunderstandings as to the nature of corporate objectives exist and should be avoided. The word 'maximise' is without meaning, as is the word 'survive'. It is vital to understand that the corporate objective is the aim; everything else is a possible means. Turnover, market shares, mergers, margins, products, factories, subsidiary companies – all these are pawns to be moved with one aim in mind, namely to achieve a return on shareholders' capital, and decisions about these are the output of the corporate planning process, not the input.

The corporate objective must be determined by or for shareholders; strategies are determined by managers. If a set of strategies is not likely to achieve an objective, it is the strategies that must be changed, or the managers, but not the objective. Ethos is decided by society, or by the managers in accordance with how they see society's views.

There are also some difficult cases, most of which arise because of multiple objectives set by one beneficiary or, worse, by several different beneficiaries. A wide variety of measures is available to the team for dealing with this problem: accept the problem as insoluble, hive off one of the beneficiaries, split the organisation itself, appoint an independent chairman, representative council or supervisory board, and so on. None is as satisfactory as having a single beneficiary with a single aim. Nationalised companies have this hybrid problem, but a solution to it is not impossible nor even very difficult, given stable political conditions. The stakeholder theory seems to raise problems, both theoretical and practical, that are very much further from solution than is generally realised.

Finally, since this chapter is philosophical, political and moral in nature, I ought to emphasise that the views expressed here are my own, formed and reformed in countless discussions with countless company directors all over the world during the past decade. What matters, of course, is not my views nor my answers to the questions, but the questions themselves and *your* answers. These are the questions that your planning team should ask; ensure that a consensus forms over the answers. In the vast majority of firms these questions have never been asked, let alone answered. The older and larger a company is, the more it will have lost its sense of direction.

In the next chapter we shall consider what level of performance shareholders are entitled to ask for. In other words we shall have to put some figures to the concept 'return on shareholders' capital'.

CHAPTER 3

Corporate Targets

The previous chapter was almost entirely philosophical in character and, assuming that one takes the capitalist view, relatively simple. Many teams will be able to reach a consensus over their corporate objective and ethos in a few hours or even minutes. The target, to which we must now turn our attention, will take much longer. There is little philosophy here. Instead, there are some tricky technical problems and a number of calculations to make, and these will occupy the team for one or perhaps two meetings as well as involve a lot of hard work for the company's financial staff and advisers.

First, however, we have to decide what is to be the time horizon of the planning exercise. Do we need a five-year target, a ten-year, or what? Since the corporate planning exercise is essentially about changing the structure of one's company to meet the changing world, the only time horizon that cannot be too short is the time required to change the structure of the company. For a giant chemical company to convert itself into a giant electronics company, for example, might take several decades; very well, that would be the correct horizon for its planning.

Few planners would accept this conclusion without question; and frankly it is a somewhat theoretical answer, since very few companies are going to have to change everything. However, at the other end of the scale I can see little point in planning for less than five years, because that is the period of many of the world's economic cycles (*pace* Kondratieff, a Russian economist, who has said that there are also twenty-five-year economic cycles). Since most companies are affected by the fluctuations within these cycles, it would be foolish not to plan over the whole cycle from trough to trough or peak to peak.

Now, five years is a long time. The errors in five-year forecasts are enormous, and they are not much worse for ten, although beyond that the future becomes somewhat blurred to say the least. Most corporate plans lie within these two limits.

Of course, no company should plan five years ahead if some

momentous event is likely to occur six years ahead. Also, in many cases the precise time horizon turns out not to be important. All that matters is that, when a strategy is selected at the end of the process, any predicted event that is of strategic importance be taken into account in the selected strategy regardless of when that event is expected to occur, even if no one knows when that may be. A glass-bottle manufacturer, for example, may well see plastics as a very real threat to his existence; and even if he believes that plastics will make no serious inroads into his business for fifteen years, he will be wise to tailor some of his strategies with that event in mind. Also, a timber grower must look ahead to the maturity of his trees. A company in a declining industry must at least bear in mind the probable date when it may start making losses.

Sometimes the horizon of the plan need not be as long as the horizon chosen for the forecast, and only very occasionally do companies need to make detailed calculations much beyond five years, even though the strategy may be intended to embrace ten or more. On balance, bearing in mind that this book is intended for medium-sized companies beginning the corporate planning process, I recommend a five-year horizon for targets and forecasts, at least to start with.

One other word to introduce this chapter: for a company a target is what it *wants* – an aim, a hope, a desire – whereas a forecast is what the company expects to happen, whether it wants this to or not. It seems to me rather important to understand that targets and forecasts are not the same things. A plan, of course, is what the company intends to do to close any gap between what it wants to happen and what it expects to happen. In the context in which I am using these words they both suggest figures; a target is usually a number, and in management a forecast also is very often a number.

Thus, a corporate target is the numerical expression of what a company wants to achieve; it is the corporate objective expressed in figures.

Three target-setting problems

The task before us is to put some figures on to the corporate objective. If this has been identified as 'generate a return on shareholders' capital', we need to select a figure that reflects the shareholders' demands. If it had been identified as 'generate a benefit for each stakeholder', we should have the unenviable task, to which I shall return later on, of setting targets for each stakeholder.

This target, then, is to reflect the level of performance that the shareholders want, demand or are entitled to expect from their company over the next five years. However, this depends on innumerable other factors. Should they be thinking of a satisfactory level of performance, a tolerable one, an acceptable one or an amazing one? Should they take account of the company's past and present record and the industry in which it is operating? How is return on shareholders' capital measured anyway?

Exhibit 3.1   The three target-setting problems

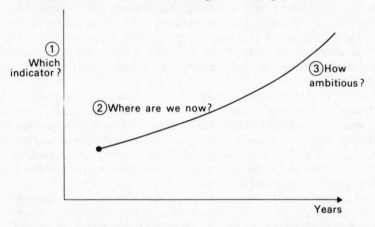

All such questions boil down to three major problem areas. Consider Exhibit 3.1, which shows in diagrammatic form the (simplified) requirements of any shareholder in any company. What he generally wants is an improving reward on his investment. If his dividend this year is £12, for example, he looks forward to, say, £13 next year. However, clearly this is not all. It is not only dividends that he wants; he looks forward to capital gains too. How are we going to measure these two different requirements? So, one problem is which performance indicators to use. Suppose that the £12 dividend this year represents a *reduction* on last year, when he received £15; this will certainly influence his hopes for next year. So, 'Where are we now?' or selecting a suitable base year is problem number two. The third problem is probably the most difficult, namely: how ambitious is a shareholder entitled to be? Should he demand rapid growth (which is often very risky), slow reliable growth or no growth at all?

These are the three problems that I shall discuss.

Problem 1: which indicator?

There are a number of candidates for the role of indicator (or index or proxy, as it is sometimes called) of overall company performance.

ROSC. The most obvious one is return on shareholders' capital (ROSC). Suppose that a shareholder buys five shares for £20 each at the start of the year, receives a dividend of £4 and then sells his shares for £106. His ROSC is 10 per cent; he has had £4 in dividend and £6 in capital gains. Notice that this is real money, not book values; nothing is estimated or written down; it is cash.

Most shareholders leave their money in a company for several years, and we can use the discounted-cash-flow (d.c.f.) method to sum several years' dividends, gains, bonus issues, and so on. Thus, Exhibit 3.2 shows a shareholder who bought five shares for £20 each in year 1, received dividends of £5 and £6 in years 2 and 3 and then received a bonus share in a 1–5 issue. He sold out soon afterwards for £120·49. His ROSC over the period was 10 per cent. So, ROSC can easily be calculated for one year or for several.

Exhibit 3.2   Calculation of return on shareholders' capital

Year	Operation	Cash flow (£)	10% discount factor	Discounted cash flow (£)
1	He buys 5 shares for £20 each	−100·00	1·000	−100·00
2	He receives a dividend of £5	+5·00	0·909	+4·55
3	He receives a dividend of £6	+6·00	0·826	+4·96
4	He receives 1 share as a bonus	0·00	—	0·00
	He sells all 6 shares for £120·49	+120·49	0·751	+90·49
			Total	0·00

Note: If in year 4 the stock market fell by 30 per cent, the shareholder could sell out for only £84, and his overall ROSC would be negative.

I believe this indicator to be so important that the team must use it in its own calculations, although one of its disadvantages is that it is rather esoteric, so not everyone outside the team will understand it. Its other disadvantage is that for companies quoted on a stock market the fluctuations in share values, which often have nothing whatever to do with the performance of a company, can severely distort the calculations. If in Exhibit 3.2 the share price dropped by, say, 30 per cent just when the shareholder was selling, his overall ROSC would swing from 10 per cent to a loss. On the other hand, if a company's shares are not quoted, this makes it difficult to establish just what the share price is at any given time.

These two disadvantages of ROSC – its remoteness from everyday company discussions and calculations, and its instability – lead us to look very carefully at the next candidate.

EpS.   Earnings per share (EpS) has the great advantage that it relates quite closely to profits, which everyone understands. In general, if profits double, so will EpS; if they go down, so will EpS (but see below). Also, since it does not include capital values, it is not affected by stock market gyrations.

I am sure that it should be used, therefore. However, note that the very fact that it does not include share values is a major defect, for share-holders very definitely do care what the price of their shares is, and the market worth of their company should always be a major consideration in the minds of managers. This defect is so severe that, I believe, the following firm rule should be made: if EpS *is* used (without also using ROSC), some other measure of the market value of the company's shares must also be employed alongside. Perhaps it is worth noting that, if a company's EpS record is average, its price–earnings (P/E) ratio also will be average; but if its record (or its prospects) is above average, its P/E ratio also will be above average. In other words there is a sense in which capital values *are* implied in the EpS indicator. However, in my view this link is too tenuous to be relied upon; and if a company adopts EpS, it should also adopt some direct method of measuring share values, as suggested above.

Profits.   This is an immensely strong candidate, because it is so widely used and understood throughout the various levels of management in all companies. However, it suffers from some truly terrible dis-advantages. It does not include capital values (like EpS). It may not correctly measure the effects of a merger (unlike EpS, which does more correctly do this; thus, a company could double its profits over-night by a merger, but this might halve its EpS!). It does not reflect share issues (which EpS does). Inflation has eroded its meaning. It ignores tax. What a list! However, it simply has to be used as an indicator, because it is so widely understood.

So, now we have three – ROSC, EpS and profits – and the whole exercise is becoming dangerously complicated. If we are not very careful, we may select three targets that are mathematically irreconcilable, for do not forget that each of these indicators is related to the others through their linking financial ratios, as exemplified in Exhibit 3.3.

Mercifully, I believe that these three are all that are needed. Each has its own advantages and disadvantages; but if they are taken together in a basket, the disadvantages cancel out. ROSC is all-embracing, profits are satisfactory for most normal uses and in discus-sions with employees, and EpS is well known to bankers and

Exhibit 3.3 The three main target indicators and their interlinking ratios*

Indicator or ratio	Year 0	Year 1	Year 2	Year 3
No. of shares issued	10,000	10,000	10,000	10,000
EpS target	10·00p	11·00p	12·10p	13·31p
Earnings	£1,000	£1,100	£1,210	£1,331
Profits	£2,500	£2,750	£3,025	£3,328
Dividends paid	£300	£330	£363	£400
Dividends per share	3·00p	3·30p	3·63p	4·00p
P/E ratio	10	10	10	10
Capitalisation	£10,000	£11,000	£12,100	£13,310
Price per share	100p	110p	121p	133p
ROSC**	—	13·3%	13·3%	13·3%

*The calculations make the following extremely-oversimplified assumptions:
that there are no share issues during this period; that the EpS target is a simple
10 per cent p.a. growth; that there are no changes in taxation rates or dividend rates;
and that profits, dividends, and so on therefore all rise at a steady 10 per cent p.a.
If there is a share issue, or a major loan is obtained or paid back, or the P/E
ratio improves, the calculations become somewhat involved.

**Calculated annually only, that is, the annual dividend per share plus the annual
capital gain in share price divided by the share price = ROSC. The d.c.f. return
for a shareholder who bought shares in year 1 and sold in year 3 is also, of course,
13·3 per cent.

stockbrokers. Furthermore, I believe that all the other candidates for
the position of overall performance indicator have insuperable defects.
The most important of these candidates are described below.

ROCE. Return on capital employed (ROCE) or return on net assets
(RONA) is a most useful and important short term management ratio.
It was never designed as a long term indicator and so several years'
performances cannot be added up to get an overall long term indicator.
This is exactly what we must be able to do in long term planning;
and although ROSC allows us to do this (using d.c.f.), ROCE does not.

Another problem with ROCE is that inflation has severely undermined the various definitions and valuations on which the capital
employed part of the ROCE ratio is based. Written-down values,
replacement costs, depreciation – the problems are well known to every
accountant in the world and need no further exposition here.

Then, there is the question of exactly what ROCE measures.
Suppose that a company revalues its property assets; the capital
employed will rise, and ROCE will *fall*. So, this is bad news, is it?
However, surely the discovery that the company's property is now
worth more than last year is good news? Surely ROSC will go up?

Quite rightly, since a capital gain has been made for the shareholders. Yet, ROCE goes down!

Sometimes a company actually *wants* ROCE to go down, as I have suggested (page 41), but to set a *falling* ROCE target is unheard of. This is clear evidence, I believe, that ROCE is a dangerous indicator, because people are confused by it. Almost every company that uses ROCE as a corporate target sets a rising or 'improving' target. Yet, once a company's ROCE is comfortably above the cost of capital, the higher it sets the ROCE target, the fewer will be the projects that it is able to find, and its rate of expansion may slow down. This would lead to the company's becoming a static high profit earner, which is a perfectly good strategy except that it excludes the other perfectly good strategy of becoming a rapidly expanding low profit earner! I am most strongly opposed to eliminating any strategy at this early stage of the corporate planning exercise and even more strongly opposed to doing this by such arbitrary means.

Another problem emerges when one comes to try to select a suitable target figure for ROCE. Should a company aim at the ROCE that represents a comfortable margin above the cost of capital, at the average ROCE for its industry or at its own average ROCE for the past five years? The rationale behind any of these choices is often difficult to follow. There is one level of ROCE below which no target should ever be set, namely, the cost of capital. Plainly, it makes no sense for a firm borrowing money at, say, 8 per cent to aim for a ROCE of 7 per cent. As a long stop, therefore, in this context ROCE is useful, although precisely the same function can be performed by a ROSC target.

Furthermore, ROCE says nothing about growth. When a chairman thumps the boardroom table and demands that the company's ROCE be raised from 12 to 15 per cent, neither he nor anyone else knows what that implies for the growth of profits. In recognition of this defect ROCE targets are often linked with growth targets – for example, 'We shall aim at 20 per cent ROCE and 10 per cent growth' – but I know of no means of deciding whether 20 and 10 per cent are preferable to 10 and 20 per cent, or 15 and 15 per cent, or 30 and 0 per cent. Again, I believe that ROCE misleads rather than informs.

ROCE variants. In spite of its many disadvantages most companies use ROCE. Some use ingenious variants of it. There is return on working capital (ROWC), for example, used by merchants, dealers and others who employ mainly working capital. Any fixed assets that they have they recalculate in revenue terms. Thus, they nominally charge themselves a market rent on buildings, a leasing charge on equipment, and so on. At the opposite end is return on trading assets (ROTA), where all fixed assets are revalued at current market equivalents.

Then, there is return on shareholders' funds (ROSF), which is the figure shown in the balance sheet; the 'return' will be attributable earnings in this case. All these have various disadvantages. ROSF looks attractive, but note that it is book value only; the real live shareholder is looking at his share price in the stock market. If a company begins to perform very well, the P/E ratio will rise much faster than ROSF, and the market capitalisation will run ahead of 'shareholders' funds'. It may be even more dramatic if the company has a poor year; its share price and the P/E ratio may collapse, while its book values hardly change.

I must emphasise that the above remarks relate to the use of ROCE as a top *corporate* target, where I am suggesting that its disadvantages exceed its advantages. I prefer ROSC to ROCE. However, when we come to setting top financial targets to *subsidiary* companies and profit centres, ROCE is not just useful; it is essential. I shall return to this exercise much later on (see page 180), where I shall emphasise the need to treat ROCE with care even in this role. Its use demands that the parent company insist on standard accounting procedures, careful transfer pricing and allocation of overheads among its subsidiaries or profit centres before ROCE can be used at all; but even here, where its use is obligatory, it can still mislead.

Growth. Most companies aim to grow. However, at this stage in the planning process we are only concerned with shareholders' financial objectives, so consideration of the growth of all physical things – number of employees, size of factory, turnover, and so on – must be postponed. Growth of financial things must be considered, however.

Growth of what? Profits? Almost certainly, but pause just long enough to note that steady profits (in real terms, of course), so long as they are high enough, are often a perfectly acceptable aim for many shareholders. Pause long enough too to note that 'make a fast buck' is also a possibility; for example the shareholder who invests £100 in a company and receives three massive but *declining* annual dividends – say, £70, £50 and £30 – before it goes bust probably receives a better ROSC than he could from most conventional companies. Also let us not forget that some sections of society deem large profits to be highly immoral; consequently if a company's profits are already high, growth of profits will seem an inappropriate aim. So, nil growth or even de-growth is not to be rejected out of hand.

Generally, however, growth of profits is a major aim. So is growth of EpS. So is growth of ROSC, provided that it is not already too high, and it need be no higher than the opportunity cost of equity capital plus a prudent margin. Growth, then, is almost always an absolutely essential ingredient in the array of financial targets of most companies. Indeed, many companies take growth of profits or EpS for granted, and discussion will centre on the most appropriate rate of growth to select or the quality of that growth. For example, a long steady reliable record of gradual growth often impresses the stock exchange more than a dramatic spurt, and this may be an important or even over-riding consideration to a private company that is about to seek a public quotation.

Growth of profits or EpS, then, or sometimes of ROSC, is an appropriate corporate target. Growth of anything else is invalid at this stage.

Ratios.   All management ratios are invalid, I believe. Yet, time after time sales margins or market share targets are adopted by companies as corporate targets alongside or even above profit targets. I cannot understand this. Suppose that a company is making a profit of £1m. and that its market share is 10 per cent. Now imagine that two targets are set for year 5: £2m. profit and 20 per cent market share. Now imagine that the company discovers, in year 2 say, that the more it tries to increase market share, the more it has to cut margins, and the lower its profits are going to be. Which target does it abandon: the £2m. profit or the 20 per cent market share? If, as I suspect it will be, it is the latter, does not this prove that it should never have been placed alongside the profit target in importance? How silly to select '20 per cent market share' at the start of the corporate planning process! Yet, innumerable plans do start this way.

A similar argument applies to margins on sales. A target to 'increase sales margins from 8 to 10 per cent' may well be a sensible one in many strategic situations, but it is by no means universally valid. Sometimes, it is more appropriate to *decrease* margins on sales. Until a company's strategic situation has been analysed, it seems downright silly for them to plump for increasing margins, thereby excluding all strategies that would reduce them – or vice versa.

I believe that this practice of starting the corporate planning process with a set of management ratios or operational ratios as 'corporate targets' is idiotic. I once saw a corporate plan that began by setting out a pyramid of thirteen management ratios as corporate targets. These so trussed up the company that no strategic options existed anywhere!

My rule, then, is: never set a target and then tailor strategies to hit it. Never, for example, set a rising margin-on-sales target and then have to move up-market to hit it. By all means tackle it in the reverse order, however; that is, decide on rational grounds to go up-market, and then set rising margin-on-sales targets to act as milestones along the chosen route. Ratios are invaluable in this role as management control devices to keep you on the rails.

I know of no ratio that is inherently better because it is bigger. A high ROCE is not necessarily better than a low one (so long as it exceeds the cost of capital). A big value-added per employee can merely tell us that this company is more vertically integrated than a company with a low one. A high turnover–assets ratio can describe a company that is undercapitalised just as well as one that is using its assets efficiently; and horror of horrors, it can even mean that the company is overtrading and will shortly become insolvent.

I shall use dozens of management and accounting ratios throughout this book, but never as a target at the corporate level. Let me give an example of how confused everything is made by grabbing ratios out of the air and using them as targets. The company concerned set the following targets: turnover to double by year 5, margin on sales to be 10 per cent, ROCE to be 25 per cent and exports to rise to 50 per cent by year 5. These targets and the ratios for year 0 are shown in Table 3.1.

Table 3.1

Ratio (%)	Actual for year 0	Targets for year 5
Margin on sales	5·0	10·0
ROCE	14·4	25·0
Exports as % of sales	16·2	50·0

These ratios were chosen by the chairman himself, but unfortunately he had neglected to work out what they meant in actual money. Table 3.2 gives the actual figures for year 0 together with the figures for year 5 implied by the target ratios. Notice how home sales rise by less than £8m. or about 4 per cent p.a. for five years. The chairman was somewhat taken aback by this conclusion. He was equally astounded at the task that he had inadvertently set the export manager. So was the export manager.

Table 3.2

Indicator (£m.)	Actual for year 0	Targets for year 5
Turnover	48·2	96·4
Home sales	40·4	48·2
Export sales	7·8	48·2
Profits	2·4	9·6
Capital employed	16·6	38·4

However, that is not all. Table 3.3 gives my own alternative target ratios and figures for year 5 for this company. I also have grabbed the figures out of thin air. Which do you think would be best for this

Table 3.3

Ratio or indicator	Actual for year 0	Chairman's targets for year 5	My targets for year 5
Margin on sales (%)	5·0	10·0	7·5
ROCE (%)	14·4	25·0	30·0
Exports as % of sales	16·2	50·0	20·0
Turnover (£m.)	48·2	96·4	128·0
Home sales (£m.)	40·4	48·2	102·4
Export sales (£m.)	7·8	48·2	25·6
Profits (£m.)	2·4	9·6	9·6
Capital employed (£m.)	16·6	38·4	32·0

company: the chairman's set or mine? The answer is that you haven't the faintest idea. The only way to select these targets is to go all the way through the corporate planning process to examine the company's skills, its strategic situation today, its financial position, and so forth. To make these decisions and set this sort of target *before* going through the process seems to me quite absurd. The targets should come out of the process. As a matter of fact, and just to make the point another way, this particular company did go through the process of corporate planning after setting these targets, and it came out very strongly indeed that neither the sales to the home market not to the export market, nor even the sales turnover nor the margin on sales, mattered in the least. What mattered to this company was that a well-established technological change was gnawing away at the central core of its business! Some of the executives had been saying so for several years, but the true extent of the damage being done to the business had not been grasped in the boardroom.

Section Summary. To summarise this rather long section of this chapter: since we have identified the corporate objective as 'return on shareholders' capital', the search for a suitable numerical target is logically limited to financial ratios, and all accounting ratios and management ratios are best relegated to lower levels in the hierarchy of objectives, that is, the *outputs* of the planning process. The three financial indicators that look most useful at the very top are ROSC, EpS and profits; taken together as a trio they have few failings except perhaps their complexity. If one only has to be chosen, it should be EpS, which, although not directly taking account of capital values, does indirectly reflect them through the P/E ratio.

No other indicators are valid at this corporate level, although for subsidiaries and profit centres, and for nationalised companies (which sometimes are in fact simply subsidiaries of the state), ROCE is useful or essential. In some non-company, and therefore non-profit-seeking, organisations share of the market may be a key indicator, or even the only indicator, of how well or badly they are performing.

Problem 2: 'Where are we now?'

The second problem in the target-setting sequence is, using the indicators now selected, to decide whether the company's present or current performance is suitable for use as a base (see Exhibit 3.1). For many companies it is suitable, and we can then go ahead to problem number three, which is to select a suitable target level of performance for year 5, year 10 or whatever. Sometimes, however, the current year's performance is exceptionally good or exceptionally poor and so provides a thoroughly unreliable norm, benchmark or startline for the planning process.

How can you tell whether your company's current performance is satisfactory? There are three quite simple tests. The first is to examine the company's past few years' performance in respect of ROSC, EpS and profits. If they display a good smooth upward trend (after you have stripped inflation out of the sequence of figures, of course), this is an encouraging sign. If the curve is sharply up or down in the current or recent years or very flat for the past several years, perhaps the company's current performance is rather above or below norm. It is, of course, most important to notice whether this performance has resulted from some financial or other deterioration and whether it does truly reflect a genuine improvement or worsening in performance. For example, for a time it is possible for a company to show a remarkably good succession of results simply by cutting margins and increasing loan capital (this is known as overtrading), but there can only be one eventual outcome from this behaviour: it goes bust! However, it can look quite impressive for a time. Make sure there has been no erosion of dividend or interest cover.

The second test is to compare your company's past and current performances with those of competitors. Check such ratios as profits per employee, ROCE, margin on sales, value added per pound total remuneration, growth of profits, and so on as in any conventional inter-firm comparison, except that this one needs to be in rather less detail than usual and for rather more years into the past than usual. As a result of this exercise you might find, for example, that although your company made a profit of £1m. last year, a competitor with the same number of employees made £1·3m. and another competitor with twice your capital employed made £2·7m.; both results would suggest that your profits last year were perhaps 30 per cent too low. Be careful with inflation and inflation accounting when comparing other companies, especially foreign ones.

The third method of establishing a stable base is to ask the experts. Go to a banker, accountant, merchant banker, stockbroker or investment analyst and seek his opinion on the performance of your company compared to others. By using such tools as P/E ratio, dividend cover, income gearing and the quality of your assets he will be able to offer a useful opinion.

One word of warning is needed. In the case of groups, holding companies or parent companies the question 'Where are we now?' can and should be asked of each subsidiary or profit centre. Great care is needed to ensure that transfer pricing, allocation of central overheads, and so on are uniform throughout the company. I know of one company where, it was believed, the company's total profits arose from its three subsidiaries almost equally; but, it was discovered, due to biased transfer pricing between them one was in reality making a huge loss. In another case the opposite situation was revealed; the subsidiary traditionally believed to be making a small loss for several years past was found to be profitable. (In this case the products of this subsidiary were sold through another; by the time the products were sold inflation had raised their prices, and this increase was all being reaped by the selling subsidiary.)

There can be three possible outcomes to these 'Where are we now?' inquiries. One is that your company's performance is quite normal, in which case you go on to the third problem. Another is that it is not normal, in which case it is not usually very difficult, using the three methods outlined above, to pinpoint a level of current performance that can be considered normal. You will then be able to state 'Last year our profits were 15 per cent too low, and any profit target that we set must take this into account'.

The remaining outcome, which does happen occasionally, is that no agreement is possible. I recall one case where five members of a board thought that the company's current performance was not too bad at £1·2m. profits; the marketing director was adamant, however, that £1·2m. was half of what it should be, even taking account of the depressed state of the industry at that time. So acrimonious did this dispute threaten to become that, contrary to my normal procedure, I suggested that they continue the planning process without setting the target. Towards the end of the process a consensus emerged, without any further formal discussion of the subject, that the marketing director was probably right.

This, then, is an important general lesson. Although my strong advice is to proceed along the planning process in exactly the sequence being described in this book, there are certain to be occasions when it is better to jump backwards or forwards. As I have said (page 22), the process is fundamentally a straight-through sequence with frequent cycling back and forth to check and modify previous conclusions.

However, in the case mentioned above it was more than a mere cycling; it was the deliberate temporary omission of a whole step – not to be recommended lightly.

One further word on establishing the 'base camp': since we are about to set a profit target for the company for five or even ten years into the future, surely it really hardly matters whether the profits this year are or should be £1·1m. or £1·14m.? Although it is vital to know the situation within reasonable bounds of error, there is a strict limit to the amount of effort that it is worth putting in to establish the last decimal place.

Problem 3: setting the target

The difficulty here is quite simple. If a company decides to set an ambitious target for itself, not only can this place shareholders' capital at risk, but in addition the effect on morale of failing to achieve the target can be serious. Yet, to do the opposite is equally unattractive; a low pedestrian level of performance is not going to inspire managers, employees or shareholders. Not even a compromise somewhere in the middle is much use; by definition it is not going to be a very inspiring figure to aim at either.

In my view there is no solution to this difficulty, unless we break with the traditional methods of setting targets. There just is no one figure that is right for all occasions. We shall have to use two figures – a bracket of targets – to cover all legitimate opinions, for we must remember that 'shareholders' are not usually a homogeneous group of people all holding one view on how well the company can be expected to perform over the next few years. Also, we are not concerned only with the views of shareholders; the managers will certainly have something to say about the level of performance that they hope their company will attain.

Thus, suppose that a company's present profits are £1m. If we asked the shareholders what level of profits would satisfy them for year 5, they might say £1·15m. However, the managers might be disgusted with such an out-turn and not be satisfied with less than £1·3m.; some young turks might even go for £2m. How can we possibly accommodate this situation with a traditional target? *Any* figure chosen will be wrong! This is not an academic joke; those who set targets in this way find out that it cannot be done – painfully sometimes. No one likes to be seen publicly hauling down last year's tattered banner with '£5m.' on it and running up a little rag with '£2·5m.' written on it – in pencil in case it is wrong again!

My invariable practice now is to set not a single-figure target but a band or bracket of targets. Exhibit 3.4 shows a company that made a

Exhibit 3.4   A bracket target

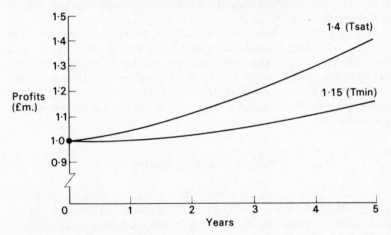

profit of £1m. in its base year and is aiming at £1·4m. in year 5, or anything above or anything below, so long as it is *not* below £1·15m.

What on earth does this mean, you may exclaim? Surely the bracket is so wide that it is not worth the trouble of selecting the figures? However, take the figure £1·15m. This represents the absolute minimum that the shareholders feel that they can accept (it is labelled Tmin in the exhibit). After all it is less than 3 per cent p.a. growth, and well over half of the companies in Europe and America should be able to beat that. 'Why,' the shareholders would say, 'that sort of performance is going to be well below average. I am not interested in keeping my money in that sort of company.' No management could possibly contemplate setting its sights at a below average target.

I attach enormous significance to Tmin. Not only is it fairly easy to identify – the question to shareholders or their advisers is a straightforward 'What is the worst performance that you would tolerate from your company before you sold your shares or sacked the management?' – but also it provides the ultimate criterion for the later selection of a strategy. The strategy then selected not only has to have a good chance of achieving a *good* performance but *in addition* has to render the company virtually impregnable against a fall in profits to below that dreaded £1·15m. in year 5.

Tmin corresponds to that level of performance which is so low as to be painful. It is to be avoided at all costs. Below it lie despair and disgrace. Thus, I believe Tmin to represent a very clearly recognisable point on a scale of performance, and it can be identified by every entrepreneur for his own little company and by all senior executives for theirs, however large.

The same is true for the other point on Exhibit 3.4, namely, the Tsat target. This is where the entrepreneur or manager feels that he has done quite well – not outstanding, not terrible, just quite well. The result is satisfactory. Both of these points – Tmin and Tsat – reflect more closely than any previous target-setting procedure, I believe, what real human beings feel about their own aims and ambitions for their companies and for themselves.

Let us return to the upper edge of the bracket in Exhibit 3.4, that is, the figure of £1·4m. This is the level that the shareholders regard as being 'satisfactory'. If it is achieved, no joyous hats will be thrown in the air, but neither will there be a beating of disappointed breasts. As a matter of fact this figure – £1·4m. by year 5 – represents an annual rate of growth of 7 per cent, which even by the standards of the 1960s is more than merely satisfactory in the opinion of many company directors. It is, of course, up to each company to decide its own figures.

Sometimes an upper figure has to be determined. This, called Tmax, is not shown in Exhibit 3.4, because it does not often need to be set. It has to be selected when there is some upper figure that represents an embarrassment of riches. I know of two cases. One is a non-profit-making charity that made a 'surplus', as it was called, of £5m. on a turnover of £20m. for each of several years. The other is a southern European company owned by a well-known capitalist family. Its products enjoy great popularity but are ridiculously profitable. Not only is the company regularly pilloried in the left-wing press, but members of the family constantly go in fear of their personal safety as well.

The need to set Tmax targets may be rare for such medium-sized companies as those for whom this book is mainly intended, but it is very commonly necessary for large companies, multinationals and nationalised corporations.

Bracket targets

The idea of a bracket target as described above does not represent a fallback compromise from the traditional single-figure target. I believe that the single-figure target is and always has been a mistake. I do not believe that anyone, whether shareholder, manager, entrepreneur or private individual, ever defines his ambitions in terms of one finite level of performance. They all have in mind a whole range of possible and hoped-for outcomes, stretching all the way from some dreaded and disgraceful level above which they must strive to aim at all costs through to some almost incredible and even embarrassing level of success. Somewhere in the middle is a level that they regard as satisfactory.

What figure should be selected for each company at each level of performance is debatable to say the least. Some people believe that they should take account of which industry or nation they are operating in. My own view is that they should not. We are concerned here with long range planning, remember, where the planning horizon is so far ahead that the options of moving out of declining industries, diversifying geographically and identifying more profitable niches are all open. Indeed, this is the whole point of the entire exercise known as corporate planning!

Hence, the correct context for setting targets is not existing return on capital, not current industrial averages, not the general level in the company's traditional nation but something much wider. It is whatever return shareholders currently expect from a worldwide portfolio. Just consider for a moment what this means.

Suppose that a company has set itself a target that it thinks will satisfy its shareholders, and suppose that it finds to its dismay that the strategy that it has chosen is not likely to hit the target. Should the company revise the target downwards? *No,* it should not! To do so would be tantamount to aiming to dissatisfy the shareholders, which is something that no director should ever contemplate. No, the correct course is to start looking for a better strategy before the shareholders start looking for a better team of managers!

Now imagine the opposite case, where it looks as if the chosen strategy will exceed Tsat. What then? There is no call to alter Tsat here either, because Tsat is the level that represents shareholder satisfaction; and if a strategy looks like more than satisfying them, well, that's fine! Tsat is Tsat. If you want to set a really challenging target, do so by all means, but the target should be labelled Tchallenging or Tfantastic.

What really matters here is that the team should discuss its aims and ambitions on behalf of the shareholders and reach agreement and consensus on Tmin and Tsat in particular.

Some companies that I know select zero growth as Tmin; that is, they feel that in their particular circumstances their shareholders will accept the same level of real profits in year 5 as in the current year as a poor but not a disgraceful performance. Other companies take 5 per cent p.a. as Tmin. Some companies in some nations traditionally declare very low dividends; in Japan, for example, dividend yields have been low, 2 per cent say, and growth rates therefore high, 8 per cent say, making a ROSC of 10 per cent. In Britain many companies yield 6 per cent dividends and growth rates of only, say, 4 per cent, making a ROSC of 10 per cent. These are currently average levels of performance, and for a management that believes that average is satisfactory these are the levels represented by Tsat. I have seen Tsat growth targets set between 5 and 15 per cent, which, assuming a dividend yield of around 5 per cent, represent a ROSC of 10–20 per cent. Sometimes a company has a particular deadline in mind; it may be the date of a convertible share, which almost automatically sets a profit target, or it may be a private company wishing to go public, which can only be achieved if its profits reach a particular level by a certain date.

Finally, I must re-emphasise how this bracket target system affects the choice of a strategy. Using a simple single-target figure, say £2m. by year 5, a company will look for a strategy that will achieve £2m. by year 5. However, using the bracket system the target may be defined as 'Tmin = £1·5m., Tsat = £2·5m.', and this means that the concept of risk is built into the whole planning process right from the start. The strategy needed to hit these targets will have to display a good chance of achieving £2·5m. by year 5 and virtually no chance at all of yielding less than £1·5m., come what may! (A further development of this concept appears in my book *Systematic Corporate Planning* under the heading 'performance risk'.)

Targets for stakeholders

If we accept the stakeholder view, presumably we must set targets for the various demands that it is legitimate for each stakeholder to make upon the company. I know of no case where this is done comprehensively, although I occasionally come across companies that have set targets for a few of these items.

The most common example (described on page 46) is the demands of the employees. One South African company that I know decided that, if it was right to set a shareholder target, it would be appropriate to set a target for total remuneration per employee. The targets chosen were: a growth in dividends of 5 per cent p.a. for shareholders; and a growth of 2 per cent p.a. in take-home pay for managers (who were almost exclusively white) and 8 per cent p.a. for workers (who were almost exclusively black). The ratio of management salaries to workers' pay was at that time approximately 20–1, and, as can be seen from Exhibit 3.5, this differential would in twenty years come down to 6–1, which is comparable to ratios in some European nations. Whether these targets were acceptable to, or even discussed with, the managers and workers concerned I do not know, and I quote the case solely because it is the only one that I have personally encountered where actual numerical targets were set for groups other than shareholders. How targets can be set for other stakeholders – suppliers, the local community, and so on – in hard practical down-to-earth figures I do not know.

The above example contains another important lesson for planners. Planners like smooth growth curves; but, I believe, Nature does not, nor does history. The disparity between the wages of the workers and

Exhibit 3.5   An example of stakeholders' targets

	Year 0 (actual)	Year 10 (target)	Year 20 (target)
Average annual salary for managers (target growth = 2% p.a.)	£2,000	£2,440	£3,000
Average annual wages for workers (target growth = 8% p.a.)	£100	£215	£470
Salary–wages ratio	20–1	11–1	6–1

the salaries of the managers in the above example was so out of line compared with other nations that I should not be surprised if a major 'discontinuity' in the curve were inevitable. In plain words, in the near future wages might jump up 50 per cent in the space of a couple of years, while salaries could well fall in real terms; or wages could treble in five years and salaries halve; or anything could happen except the smooth curves assumed by this company's target-setters.

This is true of most targets. When a company's current profits are satisfactory, it may well make sense to set a smooth growth curve such as is implied by adopting a compound growth rate of, say, 5 per cent p.a. for five years. However, when the current performance is lower than satisfactory, such elegant simplicity may not be appropriate; for example, a catch-up target for three years followed by two years at 5 per cent may be closer to what is required. One company that I know made profits of £8m. three years ago but only £3m. this year; plainly, a catch-up target followed perhaps by a smooth growth target is needed here. Another company has grown so rapidly in the past few years that it has adopted the opposite: a consolidation period of three years followed by renewed rapid growth. (Also, as we shall see in the next chapter, smooth curves are not always sensible in forecasting either.)

Finally, I should return to the problem of who should be involved in the setting of corporate targets. Obviously, the corporate planning team should play the central role; but I must repeat (see page 38) that in most companies this team will consist mainly of managers, and on a strict interpretation of the rules of capitalism their views do not count. What counts is the shareholders' views. However, it would be quite absurd today not to allow the views of these top managers to colour the views of the shareholders. Indeed, most companies today go further than that and invite the views of at least the next level of managers, from whom the next generation of top managers will be drawn. One method of seeking their views is the initial seminar (described on page 23), at which the second session will be devoted to just this question of setting targets for the company. However, I have to add that, if the ambitions of the shareholders are discovered not to be compatible with those of the managers, a serious constitutional problem will arise. This is precisely one of the advantages of corporate planning; it allows fundamental difficulties and disagreements to be exposed and discussed in a rational systematic manner.

Summary

The horizon of the plans and forecasts has first to be decided. Few companies will benefit from a horizon of less than five years, and some that have longer lead times to consider, or that expect major events to take place many years ahead, may need to look much further ahead.

Assuming that the corporate objective selected for the company is to 'make a return on shareholders' capital', it is necessary to quantify exactly what this means. We run into three problems, however. First, how can this be quantified? The answer, I suggest, is to use growth in EpS, growth in profits and ROSC as a trio of indicators of overall performance. Severe misunderstanding can, I believe, arise from using ROCE as the corporate target, and none of the other management, accounting or efficiency ratios are appropriate either. The second problem is to select a suitable base-year figure. Although this is sometimes very difficult to do, normally it is not. The third problem is to select a suitable target level of performance, and this is always difficult. Indeed, in my view it is impossible unless a range or bracket of targets rather than a single figure is used.

Three targets may be needed: Tmin, which represents the worst possible result that shareholders will tolerate and which, of course, must be exceeded; Tsat, which represents the level of achievement that shareholders, managers or both will recognise as being quite good; and Tmax, which only some companies will need to define – a level that is so high as to cause embarrassment and must therefore not be exceeded.

The setting of a bracket target has a profound and totally beneficial consequence for the eventual selection of strategies for the firm. Instead of searching for any strategy that may achieve some single-figure target, the company looks for strategies to meet a bracket target, the specification for which will include such a phrase as 'must stand a good chance of achieving Tsat *and* be virtually certain to exceed Tmin under all the circumstances that the company may face'. Thus, the ugly twin sister of profit, namely, risk, is introduced into the planning process at the start – here at the target-setting stage.

As for setting definitive quantified targets for stakeholders, the practice is rare and fraught with difficulties. Neither social accounting, cost–benefit analysis nor the science of trade-offs is, in my view, anywhere near being of real practical help in this area.

Finally, notice that deciding the corporate objectives and selecting the targets have taken up two long chapters. In my view most corporate planners and most corporate planning systems fail to understand the importance of this part of corporate planning. Either they leave it out altogether, they decide objectives after strategies – an error that surely indicates crass ignorance of the principles of management – or they adopt half a dozen assorted ratios without realising that in so doing they are negating the entire planning process.

I am convinced that a large proportion of plans that go wrong do so at this very first stage.

CHAPTER 4

Forecasts and Gaps

The position reached in the planning process is as follows. By now the planning team has a very good idea what the company is trying to do for whom, what its social obligations are and what level of achievement it is aiming for. This consensus has probably taken at least two meetings to develop as well as much discussion with people both inside and outside the company, and it contains several of the key criteria by which the chosen strategy will eventually be judged.

However, we are still a long way from the stage of judging strategies. Indeed we do not yet know if *any* new strategies are going to be needed. Perhaps the company can meet and exceed all the criteria exactly as it is now, without any new strategies. What idiots the planning team would look if it went off into cloud cuckoo land searching for some dynamic new strategy to get the company where it would be anyway! The greenest grass *is* sometimes found in the precise field that you are already in.

What the forecast is for

This is one reason why the next step for the planning team is to make a forecast of profits for the next five years on the assumption that the company continues to be managed on existing policies and strategies. So, if research and development (R & D) is habitually 2 per cent of turnover, assume that it will continue at 2 per cent. If a new product is introduced every two years, assume that this continues to be so. If top managers retire at 60, assume that they go on doing so.

Although it is unlikely that merely by continuing to run the company exactly as it is the management will achieve its targets, it may get somewhere near them. If so, a major strategic change may not be necessary or desirable; a minor change may do. Alternatively – and this is surely rather important – it may be discovered that what is needed is not a profit-increasing strategy but a risk-reducing one. On the other hand it may be discovered that a major new strategy *is* needed and urgently required, or that it is certainly going to be needed but *not* urgently.

Finding out how close to the targets the company is likely to get, and therefore what size, shape and timing the new strategy must have, is one reason why this forecast should be made. There is another reason: in order to forecast the behaviour of any organisation it is first necessary to understand it. It is vital for the successful completion of all the other steps in the planning process that the planning team understands how the company works, how it makes its profits and where its weaknesses and vulnerabilities are. To make a forecast it is necessary to learn about the company and its past. Things will be learnt and remembered that were never known or have long been forgotten – things that will have a vital bearing on the choice of strategy.

In order to make a five-year forecast it is necessary to discover what are the factors to which the company's profits are most sensitive. Many companies concentrate their attention on the sales volume, for example, believing this to be the most crucial element in the company's profit-making machinery. In some companies it is so (and in all companies it is an important factor), but in others it is less critical than, say, exchange rates, raw material prices, interest rates or inflation. What the team learns about the company's sensitivity to such changes is one of the most useful byproducts of this part of the planning process. Also, there is yet another reason why the making of these forecasts is so useful.

Memories are short. In most companies there will be no one who remembers why six years ago margins on sales suddenly fell, for example, or why ten years ago there were eight factories where now there are two. No one will have examined how the company's breakeven point has moved, how the fixed costs have risen, how product life cycles have shortened, how the last economic recession affected margins, at what rate the number of product variations has grown, and so on to infinity.

A very common reaction to the suggestion that a five-year profit forecast be prepared is sheer disbelief. How can we possibly see that far into the future? We cannot. Well, then, say the sceptics, if we cannot forecast, surely we cannot plan? On the contrary, it is when the future is uncertain that we *must* plan. A plan is nothing more than taking a systematic look at the future and deciding what is the best thing to do, *knowing how uncertain the future is*. If the future were certain, any office boy could do the planning, or a computer could. It is the fact of uncertainty that lies at the centre of all long-range plans.

The nub of planning over a long time horizon is the size of the errors in the forecasts. Now, this means two things. First, any forecast that the corporate planning team produces *must*, if it is not to be utterly worthless – and a jewel of professional incompetence – contain a statement of errors. Secondly, because these huge errors make forecasting and planning much more difficult, the complexity and level of detail in the forecasts and plans *must* be kept to a minimum. Huge errors and bewildering detail together make powerful poison.

These two things mainly distinguish a competent short-range plan from a competent long-range one. In a short term plan a statement of errors would look odd, and lack of detail would look odd. In a long range plan, however, the absence of a statement of errors would be sheer negligence, and any attempt to plan more than a few major features of the company would be ridiculous; a long-range planning document containing dozens of pages of detail would be absurd.

Errors in forecasts

Let us consider where in the forecasting process these errors arise. Start with the simplest possible forecast, namely, the straight projection. In this it is assumed that *everything* in the future continues exactly as in the past. So, if we were forecasting the profits for the company in Exhibit 4.1, we should draw a line of best fit through the last five years' profits and project it five years into the future.

Now, there are four sources of error here: two deliberate and two unintentional. The deliberate ones are the assumptions that nothing in the world outside Blackbird & Co. is going to change and that Blackbird is not going to make any strategic changes either – no

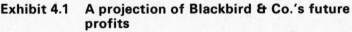

Exhibit 4.1   A projection of Blackbird & Co.'s future profits

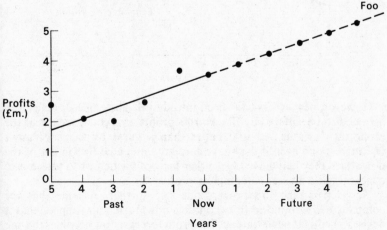

change and no response. I call this type of forecast an Foo forecast –
one 'o' for nothing changing in the environment and the other 'o' for
no response from the company.

The two unintentional errors are: (1) the trend line may not
accurately reflect the past trend; and (2) it is based on only five years'
past history (perhaps if we looked one year further back the pattern
would change). In order to reduce the size of these errors we should:
(a) examine the causes of the fluctuations in the past five-year figures to
identify any freak results that there may have been; and (b) go back as
far as possible.

Now let us turn to the next type of forecast. Here we make the
assumption that, although the company continues to be managed
exactly as it is now being managed, there will probably be changes in the
outside world. Thus, in the profit forecast for Blackbird and Co. in
Exhibit 4.2 the company now expects profits to fall due to a downturn
in the economy. I call this type of forecast an Fo forecast, because in
this case a change in the environment is assumed but a response from
the company is not – only one 'o', therefore.

Exhibit 4.2   An Fo forecast for Blackbird & Co.'s profits

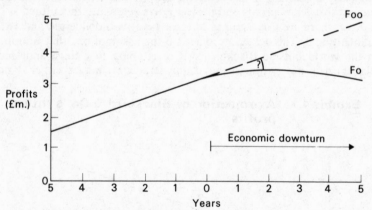

However, new errors have been introduced. The angle of deflection
assumed to be suffered by Blackbird's profits as a consequence of the
economic downturn is little better than a guess by the company's
executives; and even if they have correctly predicted the timing of the
downturn, they may have been either too optimistic or too pessimistic
concerning its impact on company profits.

Now let us take this process one step further. Assume that the
company *will* respond to this economic downturn, and suppose that it
devises a brilliant new strategy. The profit forecast now becomes the one

Exhibit 4.3   An Fp forecast for Blackbird & Co.'s profits

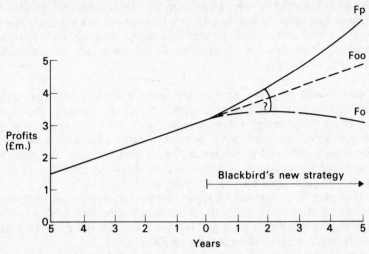

shown in Exhibit 4.3. However, again a new source of error has been introduced, namely, the effect on profits of this proposed plan. So, Fp forecasts, that is, forecasts calculated on the assumption that plan P is adopted, are even more wildly erroneous than Fo forecasts.

In this trio of different forecasts I can see little use for the Foo forecast in planning. I hope that it is clear that the forecast to be made at *this* stage of the planning process is the Fo – the no-change-in-strategy forecast. Only much later, when a strategy has emerged, will any Fp forecasts need to be made (see page 175).

Dealing with errors

Since errors play such an important and dangerous role in long range planning, we must do all that we can to reduce them. There is a considerable number of steps that we can take to do this, although most of them are little more than commonsense precautions that will do little more than eliminate the crass and careless errors. The planning team will ignore these precautions at its peril, however. Let me describe them.

Assumptions.   It is essential to ensure that everyone who contributes to a forecast is told what assumptions to build in, particularly economic growth rates, rate of inflation, dates of major events (the start-up date of a new factory, for example), and so on.

The past.   Go back in the records as far as possible. Some people suggest that this is not always a helpful thing to do, because 'everything was so different before our merger' or '. . . before the 1973 oil crisis'. However, if we are going to look five or even ten years ahead, this is precisely the order of magnitude of changes that we shall have to imagine, so let us learn of any real-life examples that have actually occurred in the past.

Understanding the past.   It should be possible for the planning team to be able to explain and account for every major movement in the profit record of the company for many years past. Why did profits fall by 15 per cent four years ago? Because a large customer went to a competitor. Why did profits rise by 10 per cent last year? Because we purchased a special consignment of steel. Look at the effect of that strike five years ago! £3m. down! And so on.

However, it is not only unique events that cause movements in profits; trends do so too. So, the planning team should be able to show how the various major costs and revenues have moved over the years and how these have influenced the profit record.

Only when the team members can explain all the major movements in profits, earnings, return on capital employed (ROCE) and even share price changes can they honestly claim to know enough about their company's past to allow them to predict its future. We may even add the further criterion that the team should be able to explain why the company's profit pattern has differed from that of each of its competitors; for example, 'We always do better at Christmas than Robin & Co.' or 'They cut margins all through the 1979 depression, and we did not'.

Do not forget to study how inflation (see below) has affected each major aspect of your company. Have wages risen at the same rate as raw material prices over the past five years, and raw material prices at the same rate as fuel prices? If not, what are the differential rates, and why? Will they continue?

Link the past with the future.   Whenever I see a forecast that starts at year 1 or at the current year, I can almost guarantee that it will be faulty. Only if a forecast shows the figures for the past few years *as a sequence* with the current year and with the future can one be sure that there is no hidden error. Two main types of error lurk at the junction between past and future.

One is incompatible methods – accounting procedures, valuations, definitions, and so on. (I was once caught out by a change from tons to tonnes.) The only way to ensure continuity is to show past and future as a continuous sequence with reconciliations where necessary.

The other is hidden angles of deflection. I frequently see forecasts showing, for example, market share rising from 18 per cent in year 0 to 20 per cent in year 5. When I ask what the market share was five years ago, I am told '18 per cent'; and when I ask what action is to cause this change from a static past to such an heroic future, there is no answer. (In any case this is supposed to be an Fo forecast, remember, which excludes any new strategies.) Thus, this past–present–future continuum is among other things a useful safeguard against the most potent enemy of long range planning, namely, unwarrantable optimism and 'numbers game' forecasts.

Cross-checks. Take every figure in every year of the forecast and check it against another figure. Do total wages rise faster than total salaries? If so, does this make sense? Do research costs rise faster than sales? Have they done so in the past? Calculate the ROCE for year 0 and year 5. Do you believe that it will really move like that? Project all the figures forwards another five years. Does anything absurd happen, such as research expenditure overtaking total salaries or the achievement of a 105 per cent market share?

In other words stand back – back from the mass of figures – and see whether they make sense.

Verification Sessions. Let the people who have prepared the company's Fo forecast face a challenge from people who have not. Having to justify any assumptions and calculations made to their colleagues is a most effective means of reducing excessive optimism (or pessimism). I must emphasise that, when forecasters are attempting to look far into the future, there is a strong tendency to lose touch with reality; anything that brings them down to earth is valuable.

Inflation. Planners have to make up their minds very clearly indeed as to how they intend to deal with inflation. In short term planning planners almost always make their forecast with inflation built into the figures, especially when the figures are going to be used for budgetary control, variance reporting and other control purposes, as most short term planning figures are.

However, in long term planning, which does not normally include the control element of the management cycle, there is the option of using constant-value or real-terms figures. In my experience these are more useful than inflated or current-value figures for long range planning. For one thing all past trends are meaningless until inflation has been stripped out of the recorded figures; it is necessary to use constant values to examine the past. Most executives are more at home talking in constant terms in periods of time exceeding one or two years. For example, the sales director, if asked what the increase in sales turnover will be next year, will probably answer '15 per cent', meaning 3 per cent real plus 12 per cent inflation; but if asked the same question for a five-year horizon, he will probably answer 'about 3 per cent p.a.'. The reason, of course, is that inflation rates are notoriously difficult to predict; and although it is relatively painless to revise a one-year forecast if the relevant inflation rate for that year has to be revised, there is much less enthusiasm about revising five years of forecasts. If confidence in the inflation rate forecast for only one of the years is lost, the whole five-year forecast has to be recalculated.

On the other hand a forecast that excludes inflation will not truly reflect a company's cash-flow position. In my opinion all forecasts have to be made twice: once in constant money and again in inflated money. The most important version for planning purposes is the former; the latter is made only to see the effects of inflation on cash flows, asset values, gearing ratios, and so on.

The constant value forecast is the most important, then, especially as, in an examination of the company's past performance, all the figures have to be converted to constant values in order to make the real trends or movements of turnover, profits, material prices, and so on intelligible.

State the errors.   No long term forecast is complete without a statement of the probable errors. This can be done by stating a central figure, say £3·7m., and indicating the error thus: ±£0·7m. (that is, the forecaster does not expect an outcome below £3·0m. or above £4·4m.); or it can be done by means of a bracket with or without a central figure, thus: 'between £3·0m. (pessimistic) and £4·4m. (optimistic) with £3·7m. as most probable'.

Notice that I have come to a bracket again, this time in the context of forecasting. Many planners today have at last come to accept the need to use a bracket of figures in their forecasts; perhaps in a decade or so they will accept the need for it in setting targets! We shall see how useful these bracket targets and bracket forecasts are when we reach the stage of 'gap analysis'.

However careful planners are in making forecasts, I cannot recall even one that did not contain at least one mistake when I was asked to check it. Frequently, the mistakes are due to not linking the future in a sequence with the past and thus allowing mere guesswork to take the place of experience. Inflation invariably causes confusion: sometimes, a company's financial year does not coincide with the twelve-month period on which an official index of price inflation is based; sometimes, a forecaster escalates wages, say, for the effect of inflation but forgets to escalate raw materials; sometimes, profits are escalated for inflation but assets (especially land and property) are not, with the result that predicted ROCE rises rapidly over the five-year period.

Sometimes, bank interest on overdraft is omitted, with the result that profits are over- or understated by significant amounts by the time year 5 is reached. The errors inherent in the very nature of the future itself are quite bad enough without man-made mistakes being added as well, yet they always seem to creep in. My advice to the beginner is to keep it simple to start with.

There is one final nugget of information to be extracted from the fact that errors exist in forecasts, for, when all the man-made slips, omissions and mistakes have been eliminated, we are still left with the inescapable fact that the future is uncertain. Suppose that we find it almost impossible to make a forecast because the width of the band of uncertainty that surrounds our company's future is so vast. We really cannot say whether our profits in year 5 will be plus £100m. or minus £50m. What then? Well, this may be a clear warning for us that, when we reach the stage of strategy formulation – still a long way off – we may have to select risk-reducing strategies rather than profit-increasing ones.

Methods of forecasting

I shall describe three methods of making the Fo forecast for a company; one is extremely simple and in view of my comments above is therefore highly recommended. In addition to this simple forecast I shall describe the budget forecast and the company model.

The Simple Forecast. To make a forecast of profits for year 5 using this method, take the sales turnover and the trading profit figures for the past five years, strip out inflation and list them as in Exhibit 4.4(1) along with the margin-on-sales ratio. Now consult the relevant colleagues and estimate as best you can what sales turnover and margins will be in each of the next five years. Then simply calculate profits for each year and list as in Exhibit 4.4(2).

As can be seen from Exhibit 4.4(2), this company believes that its sales will rise by £1m. over the period but margins will remain at 7·3 per cent. This is an Fo forecast, remember, and the assumption that there will be no change in strategy means that past trends in performance will not change significantly.

The great advantage of this method of forecasting is its simplicity. A forecast can be made in minutes. However, surely, it may be exclaimed, this forecast is so simple as to be ridiculously inaccurate? I do not think so; on the contrary I believe it to be a most useful ranging shot against which the more detailed forecasts made later can be judged. None of these forecasts will be accurate either. All long range forecasts are wildly inaccurate. We should not pretend otherwise, for no amount of detailed analysis and abstruse mathematical calculation can penetrate the future.

Exhibit 4.4   The simple forecast

---

(1) First list turnover, profits and sales margins for the past five years.

	Year−5	−4	−3	−2	−1	0 (estimate)
Sales turnover (£m.)	12.0	12.2	11.9	12.0	11.8	12.1
Profits (£m.)	0.87	0.96	0.45	0.86	0.88	0.88
Margin (%)	7.25	7.86	3.78	7.17	7.45	7.27

(2) Then forecast turnover, margins and hence profits five years ahead. This is an Fo forecast.

	Year 0	1	2	3	4	5
Sales turnover (£m.)	12.1	12.3	12.5	12.7	12.9	13.1
Profits (£m.)	0.88	0.90	0.91	0.93	0.94	0.96
Margin (%)	7.3	7.3	7.3	7.3	7.3	7.3

(3) Then establish the possible limits of error by making an optimistic and a pessimistic version.

Optimistic	Year 0	1	2	3	4	5
Sales turnover (£m.)	12.1	12.7	13.3	14.0	14.7	15.4
Profits (£m.)	0.88	0.94	1.00	1.06	1.13	1.20
Margin (%)	7.3	7.4	7.5	7.6	7.7	7.8

Pessimistic						
Sales turnover (£m.)	12.1	12.1	12.1	12.1	12.1	12.1
Profits (£m.)	0.88	0.87	0.87	0.87	0.87	0.87
Margin (%)	7.3	7.2	7.2	7.2	7.2	7.2

In view of this uncertainty it is essential to reveal what level of uncertainty any long term forecast may carry. Using the simple forecast method we can do this quite easily. Go and confer with your colleagues again. Let us assume in this case (see Exhibit 4·4(3)) that these executives agree that the most optimistic view that they can possibly take of the market is that sales will increase to £15·4m. by year 5 (an average rise of 5 per cent p.a.) and that margins will rise to as high as 7·8 per cent (they haven't been so high for four years); *if* this happens, profits in year 5 will be as high as £1·2m. Their most pessimistic view is that sales will not rise at all (they haven't over the past six years) and that margins will stay down at 7·2 per cent (surely they will not go as low as 3·78 per cent again?); in this case profits will be £0·87m. So, there is the bracket: from £0·87m. to £1·20m., with £0·96m. as a 'most likely' figure nearly in the middle.

I very strongly recommend this method as a beginner's starting point. By all means add complications and refinements, but do not do so unless the simple forecast is wholly absurd in your context. If your company operates in two totally different markets where margins are traditionally, say, 2·3 per cent in one and 18·5 per cent in the other, perhaps you need two separate calculations.

Budget Forecasts. These are infinitely more complicated. They are often so complex that there is no way of checking them except by comparing the overall picture that they present with the results obtained from the simple forecast. Part of the problem is that a large number of people contribute to the budget exercise, many of whom will be afflicted by the long term forecaster's most common ailment, namely, unwarranted optimism. Although the planning team may be able to detect this, it may find it difficult to eliminate without damping executive enthusiasm.

The procedure is as follows. Inspect the budgets that the company has produced for the past five years, extract all those items that are of major significance and merge into more general categories all those that are not. Now forecast each of these major items forwards for five years, remembering to take account of changes in the environment but, as this is an Fo forecast, proposing no new strategies.

As can be seen in Exhibit 4.5, such forecasts are often very detailed and concentrate heavily on operating costs. As suggested above, it is usually essential to go through the whole exercise again, using inflated figures to determine the consequences on cash flow and other financial, as opposed to operational, areas. The whole exercise has to be repeated with optimistic and pessimistic assumptions. In other words we are up against our old enemy again, namely, too much detail coupled with very large ranges of error. So, be ruthless; cut down the number of items again. In Exhibit 4.5, for example, it would be practical to merge all the factory costs into one category without incurring too much inaccuracy as a penalty.

In simplifying a company's cost and revenue structure for the purpose of long range forecasts a useful guideline is the '10 per cent rule'. This suggests that an item deserves a place on its own in any long term forecast if, and only if, it can affect the profit forecast by 10 per cent or more. Thus, in Exhibit 4.5 it is inconceivable that 'inspection' could ever become so large (or small) as to reduce (or increase) the company's profits by as much as 10 per cent of £1·076m. in, say, year 5, not unless there were a major change of strategy as regards inspection, which is ruled out in an Fo forecast.

The great advantage of taking the budget as a forecast is that most companies today prepare budgets, often for five-year horizons, so some of the work is already done. In a group of companies, where the group Fo forecast is the sum of all the subsidiary companies' Fo forecasts (minus group expenses), this is especially useful, because virtually

Exhibit 4.5   A budget forecast for Swallow & Co. five years ahead

Item	Year 0 (estimate)	1	2	3	4	5
Sales (000 units)	347	355	372	382	393	399
Unit selling price (£)	24·43	25·65	26·42	26·45	26·50	26·5
Turnover (£000)	8,477	9,106	9,828	10,104	10,414	10,574
Variable costs (£000):						
Labour	2,431	2,495	2,712	2,731	2,880	2,980
Materials	2,611	2,650	2,777	2,852	2,890	2,920
Electricity	310	340	380	388	401	410
Fuel	185	205	210	207	203	195
Total	5,537	5,690	6,079	6,178	6,374	6,505
Contribution (£000)	2,940	3,416	3,749	3,925	4,040	4,069
Fixed costs (factory) (£000):						
Toolroom	401	483	501	532	541	550
Inspection	42	69	83	84	88	90
Warehousing	31	38	41	52	57	60
Repairs	305	605	812	807	795	660
Depreciation	251	289	307	348	399	410
Total	1,030	1,484	1,744	1,823	1,880	1,770
Overheads, office, etc. (£000):						
Sales	286	299	318	338	347	350
Management	437	422	480	492	503	520
Accounts	125	130	102	101	100	80
General	220	230	212	255	275	273
Total	1,068	1,081	1,112	1,186	1,225	1,223
Total all costs (£000)	7,635	8,255	8,935	9,187	9,479	9,498
Profits (£000)	842	851	893	917	935	1,076

all groups prepare five-year budgets. It is virtually impossible to manage a group of companies without them. (Indeed, I dare to suggest that any company, and certainly any group, that has not already adopted multiyear budgets – not necessarily five perhaps – is probably not ready to adopt corporate planning. To leap from one-year budgeting to corporate planning is not merely stretching managerial thought patterns too far; the data needed for strategic decisions may simply not be available in such a company.)

The one disadvantage is that a budget is usually a hotchpotch of targets, forecasts and plans and so, strictly speaking, is not an Fo forecast. In particular the budget that any subsidiary company submits to its parent company will reflect a large number of decisions that the management of the subsidiary has taken, will take or wishes to take. Strictly speaking, therefore, these are not Fo forecasts, that is, ones in which the management is assumed not to make new strategic decisions.

Normally, however, in practice any minor decisions included can be ignored, any major ones can be separately identified, and, if desired, the Fo forecast can be adjusted. In fact the presence of a number of decisions in these forecasts is not a disadvantage but a major benefit.

People often ask where in the Argenti system the managers of subsidiary companies are encouraged to contribute their own ideas to the group's corporate plan. The answer is that there is or should be a large number of such opportunities starting with the introductory seminar (see page 23), continuing with close liaison between the group and the subsidiary's teams (see page 19) and carrying on here at the forecasting stage, where their ideas can be included formally and explicitly in the Fo forecasts that they put up to the group team. Similar formal opportunities appear throughout the rest of the process; and unless morale and communications are awful, informal opportunities are continuous in most companies (see also Exhibit 1.3, which shows where these five-year budgets or Fo forecasts fit into the corporate planning process (at B2) of a group).

Company models. These are undoubtedly the apogee of the art of the forecaster. I strongly recommend that beginners start with a quick simple forecast in the early days of the planning process, then proceed after a few weeks to budget forecasts and only later, after a couple of months perhaps, start building the model. In any case the model probably has greater value when used for testing alternative strategies much later on than when used for making Fo forecasts here.

The idea is to calculate profits, cash flows, ratios, stocks, loans, earnings per share (EpS), market share, the market size, selling prices – everything that planners want to know about the company *and* its environment over the next five years – all in one single coherent exercise. Using these results it is possible to calculate what effect any new or changed assumption about the future will have on every aspect of the company.

In my own version the model is broken down into sections, each of which is mathematically related to several others. Thus, section A contains the market data, section B the profits, section C the balance sheet, and so on. In section A the total market can be shown expressed in units of product and in value, broken down into segments, specialised areas or geographical zones, together with the market share of each major company including one's own. In section B one's company's turnover, average selling price, unit sales, margins, profits before and after tax, and so on are shown (see Exhibit 4.6 for Bunting Ltd, which includes some of these features).

The mathematical relationships are given in column 3. For example, it can be seen that item B7 (profits after tax) is calculated by subtracting item B6 from item B5 (that is, tax from profits before

Exhibit 4.6   Company model forecast for Bunting Ltd.

Notes on the model

Purpose.   The purpose of this particular 'run' on the model (run no. 18) was to observe the effect on profits, cash flow, and so on of the 'most likely' assumptions as to market growth, labour productivity, and so on. One major assumption that the planning team made, which was not in accordance with past experience, was that overheads might be held steady (see item B2). Another was that labour productivity would improve by 5 per cent p.a., and another was that the company's bank would allow it to use an overdraft facility up to 10 per cent of its capital employed (see item G5 and G4 respectively). Otherwise, the assumptions were based on past experience.

Conclusions.   In spite of the slow improvement in the growth of the market (A1) the operating profits rise rapidly (B3) because of the constant overheads (B2). Profits before tax rise even more rapidly (B5 and G3) due to the rapid decline in overdraft, which is in fact converted into a balance in year 1 (C10), and bank interest of £0·16m. is converted into interest on investments of £0·82m.

The very large positive cash flows are an outstanding feature, and on these assumptions item G4 suggests that Bunting Ltd will have unused short term borrowing capacity of £15m. by year 5. Another interesting conclusion, which also suggests underused capacities, is the decline in the workforce implied by these assumptions (G6). (This is an Fo forecast and assumes that the company does not invest in any new projects not already approved by the board.)

Abbreviations

a   = figure suggested by planning team.

b   = figure based on past experience.

e   = approximate figure or approximate relationship (often used to simplify calculations on tax, foreign earnings, exchange rates, depreciation, and so on).

m   = a major assumption. It is the purpose of this run to test the effect of these 'm' assumptions.

py   = previous year; for example, pyC4 – C4 means 'Subtract this year's C4 from last year's C4'.

Company model for Bunting Ltd: five years, run no. 18

Ref.	Item	Method of calculation (see notes)	Year 0 (actual)	1	2	3	4	5
A	*Markets*							
1	Total market size (000 units)	a (rising at 3% p.a.)	847·00	872·40	898·60	925·50	953·30	981·90
2	Average selling price (£)	a (constant)	355·10	355·10	355·10	355·10	355·10	355·10
3	Total market value (£m.)	A1 × A2	300·80	309·80	319·10	328·60	338·50	348·70
4	Bunting's market share (%)	b (constant)	12·30	12·30	12·30	12·30	12·30	12·30
5	Bunting's sales (000 units)	A1 × A4	104·20	107·30	110·50	113·80	117·30	120·80

Ref.	Item	Method of calculation (see notes)	Year 0 (actual)	1	2	3	4	5
6	Bunting's average selling price (£)	a (falling at 2% p.a.)	386·00	378·40	371·00	363·70	356·60	349·60
7	Bunting's sales turnover (£m.)	A5 × A6	40·22	40·60	41·00	41·39	41·83	42·23
8	Retail price index (year 0 = 100)	a (nil inflation)	100·00	100·00	100·00	100·00	100·00	100·00
B	**Profits (£m.)**							
1	Variable costs	b, 0·36A7	14·50	14·62	14·76	14·90	15·06	15·21
2	Overheads and fixed costs	am (constant)	20·84	20·84	20·84	20·84	20·84	20·84
3	Operating profit	A7 − B1 − B2	4·89	5·14	5·40	5·65	5·93	6·18
4	Interest on loans	e, 0·1 (D4 + pyC10)	0·16	0·17	+0·05	+0·29	+0·54	+0·81
5	Profit before tax	B3 − B4	4·71	4·97	5·45	5·94	6·47	6·99
6	Corporation tax	a and b, 0·52B5	2·45	2·58	2·83	3·09	3·36	3·63
7	Profit after tax	B5 − B6	2·26	2·39	2·62	2·85	3·11	3·36
8	Dividends	a and be, 0·3B7	0·68	0·72	0·79	0·86	0·93	1·01
9	Retained earnings	B7 − B8	1·58	1·67	1·83	1·99	2·18	2·35
C	**Balance sheet (£m.)**							
1	Fixed capital	pyC1 + E6 − E3 + (A8 ÷ pyA8 × pyC1)	18·23	18·31	18·40	18·50	18·60	18·70
2	Investments	a (constant)	0·30	0·30	0·30	0·30	0·30	0·30
3	Total	C1 + C2	18·53	18·61	18·70	18·80	18·90	19·00
4	Stocks	b, 0·26A7	10·46	10·55	10·66	10·76	10·87	10·98
5	Debtors	b, 0·24A7	9·65	9·74	9·84	9·93	10·04	10·13
6	Total current assets	C4 + C5	20·11	20·29	20·50	20·69	20·91	21·11
7	Creditors	b, 0·17A7	6·84	6·90	6·97	7·04	7·11	7·18
8	Taxation	= F5	1·57	1·78	1·95	2·13	2·32	2·51
9	Dividends	ae, 0·60B8	0·41	0·43	0·47	0·52	0·56	0·61
10	Bank overdraft (+) or balance (−)	pyC10 ± E12	+1·61	−0·52	−2·80	−5·30	−8·02	−10·96
11	Total current liabilities	C7 + C8 + C9 + C10	10·43	8·59	6·59	4·39	1·97	−0·66
12	Net current assets	C6 − C11	9·68	11·70	13·91	16·30	18·94	21·77
13	Net assets	C12 + C3 and = D6	28·21	30·30	32·60	35·09	37·93	40·77
D	**Capital employed (£m.)**							
1	Share capital	a (no new equity issues)	12·80	12·80	12·80	12·80	12·80	12·80
2	Reserves	pyD2 + B9	10·91	12·58	14·41	16·40	18·58	20·93
3	Total shareholders' capital	D1 + D2	23·71	25·38	27·21	29·20	31·38	33·73
4	Long term loans	a (no new loans)	0·10	0·10	0·10	0·10	0·10	0·10
5	Deferred taxation	pyD5 + F3	4·37	4·80	5·27	5·78	6·34	6·94
6	Capital employed	D3 + D4 + D5 and = C13	28·21	30·29	32·59	35·08	37·82	40·77
E	**Cash flows (£m.)**							
1	Profit before tax	= B5	4·71	4·97	5·45	5·94	6·47	6·99
2	Sales of assets, etc.	a	0·31	0·00	0·00	0·00	0·00	0·00
3	Depreciation	be, 0·04pyC1	0·68	0·73	0·73	0·73	0·74	0·74
4	Increased creditors	C7 − pyC7	0·21	0·06	0·07	0·07	0·07	0·07
5	Total cash	E1 + E2 + E3 + E4	5·91	5·76	6·25	6·74	7·28	7·80
6	Capital expenditure	be, 0·02A7	0·80	0·81	0·82	0·83	0·84	0·84
7	Increased stocks	C4 − pyC4	0·34	0·09	0·11	0·10	0·11	0·11
8	Increased debtors	C5 − pyC5	0·31	0·09	0·10	0·09	0·11	0·11
9	Dividends paid	e, 0·6pyB8 + 0·4B8	0·61	0·70	0·75	0·82	0·89	0·96
10	Tax paid	= F4	2·05	1·94	2·19	2·40	2·61	2·84
11	Total out	E6 + E7 + E8 + E9 + E10	4·11	3·63	3·97	4·24	4·56	4·86
12	Cash flow + or −	E5 − E11	+1·80	+2·13	+2·28	+2·50	+2·72	+2·94
F	**Tax calculations (£m.)**							
1	Tax this year	= B6 = 0·52B5	2·45	2·58	2·83	3·09	3·36	3·63
2	Advance corporation tax	ae, 0·52B8	0·35	0·37	0·41	0·45	0·48	0·52
3	Add to 'deferred tax' in D5	e, 0·52(0·9E7 + 0·15B5)	0·53	0·43	0·47	0·51	0·56	0·60

Ref.	Item	Method of calculation (see notes)	Year 0 (actual)	1	2	3	4	5
4	Tax paid	= E10 = F2 + pyC8	2·05	1·94	2·19	2·40	2·61	2·84
5	'Taxation' in C8	C8 = F1 − F2 − F3	1·57	1·78	1·95	2·13	2·32	2·51
6	Capital allowances	ignored e	0·00	0·00	0·00	0·00	0·00	0·00
G	Ratios, etc.							
1	Margin on sales (%)	B3 × 100 ÷ A7	12·10	12·70	13·20	13·60	14·10	14·60
2	ROCE (%)	B5 × 100 ÷ C13	16·70	16·40	16·70	16·90	17·10	17·10
3	Growth rate of profits, EpS (%)	B5 × 100 ÷ pyB5	2·90	5·50	9·60	9·00	9·00	8·00
4	Spare overdraft capacity (£m.)	m, 0·1C13 − C10	1·21	3·55	6·06	8·81	11·80	15·03
5	Labour productivity (units per man)	m (improves at 5% p.a.)	100·80	105·80	111·10	116·70	122·50	128·60
6	No. of workers	A5 ÷ G5	1,034·00	1,014·00	994·00	975·00	957·00	939·00
—	Added value, spare factory capacity, P/E ratio, share value, wages per employee, added value per average wage, etc.	—	—	—	—	—	—	—

tax). Most relationships are very simple. Tax calculations (at least in the United Kingdom) are not so simple, as can be seen from the section on tax (section F); calculations for deferred taxation are particularly difficult. Some ratios are not simple either.

I unreservedly recommend the planning team to develop a model of this sort. Start with the simplest model possible, and add new items only when they are really needed to provide a full understanding of the company or to answer specific 'What if . . .?' questions of strategic importance. Later on a computer should be programmed to make these calculations, but I strongly recommend the team to start with a manual model, so that it really understands what these calculations do and do not do. The team need not make the calculations manually itself; it is easy to 'programme' an intelligent accounts clerk to do them. One run, such as Exhibit 4.6, will take him an hour or two using a calculator. About a dozen runs, each on different assumptions about the future, will be needed to establish a bracket forecast.

Typical questions that such a model can answer are: (1) What will be the effect of inflation at 10 per cent p.a. over the next five years on our company's cash flow, net current assets and overdraft? (2) What rate of expansion in turnover can we achieve, assuming that margins remain constant, from our own internal finance, that is, with no new loans? (3) What will happen to profits if turnover and margins both decline by 2 per cent p.a. due to strong competition, and how long will our cash reserves last? (4) Ditto, if turnover and margins both increase by 2 per cent p.a.? (5) Assuming that the bank allows our overdraft to rise and remain at 10 per cent of our capital employed, how much more can we borrow on overdraft by year 5? This was one of the questions asked by Bunting Ltd, whose model is shown in Exhibit 4.6; the answer can be seen in item G4.

Clearly, this is an extremely useful device, not only when making Fo·forecasts at the optimistic, pessimistic and most probable levels, but also and even more so later on when evaluating alternative strategies, for each of which an Fp forecast is needed (see Chapter 8).

One important point to remember when making forecasts using any of these methods is that the future may not be smooth. Indeed, it is far more likely to contain jumps and discontinuities; it is only necessary to glance at any graph showing past trends to see how jerky real life is. Predicting when these leaps may occur is no easy task, but once again the idea of the bracket comes partially to the rescue, for an event that is helpful to the company can be assumed to occur early in the five-year sequence in the optimistic estimate and later in the pessimistic one – and vice versa for bad news. Most planners will attempt to reproduce the effects of the business cycle in their five-year forecasts.

Gap analysis

By now the planning team knows its bracket target and its bracket forecast. It only remains to place one on top of the other to see what the company's strategic prospects are.

Exhibit 4.7   Gap analysis showing a very urgent and serious situation

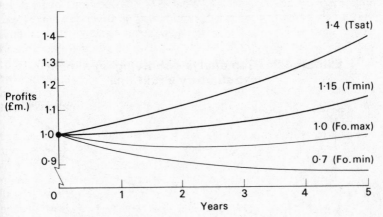

Suppose that they look like Exhibit 4.7, where not even the most optimistic forecast of profits for year 5 (labelled Fo. max and equalling £1m.) comes up to the lowest acceptable target level (labelled Tmin and equalling £1·15m.). There is even a possibility that on present strategies profits will be as low as £0·7m. (Fo. min). It is clear that a major attack on profits must be mounted; and since profits are forecast to fall significantly below Tmin in year 2, there is some urgency about it. The strategy *must* yield at least another £0·45m. by year 5 to get profits above Tmin, but preferably it should boost profits to £1·4m., that is, by another £0·7m.! Thus, the team will be alerted to the size of its task.

Suppose that the prospects look like Exhibit 4.8, however. Here the company has time to think, for no serious gaps arise for a couple of years. Furthermore, there is little chance of missing Tmin by more than £0·15m., so this company's future looks quite different from that of the last example.

Exhibit 4.8   Gap analysis showing a much less urgent situation

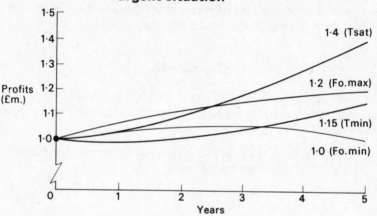

Exhibit 4.9   Gap analysis showing an almost satisfactory situation

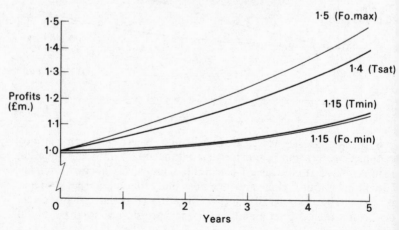

Exhibit 4.10   Gap analysis showing a satisfactory situation

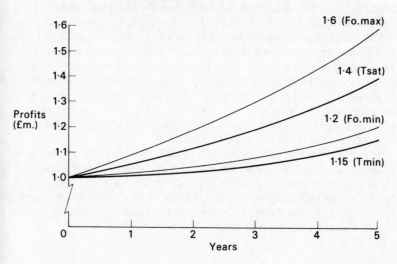

Exhibit 4.11   Gap analysis showing a situation that is too good to be true

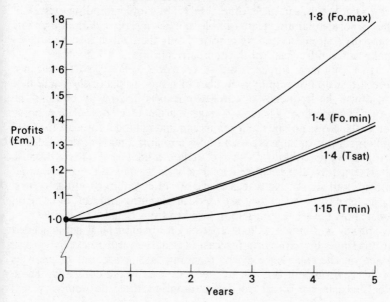

Now consider Exhibit 4.9, where it looks as though the company will exceed its targets without making any new decisions at all! In fact, however, this is a misinterpretation of what the brackets are telling us. The true position is that, although there is a negligible chance of falling below Tmin, there is also only a quite small chance of exceeding Tsat; and although a company likes to know that it is not going to do exceedingly badly (which is what Tmin represents, remember), it likes even more to know for sure that it is going to perform satisfactorily. Nevertheless, this exhibit does show a relatively happy position. Quite possibly, all that is needed is a risk-reducing strategy rather than a profit-increasing one (see page 153 for examples), but at this early stage in the process it is far too soon to be sure.

The gap diagram that represents a most satisfactory situation is shown in Exhibit 4.10. Here the Fo forecasts neatly straddle Tsat, so there is an even chance of exceeding Tsat by £0·2m. and of missing it by £0·2m. and virtually no chance at all of falling to Tmin. Of course, Exhibit 4.11 is even better. Here there is little chance of falling below Tsat – a situation not often met in the real world!

Summary

One of the most valuable sources of knowledge about the company lies buried in its past. A vital step, then, is to examine its past performance and to understand it well enough to be able to explain the major fluctuations in its fortunes. Only if this understanding exists will the corporate planning team be able to make a proper evaluation of its company's strengths and weaknesses; only then will it also be able to make rational forecasts of the company's future.

Most long term forecasts are of very poor quality, partly because forecasters do not employ a number of simple tricks of the trade that cut down the frequency of careless mistakes and partly because the future is uncertain. There is a huge margin of error on long range forecasts. Now, no one but a genius can understand a forecast that not only is subject to huge errors but also contains a mass of detail. Short term forecasts contain a mass of detail, which is required because short term forecasts are often used as a basis for day-to-day operational control, but short term forecasts are not often subject to huge errors. Long term forecasts, which are used for planning and not for control, must show the errors but seldom need to show detail.

The key is simplicity, then, especially for beginners. What is needed at this stage, therefore, is a forecast of profits over the next five years, based on the experience of the past and taking account of changes in the environment but not of any response by the company. These Fo forecasts are based on the assumption that the company will continue on its present course unaltered. This assumption has the great advantage of reducing the scope for errors, especially those introduced by optimism over some new untried idea to improve company performance. Even so, huge errors will be present, because the future is uncertain, and these must be shown, preferably by using the bracket forecast with, if required, a central 'most likely' forecast.

The team can now compare the bracket target with the bracket forecast to determine the gap, that is, the strategic task that faces it.

In the very first few days of the corporate planning exercise a crude profit forecast can be made by what I call the simple forecast method. In spite of its simplicity this will often be found to be a useful first approximation against which all subsequent and much more complex forecasts may be judged.

The next method of forecasting is to adopt the company's latest five-year budget (if it has one, and today all groups and most companies do) as a forecast. Some care is needed in doing this, because budgets usually contain not only the hoped-for effects of decisions already made but also the effects of decisions that are yet to be made, thus breaching the definition of an Fo.

By far the most powerful forecasting tool is the company model. It may be built up gradually, for, although it is useful in making Fo forecasts, it will only be really essential at the much later stage of strategy evaluation. I strongly recommend using a manual model to begin with, so that the team can understand exactly how it works, and only later programming a computer to make the calculations.

CHAPTER 5

Company Appraisal

At its fourth or fifth meeting the planning team will turn its attention away from the numerical details discussed in the past couple of chapters and towards a broad appraisal of the company. This is often called the strengths and weakness analysis – a title that correctly reflects what we are looking for, namely, those things about the company which are excellent, advantageous, powerful or beneficial and those which are feeble, deleterious or debilitating. We have to be a little careful of trying to categorise everything about a company as either a strength or a weakness, because some things may be neither yet nonetheless important. Yet, these two categories are useful mental guidelines, and I shall use them here.

Sometimes this exercise is called the internal appraisal, indicating that the search is limited to strategic factors found inside the company itself as opposed to external factors (considered in the next chapter) over which the company normally has no control, such as government actions and changes in technology.

Remember that we are looking only for the features of the company that are of strategic importance. It is unlikely that any company, however fortunate, will be able to claim to be outstanding in more than, say, half a dozen ways; nor will a company, however distressed its condition, be defective in more than a limited number of areas.

Who makes the appraisal?

Many large companies invite consultants or other outsiders to make the entire appraisal for them. In this, I believe, they are terribly mistaken, although this does not mean that there is no role for such outsiders here. Far from it; they can be most useful. I believe that the analysis of strengths and weaknesses should be conducted by the team itself but with the assistance of many other people. These other people should certainly include consultants, especially if the company already has a long-standing and close relationship with one, but there are many others whose views should be sought – not just on strengths and weaknesses either, but also on threats and opportunities, alternative strategies and, as mentioned above (page 68), the target-setting exercise.

These other people may include the company's bankers, merchant bankers, stockbrokers, legal advisers and auditors – anyone who knows the company fairly well. However, do not forget all those people inside the company as well as outside it whose views may be worth hearing: lower levels in the management, even the shopfloor, the trade union representative, the supervisory board, part-time non-executive directors, and so on. The views of all such people should be systematically solicited, gathered and collated.

However, having made this most important point I must return to the suggestion that the main burden for the analysis of strengths and weaknesses fall on the team. No one else in the world knows as much about the company as the members of the team do, and there are only two dangers in relying on their views alone. One is that they may miss some vital fact about the company, but this defect will soon be put right if the views of outsiders are sought. The other danger is that, although they may recognise all the facts about the company, they may prefer not to give them sufficient emphasis. There may be a lack of candour. There may be bias.

The views of outsiders will help to correct this bias too; but even more potent, I believe, is a four-stage appraisal system, which can be described as follows. First comes the identification stage, where lists of strengths and weaknesses are made, discussed, remade and eventually agreed as reflecting all the features of the company that are, or are thought to be, of strategic importance. In the next stage, called examination, the planning team examines the exact nature of each item in the lists in considerable detail, so as to describe it with considerable accuracy together with its history and its extent where necessary. A report several pages long together with graphs or calculations may be needed to describe each strength and each weakness. The third stage, called distillation, is where the team attempts to boil down each strength and weakness into a few pithy sentences. Sometimes a fourth stage is useful, namely, ranking. Here the team members attempt to arrange the items in each list in some order of ranking, so as to clarify their minds on the relative importance of each item.

As in so many other parts of this process the team members will come to believe that a consensus has emerged between them quite early on in this analysis. Then, one of them will suddenly make a remark, discover a long-forgotten fact or explode a company myth, and the consensus will be shattered, only to reform much later on around a new and somewhat different set of strengths and weaknesses. 'Oh,' they may exclaim, 'so it is not our foreign operations that have been dragging us down; it is the failure of the Engineering Development Department to give us new products!' Eventually, a consensus will be reached that, not only remains constant for many months and gives a feeling of confidence to the team members that they have got it right, but also portrays a simple *and* coherent profile of the company itself.

We must remember that the strengths and weaknesses with which we should concern ourselves in a corporate planning exercise are those which may decide the whole future course of the company. Most planners love to make 'comprehensive' lists or lists in 'meticulous detail', as I have seen them described. No wonder they cannot see the wood for the trees! No, let us try to make not the longest list but the shortest.

How should they do it?

Let me describe the four-stage appraisal in some detail. The first stage is identification. The best possible start for this stage can be made at the introductory seminar with which, remember, the entire Argenti planning process should normally start (see page 23).

The whole of the second part of this seminar is devoted to running quickly through the corporate planning process applied to the company in order to demonstrate to the participants what is involved and how they will each be able to help the planning team when the exercise begins in earnest. In the first session the participants attempt to set a target. Although this may be a useful demonstration, it is rare for sufficient time to be available to allow any really practical conclusions or solutions to emerge, but it does provide a useful warning to the planning team of the problems that it will meet when it starts the target-setting task in earnest.

In the second session, however, the participants (who represent, remember, virtually the whole of the top management of the company) are asked to identify key strengths and weaknesses. Their response to this question will be better informed than that of any other group of people that it is possible to imagine! This session, then, is important and will have invaluable messages for the planning team.

One useful way to reduce bias and prejudice to a minimum is to break the participants up into syndicates in separate rooms for, say, 45 minutes. Each syndicate – three or four is a practical number – should contain between two and six (certainly not more than eight) participants carefully selected from different levels and sections in the company. They discuss, list their conclusions and report back to the full seminar.

These reports and subsequent discussions take the remaining 45 minutes of the session, at the end of which a small number of strengths and weaknesses will have been identified by all the syndicates and a greater number will have been mentioned by only one or two of them. Thus, a first slightly ragged consensus will have emerged. However, be careful! This early focus sometimes proves false or distorted; and although the planning team must treat it with great respect, it is the team's job over the next few weeks to test it rather than merely to accept it.

When the planning team starts work on strengths and weaknesses in its fourth or fifth meeting, several months will have elapsed since the seminar, and it will be surprised at some of the items that found their way into the list at the seminar. So, the team's immediate task is to redraw the lists and then move on to the second stage, namely, examination. Each item should be subjected to careful examination by the team, by outside experts if necessary, by special committees drawn from the company's staff, and so on; all methods should be considered. At the end there should be a detailed report on each strength and each weakness, complete with any charts, figures, objective facts and evidence – a careful and professional job.

Thus, if at the seminar the statement 'Our products are the best' was proposed as a strength, the team should now attempt to adduce objective evidence – from market surveys, consumer reports, consultants' opinions, and so on – that this is truly so or is not so. At the end of this second phase the team will have accumulated a mass of data on each of a number of possible strengths and weaknesses.

The team's task in the third stage, namely, distillation, is to refine these data down to the bare essentials – to obtain a new consensus, a new focus. This it can best do in one of its meetings; and when the team members believe that they have attained it, they should list the items that they believe to be strategic with a paragraph or two on each. The entire appraisal will now have been distilled down to a page or two (for an example, see Exhibit 5.1). Approval of this by the team's colleagues ends the appraisal.

Discussion among the team in one of its meetings is probably the best way to make this final distillation. However, it may be found useful to attempt to rank each strength and each weakness according to importance. Although the actual scores may turn out not to be very useful in themselves, the act of attempting to rank in this way often helps to eliminate disagreements and facilitates the emergence of a consensus. Two methods are common; Exhibit 5.2 shows a list of strengths ranked from 0 to 10 in importance and a list of weaknesses ranked from A to C. (In my view it is quite hard enough to classify strengths and weaknesses into three classes of importance, let alone 10.)

In searching for strengths and weaknesses it is useful to have a checklist. The one that I use contains nine areas of a company in

Exhibit 5.1   The final list of strengths and weaknesses for Drake & Co

Strengths

Finance	Cash flow is strongly positive, gearing is low, and we could borrow £4–5m. without any difficulty at any time in the next two years.
Marketing	Marketing is extremely effective, especially in the machine tool industry, where our reputation is virtually unrivalled for service.
Position in Industry	Market share is rising rapidly towards 50 per cent.

Weaknesses

Products	The entire reputation of the company rests on one ageing product. It is very reliable and very well known, but ageing.
Research	The team was broken up by retirement and illness some years ago and is no longer the leading team in our industry.
Production	The factory is very old and has obsolescent plant and equipment.
Employees	Unions are strong. We have had many disputes but no strikes yet.
Marketing	Nearly 30 per cent of our total output goes to one customer. We export 5 per cent of output.
Management	Top management is traditional and elderly.

Exhibit 5.2   Examples of ranking systems: Auk & Sons

Strength	Rank	Weakness	Rank
Cash flow	7	Marketing expertise	A
The new product	9	Labour disputes	C
Strong top management	5	Ageing top managers	C
Professional middle managers	5	Foreign markets	B
Our traditional markets	9	Non-voting shares	A
Advertising skills	4		
R & D	6		
Stock control	1		

Note: Here the team has attempted to rank the strategic significance of each proposed strength on a scale from 10 (highly significant) to 0 (not strategically significant).

Note: Here the team has attempted to rank strategic significance by classifying the items into three categories only: A (highly significant), B (probably strategically significant) and C (not significant).

which they may be found – finance, production, marketing, research, buying, employees, management, position in industry, group – but no checklist is equally applicable to all companies, and the team must make its own search rules.

Most of the rest of this chapter is devoted to describing examples in these nine areas.

Finance. I intend this word to cover not only such strictly financial matters as profits and cash flow but some legal ones too. Let us take the financial ones first. Fluctuating profits can be most debilitating and are a serious weakness for some companies operating in industries that are subject to cycles. These cycles are sometimes of long duration (shipbuilding, for example, seems to have a decade or more of upswing followed by decades of decline) and sometimes ridiculously short (for example, umbrellas and fireworks).

High gearing is a weakness and low gearing a strength; sometimes, gearing is so high or so low as to be of strategic importance. Some companies pay very high dividends and some very low. Some companies own property. Sometimes, stocks or work-in-progress is an exceptionally high percentage of capital employed or turnover; in the animal skin industries, for example, stocks are frequently 100 per cent of turnover, because some skins can be bought only once a year. Some companies enjoy special tax concessions. Some companies lease their plant or buy on hire purchase. Some companies sell on hire purchase. All these can be of strategic significance.

Now let us turn to the legal aspects. Some companies have peculiar clauses in their articles of association. Others – many others – have gearing limitation clauses in their debenture deeds, some of which may be strategic. Some companies have long term contracts with suppliers, customers or employees. Some companies have non-voting shares that must soon be enfranchised. Others are private companies hoping to go public. Others are already public but have their control still in the founder family's hands. In some the present controllers are likely to lose control if the company issues the new equity that it so badly needs for expansion. Many small quoted companies suffer from low price–earnings (P/E) ratios.

Examine the balance sheet. Is the asset-backing adequate? How soon can you refund those short term loans? What has inflation done to your property values? Have you raised any capital in a foreign market; and if so, how would an exchange rate shift affect you? How would your imports and exports be affected by such a shift?

I hope that it is now clear how searching this internal appraisal has to be. Many strengths and weaknesses will be unearthed, which may or may not turn out to be among the strategic few. In any case all this self-knowledge is invaluable. I know one company whose four top men were so appalled by the number of weaknesses revealed in their company, and so dismayed at the errors and omissions that they themselves had permitted over the past few years in their own departments, that they suspended the corporate planning exercise for six months while they 'put our house in order', as they described it.

The company model, described in the previous chapter, is also a useful source of data on financial strengths and weaknesses. It can be asked such questions as: how rapidly can we expand turnover without exceeding our loan capacity? Another vital source of financial data is the examination of the company's past record (see page 82), where such statistics as a decline in return on capital employed (ROCE), a rise in break-even point, a fall in sales margins, and so on may be revealed. So are the financial and accounting records and the chairman's annual reports for the past five or ten years.

In virtually every case something of strategic importance will emerge in the finance area. Very well; first write it up in detail with figures, and then boil it down to a few carefully-worded sentences that represent a consensus of opinion at the top.

Here are some examples of distilled strength and weakness statements in the financial area:

'Parts of the company are making losses. Individually, these are small, except for the subsidiary in France (£0·1m. loss last year), but collectively they total £0·3m. This is massive compared with our group profits of only £1·2m.'

'Our share price is low. Our P/E ratio is half of the average for our industry sector. Our market capitalisation is half of our book value, and some of our property is undervalued in the books!'

'Our total loan capacity is probably £5–6m. at present. We only have one long term loan – a 10½ per cent debenture of £1·8m. – and the overdraft is £1·1m. and falling. So, if it were needed, we could increase borrowings by £2m. or even £3m. right now.'

'We have been overtrading for the past three years. Turnover has nearly doubled to £118m., but profits have risen by only 25 per cent to £3·1m. Fixed assets have fallen in real terms, but working capital has more than doubled (227 per cent). Gearing is approaching 60 per cent; the situation is now dangerous.'

'Due to our excellent dividend record our P/E ratio is far above the industry average.'

'Our ROCE is very low. It points to an urgent need to improve profits from existing capital resources. No one will lend us any more until we do this.'

'Following our turn-round from heavy losses six years ago the company's reputation in the City of London is now high and rising. We are frequently "tipped" in the press as a recovery situation. Our P/E ratio is above our sector average. While the family holding will deter a bid for us, we are well positioned to bid for companies in the United Kingdom. Because we now import as much as we export from Germany, exchange rates are no longer the problem that we thought that they were; the loan to our subsidiary in Belgium is at risk, however.'

'If we have to enfranchise the non-voting shares – and we shall probably be forced to do so within a decade or so – the family will lose control.'

Production. Under this heading I include not only factories, plant, equipment and machinery but also offices, warehouses, transport fleets and shop premises – all physical things – as well as all production know-how (production planning, quality control, distribution scheduling, and so on).

Consider your company's factories. How many does it have? Are there too many small uneconomic ones? Are any of them so large as to be dangerously close to the limits of man management or to be dangerously prominent politically? Where are they located? Are they in high cost areas, in high unemployment areas, a long way from railheads or motorways, or in areas of scenic beauty? How modern are they? How old are the machines in them, and how up-to-date are the services? How do manning levels compare with those of competitors? Is there excessive work-in-progress?

You may feel that these items are too insignificant ever to be strategically significant and therefore that I am breaking one of my own rules, namely, the one about excessive detail. However, I am not suggesting here that the planning team make a detailed examination of every corner of the company's production facilities – only that it examines any corner that may conceal a strategic elephant. All other corners can be ignored. I should add that some of these items are very definitely strategic for some companies; for a company in civil engineering or for a manufacturer of generating sets for power stations, for example, work-in-progress is decidedly strategic. Every company is different – so different that it is hardly worthwhile attempting to list all these possible areas of strategic importance.

Commercial companies, banks, insurance companies, and so on do not have factories, but they do have offices. Very well. Are these modern or ancient? Where are they? Who owns them? Is the computer up to standard?

The company may be a high street retailer. How many shops does it have? Where are they? Are they too small? Are they in the wrong part of the high street?

I normally also include physical distribution under this heading: warehouses, depots, dockside facilities, transport fleets, ships, aircraft, and so on. I also include the technical side of production know-how: production planning, stock control, quality control, method study, materials efficiency control, value engineering, workshop layout, process control, safety and health, and so on endlessly.

The following are typical examples of strength and weakness statements in the production area:

'The whole of our production side is poor. We have invested virtually nothing in plant or equipment for six years during the recession, and our machine tools compare badly with those of our competitors in the United States and Germany. Our incentive scheme is totally out of date and is the cause of much friction. Labour productivity is low. Stocks are high, and much of the excess stock is obsolete and redundant. We believe that it will take three years and £2m. of capital to move all this up to German standards. The factory buildings and the site itself are good, so a move to new premises is not relevant.'

'We divide the factory into two for this report: the stamping shop, which is excellent, contains the new Heron machines (we have six out of the ten so far in operation in Europe) and is probably the finest shop in Europe; and the dipping, paint and finish shops, which are very traditional. We believe that these should eventually be modernised, but they are not a major cost centre, and the quality of their work is high by modern standards.'

'One of our key strengths is our depot system. Because our product is so bulky, merchants do not like keeping our full range on their own premises, and being able to obtain prompt delivery from us is a service that they unanimously applaud. None of our competitors have any depots.'

'Of the chain of 140 retail shops that we operate, we own 63, of which 28 are large modern premises in prime high-street sites and 22 are small. Of the others, 41 are rented in prime sites and 18 are small. Most of the small shops, both rented and owned, are making losses at present. As most top executives are well aware, we operate twice as many shops as any of our competitors, and our average floor area per shop is well under half of that of Cranes & Co., Rails, and

Crake Ltd. We therefore believe that for our present merchandise and our present customer profile we have far too many small shops.'

'Our procedures are well up to the standards of the leaders. We operate the latest automatic telephone switchboard into 130 visual display stations with instant access to computer files. Accounts can be examined, minor claims settled and fraudulent practices identified almost in seconds. We are not ahead of the field, but we know what we are doing in this area.'

Marketing. Here I include marketing, advertising, promotion, customer relations, public relations, selling, distribution, after-sales services, and so on – all the skills expected under such a heading. However, I also include customers, products, services, quality, pricing, merchanting, franchising, leasing, packaging, delivery, retailing and product range – absolutely everything related to the company's products and to how, where, to whom they are sold.

Consider first the various marketing skills. In particular consider whether your company has crossed the great divide between companies that produce a product and then go out and sell it and companies that find out what customers want and then produce and sell that. Some anxiety must be felt for those in the former class; they are two or three decades behind the times!

The correct identification of strengths in the marketing area is difficult. Take a company whose share of the market is increasing rapidly. This may be due to its excellent advertising, its low prices or its strenuous sales force; or it may be due to factors entirely outside the marketing area, such as that the product is superbly made, well designed or technically advanced or that its competitors have lost their best managers – or almost anything! Since we hope to erect a major new strategy on the strengths that we identify in the company, it is clearly important to identify them correctly. Perhaps, then, marketing is one area where the planning team should especially invite the views of such objective observers as marketing consultants, customers, independent laboratories specialising in product tests, and so forth.

Product comparisons are not normally difficult to make – remember that this is not a marketing audit but corporate planning, where only major defects or advantages are significant – nor are pricing or quality comparisons. Product range comparisons are more difficult. Go and look at the product range of, say, Fiat, and try to reach a rational conclusion as to whether it is 'better' or 'worse' than, say, Ford's.

Consider also the various methods of selling: retail outlets, merchants, franchises, leasing, and so on. Which of these do you use? How good at selling are you? If you rely on others to sell for you (merchants or agents, for example), how good are they? Who are your customers? Are there too many of them, or too few? How do they decide to buy your products?

Perhaps the best way to illuminate this huge section is to record some examples of strength and weakness statements in the marketing area:

'Over the past two decades there have been so many mergers among our customers that we only have three left in our home market and twelve overseas. Most of them are either very large or part of groups that are even larger; we are small compared with most of them. Five take 60 per cent of our total output between them. Four are in politically unstable nations.'

'The patent on one key feature of our only product runs out in three years, and competitors in Japan are already selling identical copies under very similar trade names. We cannot see any special advantage in our product once this patent expires.'

'The life cycle of our products is far longer than that of our competitors' products. Our prices are higher, and so are our margins. Turnover is lower for most of our products than for our competitors' equivalents. We are the Rolls Royce of the industry. Our advertising, design, packaging, service, sales staff – everything – are geared to maintaining this up-market image.'

'The main cause of our dreadful performance in the past five years is that we have lost touch with our customers. They have been moving up-market as the nation's economy has boomed and demanding better quality, while we have still been selling shoddy merchandise on price alone. They are just not interested in this any more.'

'We are market leaders in Australia and have been for a decade. We lead on design, quality, performance and reliability. Our prices are 15 per cent above the industry average, yet we enjoy a 36 per cent share of the market. Marketing, promotion, advertising and selling are excellent and highly professional and fully exploit the advantages of our product range.'

'The whole marketing side of the company in the United Kingdom is good or excellent. This includes the sales organisation, salesmen themselves, stockists, transport, distribution (not for the government sector however) and central advisory services, There is a good deal of spare capacity here, which could cope with more products of the same type or even a whole new range.'

'Half of our turnover is abroad. We are particularly successful in organising small subsidiary companies in foreign countries, managed and partly financed by nationals, to sell (and in some cases to manufacture) our product range. Only two attempts at this have failed. Seventeen are making profits that are as good as, or better than, those of our home-based operations.'

'There are no major strengths or weaknesses in this area of our company.'

Research.   Under this heading I include not only scientific research and technological development (R & D) but much more besides. Companies have to undertake not only scientific work to develop new products or processes but also many other kinds of research to develop new services and procedures. A bank about to introduce a new credit card or cash security service, an insurance company about to launch a new type of policy, a retailer about to offer new hire-purchase procedures – all these must be researched in almost the same way as, say, a new product based on laser technology.

In my definition research means all the studies, experiments, tests, designing and discussing – but not the executive actions – that have to be done to bring about a change in a company to keep it up to date. To rephrase this into a question: how good is your company at keeping itself up to date in products, processes, materials, procedures, markets and customers? This is 'R & D' in my checklist.

First take traditional R & D. Here the relevant questions are: Are your products technically advanced? Do your competitors envy your R & D facilities? Can you sell know-how, or do you have to buy it from others? Can you actually point to several innovations in your industry emanating from your company's R & D? Do your specialist trade journals often feature your work? One point worthy of attention: it is useless to state a strength in such general terms as 'Our research team is acknowledged throughout the industry'. It is essential to identify exactly what the team is noted for. Is it for work on the product itself, the process by which it is made, the materials used, the new uses found for an existing product, or what?

Turning to those other types of research, I include market research, consumer research, motivational research, materials availability studies, and so on. All these activities are devoted to making sure that, when a major decision is taken, it is right – that it is based on a firm footing of fact. One of the major sections to be discussed below is 'Management'; there we will be examining the strengths and weaknesses of line executive managers, but here we are discussing the other major constituent of a company's top levels, namely, its staff side – specialists, advisers, commentators, experts. Some companies employ hardly any of these and rely on entrepreneurial flair. I should be among the last to criticise this style of management; but if that is how your company is run, let it be stated so clearly.

Examples of strength and weakness statements in the research area that I have seen include:

'We have virtually no R & D at all. Both of our competitors in the home market (there are no imports or exports), which are four times our size, have large R & D departments. In both cases their research directors enjoy worldwide reputation.'

'We manufacture all our products under licence from competitors abroad, and have no development facilities at all.'

'We have no R & D. However, there are no signs whatever that our products or our processes are backward.'

'Our product is still the acknowledged leader. Continuous development of it is supervised by the technical committee, which studies user reports and complaints, technological trends in our industry, all the trade journals, competitor products, and so on. It is very thorough and very successful in keeping us in front.'

'We have failed to introduce any new products for five years. This is not because of the quality of the engineers in the development team but because they are responsible to the three divisional directors, who each demand fire-fighting, problem-solving and other immediate activities. If R & D were placed under the group director, some of its activities could be steered towards long term development of new products.'

'Our market-research department has not made a single useful comment for years. It certainly has not identified any new customers, new customer needs, new markets or new segments of old markets – nothing.'

Buying. Buying means buying, procuring, sourcing and purchasing. In some companies it includes stock control, quality control of purchased goods, receiving facilities, shipping, transport, credit control and chasing. Some of these may well be of strategic significance, but what I have mainly in mind is the purchasing situation itself.

What does your company buy? Make a list of, say, the ten most important components or services or materials. From where do these come? Who supplies them to you? From how many suppliers do you buy each of these materials? Can any of these suppliers deny you your materials, or can any event interrupt supplies from them? How big are the suppliers compared with you? Are you the biggest buyer in the world (or in your nation), or are you only average or very small? In other words, who has the upper hand: you or your suppliers? Does it matter?

In making your list of key purchases do not forget services, fuels and water nor any very minor item that, although small in value or quantity, is obtainable from only one remote, esoteric or risky source. Do not forget all the infinite ways in which supplies can be interrupted, prices distorted or quality reduced: strikes, political (especially tax and duty) decisions, technical advances, nationalism, crop failures, bad weather, earthquake, exchange rate crisis, war, revolution, acquisition of your supplier by one of your competitors, and, finally, depletion of that particular natural resource. Of course, many of these can be reversed to bring good news as well: bumper crops, removal of import duties or taxes, and so on.

Below are some examples of strength and weakness analyses in the buying area. (Notice, incidentally, that in all these sets of examples I often include an extract that proclaims 'There are no strengths or weaknesses in this area'. Some firms believe that the absence of a strategic strength or weakness in an area is an important fact. In any case such statements do seem to me useful, because they confirm that the planning team has looked in this area, not just forgotten it.)

'Due to our close link with Eagle Multinational Corporation we are able to purchase newsprint and newsprint machinery on extremely favourable terms.'

'None of our materials are imported. This puts us at a major advantage over all our competitors every time there is a dock strike here or in their suppliers' dock systems, which happens once every two years or so, and every time there is an exchange rate crisis.'

'The vehicle bodies that we build are all designed for a commercial chassis made by Teal Trucks Ltd, but Teal is a major competitor in all our markets over our entire range of vehicles. All other chassis manufacturers are also major competitors. When demand increases, Teal naturally satisfies its own needs first. Compared with us Teal (and the others) is huge.'

'Two of our key materials are obtainable only from politically unstable, highly nationalistic, anti-capitalist, developing nations. We should never have allowed ourselves to get in this position, but in it we definitely are:

'There are no key strengths or weaknesses in this area.'

'Our sole supplier is a huge nationalised monolith that seems unable and unwilling to meet our needs.'

'We purchase worldwide. This reduces some of the fluctuations in supply and price, but the price can double or halve in six months. We seem to be very skilful in predicting price changes, but, of course, we do not have the cash available to back these hunches, and we got it wrong last year. So, the risks are substantial.'

Employees.   Under this heading I include everyone employed by the company and everything relating to them.

How many employees are there? Where are they employed? Are they mainly male or female, black or white, skilled or unskilled? Have you measured their productivity in terms of turnover, value added and profits per employee and compared these figures with those of other relevant companies, with the national averages for all companies and with the same figures for five years ago?

What about morale? Can you say whether the employees are generally content or discontent? How high is labour turnover? How often do you have strikes, disputes or accidents? Have you compared these figures with those of five years ago, with those of other companies and with the national averages? What about age distribution? What about pay and conditions? Do you have any really awful conditions of work (noise, smell, danger) or any really excellent ones (superb research facilities, magnificent computer department) that contribute to poor or good morale?

What about skills? Do you perhaps employ the leading team of oleo-physicists in western Europe or the largest number of welders? Is there one man, or a very small team of men, on whom much of the future success of the company rests: a chief designer, perhaps, or a brilliant finance man?

Consider trade unions, of course. Are the unions strong? How many are there? Are there interunion disputes? Do the unions exploit pay anomalies or anomalies between two or more of your sites? Where do your employees live? Is the local community a close-knit one in which your firm plays a major role?

Finally consider all your employee-related systems: pensions, retirement policies, recruitment, induction, training, promotion, disputes, strikes, participation, works councils, worker–directors, worker–shareholders, pay structures, incentive schemes, and so on. Is there anything here that contains something of strategic significance, either good or bad?

Here are some typical examples of strength and weakness statements in the employee area:

'Employee relations are excellent. Most of our jobs require skills, and job satisfaction is high. We have always taken great care over our employees' needs and still do.'

'The company is by far the largest employer in the town; in fact the company virtually *is* the town. We have an excellent reputation and intend to maintain it.'

'Our offices are just like most other offices in this essentially modern-office town. Employees come and go. Most of the jobs are rather dull, just like most of the jobs in everyone else's offices in this area.'

'Strong trade unions are a tradition in this heavily working-class area. Most of the work here is heavy and dirty; ours is hot and dusty too. We employ so many people that disputes are frequent (but fairly brief). The entire work community is so steeped in tradition that, in spite of our efforts to improve things, it would take a generation to modernise work methods, attitudes, conditions and pay structures. Meanwhile, new industries are springing up around us, and our factories look more and more like an oasis of the past in a modern world.'

'Labour relations are good or exceptionally good. The importance of this can hardly be exaggerated, since reliability of supply is one of our very few major advantages over our competitors.'

'Mr Smith's close family relationship with the chairman of Grosbeak International – our largest customer by far – is plainly of strategic importance.'

Management. Under this heading I include the managers themselves, their skills and how they all fit together in the organisation.

There is one key difference between this area and all the others. It is difficult enough for managers to obtain an objective and unbiased view of their company's products, for example, or its buying position or its employees, but it is even more difficult for them to obtain such a view of themselves. Although I still believe that it is better for the managers to make this study themselves than for an outsider to do it for them, I do accept that there is a strong case for bringing in some outside view at some stage. As confirmation perhaps, or a second opinion, or to adjudicate in cases of disagreement, such a view would be invaluable, and perhaps this is a suitable moment to remind ourselves of the value of those outside-insiders, namely, the non-executive directors. They often not only have wide experience of industry but know the company intimately as well – exactly the sort of view of the company that we need to make an informed unbiased strength and weakness analysis.

What we need to know is whether the management is capable of handling the company's problems now and over the next few years, just as in the strength and weakness analyses above we have tried to decide whether the company's production facilities, marketing skills and financial situation are going to be adequate. As we have seen in countless examples, most companies find such severe weaknesses in one or more areas of their activities that they cannot imagine making a successful onslaught on future problems until these have been put right. Some companies, on the contrary, conclude that they can launch an attack on the future with confidence. Plainly, the management's skills are one of the most important areas of all in this analysis, and therefore a vital part of this exercise is often a very personal one; the top half-dozen people are going to have to discuss their own personal strengths and weaknesses quite openly with their colleagues and even with, or in front of, their subordinates. I believe that this delicate-sounding exercise is best carried out, or at least begun, in the introductory seminar (described on page 23), where each syndicate discusses and reports on the company's strengths and weaknesses. There is so little time in these syndicate sessions that no one has a chance to put up an elaborate defensive smokescreen; and if anyone does try to do this, the result is so blatantly biased that his views and those of his syndicate are instantly dismissed, sometimes accompanied by derisive laughter from the other syndicates. So, even in this part of the strength and weakness analysis, where they have to discuss the most sensitive area of all, namely themselves, the managers can usually achieve valid answers without the aid of an outside view.

However, it can do no harm and may add considerably to confidence if an outsider's view is also sought from among the company's bankers, legal advisers, management consultant, or whatever. This is particularly appropriate in a company run by an autocrat, for in this type of company it is very difficult for even the top managers to offer any criticism of the autocrat, and it may just tip the scales in favour of an honest and open conclusion if one or more respected outsiders add their voice to the muffled protestations of the employees.

Among the features that we need to identify in this management area are: whether there are any great strengths or weaknesses in the lower levels, in the middle levels or at the top of the management hierarchy; and whether the company is particularly good at some special area of management: production-scheduling, project management, financial control, labour relations, international contract negotiations, or whatever.

It is often important to look at the age distribution of the management team, succession, training, recruitment from outside and career-planning. Discussion of the company's current organisational structure is virtually always relevant, with such questions as whether the company should be divided functionally, geographically or by product groups coming up frequently.

Because this is such a sensitive area, disagreements are frequent, and a consensus takes some time to achieve. I see no point in hurrying it, unless the corporate plan has to be ready before some vital deadline – never a desirable background to the corporate planning process, as I have stated before. We must remember that someone at the top of the company (it may be you!) is going to have to admit something about himself or his department that he may prefer not to have to admit – certainly not in public. One of the reasons why corporate planning takes so long – or rather, one of the reasons why I believe that it should take so long – is that time must be allowed for difficult mental and emotional adjustments to take place.

Among typical results of analysing the strengths and weaknesses of the management area are the following:

'The top team is a most harmonious one with each director playing a vital part that interlocks smoothly with the parts of his colleagues. There is a great crevasse, however, between these six men and the next level of managers. None of the latter are professionally qualified; few have had any formal management-training; none can aspire to directorships; all play the part of assistant to directors. No succession plan exists. Although the company is run extremely competently now, illness or accident could have serious consequences.'

'No strategic strengths or weaknesses exist in this area. The company is professionally managed; it copes as well as any of its competitors with current problems; it can cope with any foreseen. However, if a major expansion were attempted, especially if an element of diversification were involved, the present management could be severely stretched.'

'Severe strains have appeared at the top in recent years. This is because the company has expanded rapidly into the Middle East and many of our top managers have been abroad for up to 30 per cent of their working days. Deteriorations in control of our home-based operations are observed almost daily; labour relations have been neglected.'

'Both the chairman and the chief executive will retire within five years, and no successors exist. The finance director is, as he himself admits, "only an accountant" and is not *au fait* with modern financial techniques. Several excellent middle managers (Blake, Watson, Smith and Patel) are ready for promotion.'

'After several months of discussion the cause of our company's poor performance over the past decade is now believed to be as follows. The company expanded very rapidly under the direction of the late John Pochard, who introduced his four sons into the top levels of management without any formal training. During his long illness and since his death a number of major diversifications have been undertaken, most of which are still not profitable. Only two members of the board have had any experience outside this company, and it has to be admitted that more directors of their calibre are urgently needed now.'

I have stated (page 99) that, although during analyses of this kind it is possible to obtain a clear consensus quite quickly, this is subsequently found to be false; a new focus then emerges. One example of this occurred to a particular company in this management area. At their introductory seminar the eighteen participants broke up into four syndicates, each composed of one or more directors and three or four second-level managers. One weakness on which all syndicates seemed to be agreed could be summarised as follows:

'Although the company's recent performance has not been too bad, we have left undone a great number of things that we should have done. We have launched no new products, spent very little on modernising the factory and allowed several markets to decay. We believe this to be because the top managers have been too busy with day-to-day affairs. The reason for this is that the managers at the lower levels are extremely poor, so it would be dangerous to delegate more decisions to them.'

Some weeks later the corporate planning team (five directors and their corporate planner), having reached the strength and weakness analysis stage, began to discuss this conclusion. Two of the directors said that they no longer believed it. The corporate planner, who had recently been recruited into the company, conducted a series of private interviews with all eighteen people who had been present at the seminar, and several others, and confirmed that this description was almost certainly incorrect.

The error lay in the last sentence. The problem lay not in the poor low-level managers (who were generally perfectly adequate) but in

he fact that the chief executive had been failing to give a lead, especially
n such forward-looking areas as new products. He had demanded
mmediate results, detailed improvements, instant cost-cutting. (I have
o add, just to complete the story, that the chief executive at once fully
accepted this conclusion and that the company then began to move
ahead. It was like unblocking a drain, someone commented.) It will be
appreciated that, with the chief executive at the seminar, it was not
possible to reach the true conclusion there, so a smokescreen rationalis-
ation was proposed as a subconscious evasion.

Be wary of all first conclusions. I frequently see 'We are a young
aggressive management team' and I occasionally see 'The company is
fortunate in being led by a man of great strength and experience'. It
s often better to reach a correct, accurate and meaningful consensus
but *not* to write it down rather than to write down a sycophantic
euphemism.

Position in Industry.   Here it is useful to state the company's position
as a member of its industry, sector or national economy.

Are you, for example, the largest company in your industry or
sector, or the largest company in Europe, New Zealand or Northtown?
Where do you rank in size with all the companies that you classify as
your competitors? Are you the price leader, the technology leader or
the market leader? Do you have any political influence in the United
Nations, in Parliament, in Brussels or in Northtown? Are you so small
that none of the more onerous items of national and international
legislation affect you? Can you run rings around the larger
competitors?

Here are some examples of strengths and weaknesses in the area of
industrial position:

'We are number three out of three in our industry. The other two
are larger and more technically advanced but cannot oblige
customers with short runs of "specials". We have virtually no
control over our destiny; they pre-empt us in price, large customers,
technical innovation and supplies.'

'We are well into Britain's Top Hundred; and although we have to be
very careful about what we do and how we do it, we also have the
ability to swing matters our way when we really need to. Our name
is a household word.'

'We are a very small company indeed, but our product is a medical
one to which the press is extremely hostile. What is worse: the
National Health Service, the medical profession and the Department
of Health all look upon us unfavourably.'

'We are the biggest employer in Northtown. Everything that we d
is front page news in the local press and headline news on radio an
television.'

Groups.   All my examples so far have been drawn from the variou
functions found in companies – production, marketing, personnel
and so forth – but many companies are divided not functionally bu
into subsidiary companies or profit centres. How do we identif
strengths and weaknesses in groups, parent companies and holdin
companies?

In my experience the best way is the one described above; that is, g
through the group's main activities using the functional checklis
described above. After all, it can be just as true of a group o
companies as of a single company that, for example, 'Our produc
range is the leader in its field' or 'Our top management could no
cope with any further expansion'.

However, there are two other areas for groups to examine in additio
to those in the checklist. One is to look at each subsidiary in turn an
see if there is anything outstandingly good or bad about it *as*
subsidiary. Thus, perhaps a group has three subsidiaries, but one o
them contributes no less than 80 per cent of all the group's profits
Perhaps one subsidiary for historical reasons is capital intensive
whereas all the others are labour intensive. Perhaps one is in high tech
nology, whereas the others are not. Perhaps the group's most impressiv
managing director happens to head the subsidiary that, for reason
beyond anyone's control, has the least promising future.

The other area of search for a group is the strengths and weaknesse
that arise *because it is a group*. Thus, one possible weakness is th
inability of the people at the centre to control the activities o
managers of far-flung subsidiaries, or there may be failure on their par
even to understand the basic facts in some subsidiary's specialise
business areas. On the other hand some groups may have the advantag
that their subsidiaries cover a wider band of business areas than thei
non-group competitors; or there may be the advantage that, if any
subsidiary discovers a particularly promising field of business, all th
financial and management resources of the group can be poured into it

Typical examples of strength and weakness statements for group
are:

'Because of our group structure we are able to operate in a very wid
range of business areas. We should have no difficulty in expanding
or diversifying almost without limit over the next few decades.'

'On several occasions in the past five years a subsidiary compan
has reported results that were very substantially lower than it

monthly reports had suggested. It is doubtful whether our information systems are adequate for our existing spread of interests, let alone any extension.'

'Our fourteen subsidiary companies span a wide range of mid-technology mechanical-engineering products. Several subsidiaries sell into the same markets, but otherwise there is little that is common to them. They share no major suppliers, supply no major customer and are dependent on no single economic or technical trend. Indeed, several are countercyclical to several others.'

'One major weakness pervades virtually all our subsidiaries, namely, that their products are obsolescent.'

'The stock exchange and international bankers have great trouble in classifying our company. We are mainly in engineering, but we also have major commodity-trading interests. Also, we operate across the world, but 80 per cent of profits arise in the United Kingdom. Furthermore, our biggest subsidiary is owned 50 per cent by an American company, which is now in some financial difficulty.'

Summary

The analysis of strengths and weaknesses is an extremely interesting and revealing stage in the corporate planning exercise. For small and medium-sized companies it is probably the most important stage (for bigger ones the environmental appraisal is more important). Some absolutely vital conclusions almost always emerge from this analysis, and these may well change the whole atmosphere in the company and switch the thinking of its top executives into quite new paths.

In theory this internal analysis should be quite straightforward. All that we need to know is what the company is exceptionally good at and bad at, so that these features can be woven into the strategy; there cannot be too many features of this calibre in any company. Furthermore, as no company today can exist for more than a few years unless it is remarkably good at something, surely it cannot be too difficult to identify what this is? In theory, no.

In practice we meet the crux of the problem as soon as we ask 'Who is going to make this appraisal?' An outsider would do it objectively and dispassionately, but in my view no one outside a firm can possibly know it as well as an insider. Yet, the view of the insider will be subjective, clouded by detail and biased by departmental loyalties and rivalries.

I believe that the four-stage sequence described above overcomes all these problems. The first glimpse of the main strengths and weaknesses is obtained from syndicate sessions in the introductory seminar, at which the top two or three levels of management are invited to give their views. Then, the planning team studies a selection of these features in detail, backed up wherever necessary by the views of outsiders, independent studies, examination of past figures and current comparisons. Thirdly, the whole exercise is boiled down to a brief concentrated statement of three or four strengths and three or four weaknesses which represents the consensus view of the essential features of the company.

No checklist for the areas where strategic strengths and weaknesses can be found is adequate. I use one with eight or nine headings, but others with eighty headings exist.

Also, it must not be thought that the final consensus is ever final. As the months pass and other examinations of the company are made, new facts or shifts of opinion will appear. Only when the consensus appears to have settled down to a steady state should any great reliance be placed upon it.

One last question for the planning team: what is it that a company in your industry has to do especially well in order to succeed? When you have identified the answer, check your completed list of strengths and weaknesses to see if you have already included it. If not, what else of fundamental importance have you missed?

CHAPTER 6

Appraising the Environment

In the internal appraisal the planning team is concerned with identifying those features of the *company itself* which will have a major bearing on the choice of strategy – features that the company itself has deliberately developed or that have been endowed upon it by past events, features that can be said to be part of the company itself. In the external appraisal the team looks for those features of its *environment*, both present and future, which also must shape its strategic future – features outside the company, in its external environment and often, but not always, outside its control.

I often refer to this appraisal as the threats and opportunities analysis. What it is called is not important; what is important is that a planning team should never reach a strategic decision until both the internal *and* the external appraisals have been completed. Deciding a strategy on the internal appraisal alone (sometimes called the 'inside-out' approach) is as dangerous as the 'outside-in' approach, where the decision is made on the basis of the external appraisal alone.

While repeating my warning that no checklist is really adequate for any given company, I use one in this appraisal that has only five categories: (1) What are the main trends in your competitive environment; that is, who are your main competitors now, and who will they be in five years' time? (2) What political trends, (3) what economic trends, (4) what trends in society and (5) what trends in technology will affect your company?

It may also be useful to subdivide these five categories using another dimension: local, national and world. That is, the search for strategic political trends, for example, should be made at the level of local politics in the company's native town or community, at the level of national political trends including, say, legislation and at the level of world or foreign political trends.

When some people, myself included, refer to this environmental appraisal as the threats and opportunities study, we do so because what we are looking for essentially are those trends and events in the future environment of the company which may present a threat to the company's prosperity or an opportunity to be exploited.

I believe it to be wise in this appraisal to follow a sequence almost identical to that followed in the internal one. The appraisal should start at the introductory seminar, where a small number of major trends will be mentioned by all the syndicates and a larger number by one or two. Next, the planning team must boil these down, add any that it believes were omitted at the seminar and then write detailed reports on each of them. In this appraisal the team will almost certainly have to draw much more heavily upon outside consultants and experts, since, although no one will know the company's own special sector of its market better than the team, it will be wise to extend all these environmental studies well beyond existing market interests. Thirdly, the team should distil these long detailed reports into brief concentrated ones like those exemplified in the previous chapter and throughout this one. Some planners like then to attempt to rank these threats and opportunities in importance. So, we have the same sequence: identify, examine, distil and rank.

This study will take many months. It is far greater in extent than any of the other phases of the planning process, because the question that we are asking here is in effect 'What is going to happen to that bit of this planet which concerns us over the next five years?' It is a big question! It may call for a major market study; a team of scientists may have to be formed to study possible changes in technology; economists will have to prepare estimates of inflation rates and disposable income. Indeed, the whole thing can get completely out of hand!

There are at least two ways to keep the duration of this appraisal within reasonable bounds. First, follow the advice that I have repeated so many times: remember that this is corporate planning, not marketing, and that you are looking for strategic elephants only. Indeed, as stated before (see page 11), a company's corporate plan may hinge on only one or two absolutely enormous features in its environment rather than ten or twenty.

Secondly, there are today so many organisations devoted to the making of forecasts that few medium-sized companies need to make their own. This is certainly true of economic forecasting in well-developed Western economies, where almost daily one organisation or another – private, government, bank, stockbroker, university – publishes its latest prediction of economic trends. (It is much less true of less-developed Western economies, such as the Mediterranean ones in Europe, and even less true of, say, Africa.) Technological trends are trumpeted from every page of trade and technical journals. Social trends are discussed at length in the press and current affairs programmes on television. So, the problem is usually not how to make these forecasts – most of them are readily available free of charge –

but how to identify which of them are going to affect your own business.

Uncertainty

We have met uncertainty once before in the corporate planning process: at the profit forecast stage discussed in Chapter 4. We dealt with it there by the simple trick of not sweeping it under the carpet but boldly recognising that all Fo forecasts are really brackets of confidence or wedges of probability.

We meet it again here, where we study the company's future environment. Our response to it will again include the bracket idea. For example, if Professor Duck forecasts that the national economy is going to expand at 3 per cent next year but Dr Drake says that the figure will be 5 per cent, we shall accept both figures into our bracket of forecasts and then (in Chapter 8) use a powerful evaluation tool to test our proposed strategies for all these eventualities. However, I am going to propose an even better weapon as well.

Over the past decade or two, as the levels of uncertainty in the world have risen – partly as a result of that momentous event in 1973 when the price of oil quadrupled – professional corporate planners have developed more and more sophisticated methods of forecasting and more and more sophisticated techniques for handling uncertain data. For a while I believed that this approach was the right one – I even wrote a very successful book on management techniques (in 1969) – but I gradually lost faith in these techniques, particularly the more advanced ones. Most managers now feel the same lack of confidence.

So, while most other corporate planners have been adding to their armoury of advanced techniques for dealing with masses of uncertain data, I have been reducing the volume of data that I handle. They still attempt to develop detailed plans produced by means of advanced techniques; I now produce plans that are totally devoid of detail by means of very simple techniques.

In my view their techniques quite simply do not work; that is, I believe that all detailed plans, however cunningly contrived, will be wrong. Because they are detailed, they will be invalidated by the speed of change. Because they are detailed, the really important decisions will be either not included at all or buried under the detail. Because they are detailed, they will have to be revised so frequently that confidence in them will evaporate. Because they are detailed, a huge corporate planning department will be needed.

So, my message here and throughout this exercise is not to use advanced techniques to forecast the future but to cut down the amount of detail until you can forecast it without advanced tools. Stand back further, so that you can see only the highest peaks of importance. If you identify three or four crucial threats to your business, you will do a better job than if you identify thirty or forty.

I should mention two other features of the Argenti system in this context. We shall meet the problem of uncertainty again in Chapter 8, where the strategy that we choose will be vigorously tested to see how it stands up to uncertainty – to find out how robust our chosen strategy is in case our forecasts are wrong. The second feature to notice is the stress that I have placed (in Chapter 7) on risk-reducing strategies as being most useful devices for reducing a company's exposure to risk.

Now let me describe the checklists that many companies use to help them to identify threats and opportunities in their future business environment.

Competitive trends

I include here not only the actions that each of a company's competitors will take over the next five years but also the entire market situation over that period.

Theoretically, what I should like to see is something similar to Exhibit 6.1. It is virtually impossible to complete such a jigsaw, I believe, but every piece towards it is useful. As can be seen, the planning team here has listed the company's main competitors (two in this case), shown how it thinks the various shares of the market, turnover and profits will move, and briefly explained its rationale for each.

What we need to know here is how the entire market will grow, how it will develop into new segments, how new technologies will affect it, whether any major new competitors will enter the market, whether there will be mergers or failures, what will happen to any substitutes that there may be now or in the future, which competitors will alter course and in which direction – to compete more directly with our products or less directly? – and so on to infinity. This is a massive inquiry – one that no firm can undertake as a single exercise. What it can do, however, is to start the exercise – to make a beginning, however modest, and then let the systematic collection and documentation of data continue onwards. Sometimes the corporate planner should be given this task; sometimes it is better given to the marketing department.

Most firms collect some of these data some of the time, but they are normally concentrated on a relatively short time horizon. The salesmen know every detail of every competitor's current price list; the buying department knows all the latest rumours about Tern & Co.'s recent inquiry for a new type of component, which can only imply that this competitor is contemplating a new product launch; and so on. All these

Exhibit 6.1 An ideal 'competitive trends' summary

	Year −5	−4	−3	−2	−1	0	1	2	3	4	5	Notes
Our company												
Turnover (£m.)	41	39	39	41	46	48	50	53	55	60	60	(1)
Profits (£m.)	3·4	2·3	2·2	2·9	4·4	5·1	5·5	6·0	6·5	7·0	7·5	(2)
Share (%)	10	10	11	10	11	11	11	12	12	13	13	
Notes	1	1	1	—	2	2	2	2	3	3	3	(3)
Tern & Co.												
Turnover (£m.)	139	132	141	140	139	143	146	144	147	150	153	
Profits (£m.)	10·1	6·1	8·1	8·2	7·4	7·9	8·5	8·8	9·1	9·4	9·7	(4)
Share (%)	34	34	36	34	33	33	33	32	32	32	32	
Notes	4	4	4	4	4	5	5	5	—	—	—	(5)
Skua & Sons												
Turnover (£m.)	74	70	59	62	63	60	58	58	55	52	48	
Profits (£m.)	5·3	5·1	0·8	0·2	−1·1	0·7	1·0	1·0	1·0	1·0	1·0	(6)
Share (%)	18	18	15	15	15	14	13	13	12	11	10	
Notes	6	6	6	7	7	7	7	8	8	8	8	(7)(8)
Others												
Turnover (£m.)	—	—	—	—	—	—	—	—	—	—	—	
Profits (£m.)	—	—	—	—	—	—	—	—	—	—	—	
Share (%)	38	38	38	41	41	42	43	43	44	44	45	(9)
Notes	9	—	—	—	—	—	—	—	—	—	10	(10)
Total												
Turnover (£m.)	411	388	391	413	420	432	443	450	460	470	480	
Share (%)	100	100	100	100	100	100	100	100	100	100	100	

Notes

(1) Poor quality and low selling prices.
(2) New 'P' range introduced at much higher margin. Very successful launch.
(3) New proposed 'Q' range launch.
(4) The market-leader, but no new products until now.
(5) Launched the 'Z' range, but it is poor quality.
(6) Successful down-market image company.
(7) New up-market product; total failure?
(8) No cash for new launch.
(9) Many small specialised firms.
(10) We believe that they supply just what the market needs.

data are short term and detailed; what we want are long term and strategic data. These are not so easy to obtain.

It is occasionally possible, by analysing competitors' strengths and weaknesses, to identify trends in their style of management, which may help in predicting how their strategy may develop over the years. To take a very obvious example: it seems unlikely that Rolls Royce will *ever* launch a popular minicar. On the other hand it is not possible to predict that Woolworth will never sell caviare; if the standard of living rises so that there is a mass demand for caviare, no doubt Woolworth will sell it.

The study of competitive trends can begin as soon as the planning team is ready to start it after the seminar. It cannot be completed until the other environmental studies are completed, however, because economic trends, to take an obvious example, will condition the market forecasts. Starting with competitive trends is often useful because it helps the team to narrow down which economic, political and other trends are likely to be of strategic significance.

Examples of competitive trends include the following:

'Half of our turnover comes from abroad, the rest from our home market. We have consulted the managers of all our overseas subsidiaries and agencies and reached the following conclusions. (1) The market will expand by very approximately 4 per cent p.a. for the next five years. Some managers can point to national economic forecasts of only 1 per cent next year, others to forecasts as high as 8 per cent. Some see a peak in world trade in year 3, falling to year 5. However, we think that a good average view of these thirty-eight reports in four continents is 4 per cent p.a. (2) None of these managers see any new threat from competitors. Profits in our industry are not so high as to attract new competitors, and our own reputation continues high and stable. Three managers mention that Sora of Japan has recently entered the market.

'Turning to the more important home market, we also have some anxiety over Sora, which has opened depots in the South-West and North-East. We must take this firm seriously. We know of no other new competitor at present; indeed, we are still picking up more business from Coot's collapse a year ago. We believe that the home market will rise at well above the world average – 6 per cent p.a. in our case – and that our share of the market will rise from 29 per cent today to 35 per cent in year 5. We think that Plover's share will fall from 32 to 28 per cent, while Courser's holds steady at 18 per cent.'

'We are completely overshadowed by the government-owned Corporation. Assuming no change in government policy we see a growth in the market of less than 2 per cent next year, 4 per cent in years 2 and 3 and then 2 per cent p.a. again. Market shares will remain much as they are, with 25 per cent for us and 75 per cent for Quaile in the private sector. However, all this is overwhelmed by any minor deviation in government policy towards the Corporation. In the total market, as opposed to merely the private sector, the Corporation has a 98 per cent share, Quaile has 1·5 per cent, and we have 0·5 per cent. It is unlikely that the Corporation's share will rise unless Quaile and we are legislated out of existence, but their share could fall. To what level? To 96 per cent would double our market; to 94 per cent would treble it! We believe that the political atmosphere now lends itself to such momentous events.'

'Disposable income will rise rapidly (7 per cent) in the early part of next year and settle down to an expansion of 4 or 5 per cent thereafter. However, our main interest is in the C_1C_2 socioeconomic category, and here we believe that demand will increase by 9 per cent next year and then by 7 per cent p.a. in our sector of the consumer market. Changes in VAT rates will further assist our sector.

'Our main anxiety arises from the activities of the large consumer groups and multiples, whose professionalism is taking market share not only from the small family businesses but also from us and other medium-sized companies. Furthermore, there are two groups, namely, Baillon and Allen, that have not yet entered our sector but must certainly do so. As can be seen from Exhibit 6.2, the message is not encouraging.'

'We are without doubt the leader in our very small and very specialised field. We have probably 30 per cent of the world market and are five times the size of any competitor, all of which operate on a purely national scale. They, not us, are the ones suffering from the long decline in the industry. We expect to end up with 100 per cent of the market in a couple of decades, by which time it will be less than half of its present size.'

'In Europe there are only two competitors, in America another three. The market is expanding extremely fast; 15 per cent p.a. is the average rate. No other consortium at present in existence has the resources to enter our market; indeed, it is extremely unlikely that consumers would welcome yet another similar product. The battle, we firmly believe, will be between the five existing giants for a decade or more. Indeed, we see our presence in this market as a matter for profound self-congratulation; for if certain technological events occur, our product will move into the centre of three other markets that are ten times the size of the current sector.'

Exhibit 6.2 A planning team's 'competitive trends' summary

Optimistic version	Year −1	0	1	2	3	4	5
Index of disposable income:							
All socioeconomic groups	101·9	100·0	107·0	111·8	116·8	122·1	127·6
$C_1 C_2$	101·2	100·0	109·0	116·6	124·8	133·5	142·9
Total market (£m.)	1,471·0	1,486·0	1,620·0	1,733·0	1,855·0	1,984·0	2,123·0
Market share (%) for:							
Five groups and multiples	31·7	32·2	33·0	33·5	34·0	34·5	35·0
Six medium-sized companies	39·0	38·7	38·5	38·2	37·7	36·5	35·4
Small firms	23·1	23·0	22·5	22·2	21·9	21·2	20·7
Baillon or Allen	0·0	0·0	0·0	0·2	0·6	2·2	3·5
Our company	6·2	6·1	6·0	5·9	5·8	5·6	5·4
Therefore our turnover (£m.)	91·2	90·6	97·2	102·2	107·6	111·1	114·6
Rate of growth of our turnover (% p.a.)	−2·1	−0·6	7·3	5·1	5·2	3·2	3·2

Assumptions:
(1) Overall disposable income rises by between 7 and 4·5 per cent and disposable income of $C_1 C_2$ rises by between 9 and 7 per cent.
(2) Groups rise to 35 per cent market share and Baillon to 3·5 per cent, while medium-sized companies, small firms and our company all lose approximately equally.

Pessimistic version	Year −1	0	1	2	3	4	5
Index of disposable income:							
All socioeconomic groups	101·9	100·0	107·0	111·8	116·8	119·7	122·7
$C_1 C_2$	101·2	100·0	109·0	116·6	124·8	130·4	136·3
Total market (£m.)	1,471·0	1,486·0	1,620·0	1,733·0	1,855·0	1,938·0	2,026·0
Market share (%) for:							
Five groups and multiples	31·7	32·2	33·3	34·5	35·7	36·8	38·0
Six medium-sized companies	39·0	38·7	38·0	36·6	34·6	32·3	29·9
Small firms	23·1	23·0	22·5	21·6	20·4	19·0	17·6
Baillon or Allen	0·0	0·0	0·2	1·6	4·0	7·0	10·0
Our company	6·2	6·1	6·0	5·7	5·3	4·9	4·5
Therefore our turnover (£m.)	91·2	90·6	97·2	98·8	98·3	95·0	91·2
Rate of growth of our turnover (% p.a.)	−2·1	−0·6	7·3	1·6	−0·5	−3·3	−4·0

Changed assumptions:
(1) Overall disposable income rises by only 2·5 per cent in years 4 and 5 and disposable income of $C_1 C_2$ by only 4·5 per cent.
(2) Groups rise to 38 per cent market share and Baillon to 10 per cent, while medium-sized companies, small firms and our company all lose more than in the optimistic version.

Political trends

Political trends are trends inspired by politicians, political parties, governments and government agencies. Not all such trends emerge as legislation, although in democracies they frequently do.

Let us consider first politics at the level of a company's native town or the area in which it operates or has factories or offices. A very obvious example is the case of a factory discharging effluent into a stream or smoke in the atmosphere. There can be few local government authorities that tolerate this today, and legislation to control such practices is one example of political trends. Alterations to roads, parking for cars and lorries, new housing areas, quarrying regulations – for some firms these are trivial, for others life or death (see the examples below).

At the national level most companies will be severely affected. Legislation on trading, pricing, dividends, safety, noise, tax, employment – the list is endless – will affect everyone, although not always strategically. More subtle and more important are politically inspired shifts of power and influence. A very well-known example is the movement in the balance of power away from managers towards the shopfloor trade unions in many European nations during the 1970s. On the other hand there was a different but favourable trend during this period, namely, the gradual liberalisation of international trade, including the modest opening of trade with the Eastern bloc.

Other trends to watch at the national level include government quality standards (on food, drugs and car exhausts, for example), pollution, safety from explosion or escape of toxic substance, training, conditions of work (not forgetting noise, which has so far been forgotten), employee participation and shareholding, trade descriptions, monopolies, trade restraints, tariffs, exchange control, export subsidies and boycotts, taxation (including allowances, depreciation and deferrals) and nationalisation. Also, no one should forget that in most nations today the government controls half of the economy and is the nation's largest supplier, largest employer, largest customer and largest investor. The slightest shift in political emphasis can decimate a market overnight. Some industries, aircraft and defence for example, are dominated by government.

Among international political trends the one most worrying to many companies is nationalism. Most companies that are large enough to contemplate corporate planning are large enough to be exporting or importing, and some will be borrowing or lending in foreign financial markets. It is not only in the developing nations that nationalism is threatening all these activities; even mature democracies are obsessed by it – for example, Scotland and Quebec – and are determined to produce their own goods, to provide their own markets, to raise their own capital and, above all, to manage and staff all enterprises with their own nationals. The number of expropriations is growing, as is legislation banning the repatriation of capital and dividends and calling for controlling interests to be ceded to nationals from foreign owners. Multinational companies are losing control and ownership at an alarming rate under such measures as Nigeria's Indigenisation Decree and Malaysia's Bumiputra Policy.

However, apart from nationalism a number of other political trends must be considered at this world level: trade barriers, international legislation (on the sea, for example, and on marine resources), the pronouncements of a growing number of international bodies (for example, the European Economic Community and the European Free Trade Area), and so on. International terrorism should not be forgotten.

Every company is different. Every company's list of strengths, weaknesses, threats and opportunities will display a unique combination, but there can be few companies of any size in the Western world that should not include some political trend in their list of strategic considerations. I think that it is fair to say that in the failures of Rolls Royce and Penn Central – two of the largest bankruptcies in history – political considerations played a significant part. My own belief is that in fact the electorates in many Western democracies are no longer seeking an expansion of political power and government influence into the business arena, or anywhere else. On the contrary, disillusion seems to be leading in the other direction, and low-tax, low-government expenditure economies are now being heralded as desirable not only for our prosperity but also for the sake of freedom itself.

It is worth remembering that political trends are only one aspect of the future; there are political crises as well, and these can blow up suddenly without warning. Some hair-raising predictions have been made: a China-Russia war, the democracies' losing control of their democratic processes, an Arab–Israeli war, a North–South cold war, the collapse of the Russian empire in Europe, and so on. Many companies will be wise not to take account of such events in their plans, but some care is needed before dismissing them as irrelevant. The price of oil might be severely affected, for example, in the event of almost any of these crises.

Examples of political threats and opportunities include the following:

'Both of our factories are under threat due to the fact that the main feature of our process depends on massive oil-fired and electricity-boosted furnaces.

'At site A, in Northtown itself, the problem is long term. The company has operated here for forty years, during which period new housing estates have been built all round us. To make matters worse Northtown has emerged as a tourist attraction; we are clearly visible from the Hill. Even if we are not asked to move (a demand that could lose 1,500 jobs in Northtown), the cost of meeting the increasing cosmetic measures being demanded of us are placing us at a competitive disadvantage.

'At site B, outside Southtown, the problem is more urgent. Southtown's local government has given a well-known food company permission to build a biscuit factory only half a mile from our factory – directly down wind! We have to think in terms of £1·5m. over the next five years to meet rising standards of environmental appearance. This is equal to 20 per cent of our proposed capital-expenditure programme for the period. Our competitors are not similarly placed.'

'Any strategy developed for this company must take into account the fact that government credit restrictions are almost unpredictable and extremely illogical and can affect our hire-purchase profits by 40 per cent.'

'We must clearly understand that all our subsidiaries in all developing nations are eventually going to be owned and managed by their host governments and nationals. The only question is how to minimise the damage that this is going to do to our business over the next two or three decades.'

'The markets that we enjoy in the developing nations will disappear gradually as they all begin to make our products for themselves. Because our products are simple, low in technology and high in labour content, we can be quite certain that the normal economic trend in this direction will be given a strong political shove by the governments of these nations. We shall be surprised if this process does not start soon, that is, in a year or two. It may reduce our business by, say, 10 per cent within, say, five years. Then, the pace will accelerate.'

'The process of obtaining approval for any new pharmaceutical product will continue to become more complex, more costly and longer. It is possible that decisions will become less scientific and more political in character, with extreme consumer groups, environmentalists and health cranks having a growing influence.'

'Shipping freight rates normally stay fairly stable, but once every few years there is a political upheaval somewhere, and freight rates shoot up. We need to remember this when we devise our shipping strategies. Thus, "Worldscale" rates have risen above 100 on only six occasions in the past thirty years, including the Korean war (1950–2), the Suez war (1956), Six-Day war (1967) and the oil crisis (1973). On all these occasions it trebled to over 300 before sinking back below 100 again.'

Economic trends

The 'local, national, world' classification is often a useful guideline in the identification of strategic economic trends.

Take the company's native town or region. Is it a growth area full of modern thriving industries or an example of urban decay populated by the unemployed, the unskilled and the forlorn? What is the economic future of the region, and how will this affect wage rates, disposable income, unemployment, the provision of roads, shopping facilities and infrastructure generally?

On the national level, what are the prospects for growth, *per capita* income, inflation, unemployment, terms of trade, balance of payments and taxation levels? I should make two comments here. First, corporate planners always behave as though economic conditions are a vitally important part of their company's business environment. This may be so for very large companies, but I am not sure that it is for smaller ones. Take a company whose share of the market is small, say 5 per cent. Now, an increase in the total market of a few percent due to improved national economic performance would add a few percent to that company's sales. This would be very welcome, but nothing like as welcome as an increase in market share from 5 to 6 per cent. For a huge company with 70 per cent of the market the opposite is true, so for them economic forecasts are useful.

Secondly, I am less than impressed by the accuracy of many of these forecasts. They are seldom correct for one year ahead and can be wildly inaccurate over a five-year horizon. The various forecasting bodies in Britain, for example, seldom agree among themselves, estimates of growth for one year ahead varying by a factor of as much as 2. (Some forecasters assume no change in government policies when they make their forecasts – an Fo forecast in my terminology – whereas others, to everyone's confusion, assume that the government will take action – an Fp forecast.) If these forecasts are so useless, why do we go on using them? The answer is that they are not useless; they are only inaccurate, and they have a most useful psychological value. We can base our plans on them; and if the next forecast tells the same story as the last, we gain confidence in our plans and perhaps take a few more practical steps to put them into action. If the next forecast tells a different story, we delay further commitment. Moreover, the forecasts are in figures, so we can judge *how much* more confident we are – how much further to go in our chosen direction. So, they certainly have their value, even if it is not quite what the professional forecasters think it is.

Of much greater use to most companies than these rather general forecasts of an entire national economy are forecasts of the company's market or market segments: construction, food, cars, and so on. The closer a forecast comes to a company's precise product or range of products, the more useful to the company it normally becomes, the more relevant become the views of its executives, and the less relevant become the views of the economists. However, now we are moving from economic forecasts to market forecasts.

Let us turn now to world economic trends. The international trade cycle is an important factor for very large firms, but again it may be rather remote from the smaller firm, although it does influence business opinion in all sectors. It seems to me more sensible for medium-sized companies to concentrate their limited resources on identifying those economic trends which more precisely affect them; I have tried to select the examples below with this in mind.

However, I doubt that this exercise – that is, identifying specific trends that are relevant to one's business – can be done realistically without an understanding of the broad economic trends that pervade the world. At present, for example, it looks as though the world's nations can be divided into four economic categories. First, there are the Western democracies (including Japan), where economic growth is relatively sedate and stable in a relatively stable political setting. These are characterised by low growth of population, low growth in basic manufacturing industries (steel, cement, and so on) but high growth in service industries, in high technology industries and in leisure and personal care industries, with increasing market segmentation and choice everywhere. The Eastern bloc is in an economic situation similar to that of the Western democracies but a decade or so behind. Thirdly, there are the underdeveloped nations, where standards of living are similar to those prevailing thousands of years ago and where there seems little hope of improving matters for some decades, due largely to rising population and low standards of education and infrastructure generally. Finally, there are the developing nations, where gross national product is now rising very fast indeed (as for a time is population) due largely to injections of capital and know-how from the richer Western, Eastern and oil-rich nations. In these nations wage rates are still very low (one-tenth, say) by Western standards, consumer goods are still scarce, the infrastructure is being provided very rapidly, income and wealth are uneven, and political stability is precarious.

Unfortunately, the balance of trade between these various groups is severely distorted and threatens the whole world economic order – a situation greatly exacerbated by the oil crisis in 1973, when the whole world economic pintable was tilted away from the developed nations. Currency fluctuations are now massive. The United States' economic supremacy is under challenge.

These developing nations represent a massive threat to Western economies because of their low wage rates and high industrial discipline, but they also represent a massive opportunity. Just imagine a billion people (equal to all the Western developed nations) whose standard of living may reach that of the West in a few decades. Lucky is the firm that gets in on the ground floor of that!

Further economic trends or events may come to mind if the planning team now refers back to the list of strengths and weaknesses and asks itself what special economic trends may affect the company's finance, production, marketing, and so on, right through the list described in Chapter 5.

One factor seems of particular interest to small and medium-sized companies, namely, size. How will economic trends over the next decade or so influence the size of any given company? Two trends seem fairly general. On the one hand there are industries that provide a product for mass markets, such as cars, bread, window glass and bricks – all rather standard goods that sell mainly on price. Companies that produce these need to be large, and it is fair to predict that in a few decades from now there will be only a handful of, say, car companies, which between them supply the entire world demand. At the other end of this scale there are products and services with personal appeal, where there is product differentiation and strong market segmentation. Here companies may well become progressively smaller and more specialised. The questions for any given corporate planning team, then, are: Do we have to get much bigger or much smaller to stay alive in our industry over the next few decades; or are we, quite by chance, just about right? Is our industry one of the odd ones where it is valid to be medium-sized?

Here are some examples of economic trends:

'Because we are the only large employer of skilled labour for many miles, our wage rates are more than 20 per cent below those of any of our competitors in Britain and far lower than those of most of our European competitors. The labour content of our product is 50 per cent of its ex-factory price – our policy has been to concentrate on products with a high skilled labour content – and our prices are 10 per cent below those of any other competitor. Except for our own prosperity we can see no local economic trend that will undermine this useful advantage.'

'The construction industry throughout the Western world has slowed almost to a standstill, and none of our advisers see any major growth prospects here or in the capital goods industry for years; some say two, others six or more. The position in the developing nations, where we do not have any experience at all, is quite the opposite. Certain growth-spots in Africa, South America, the East and the Middle East look like maintaining dramatic rates of expansion (10–25 per cent) for a decade or more. Competition is fierce for this business, which can be obtained only via national government agencies and even then only when the company is large, has at least one important reference-client and, often, is ready to offer inducements. We can qualify on none of these grounds.'

'Wines and spirits (and cider) consumption over the past decade has increased at 8·5 per cent p.a., while beer consumption has averaged 3·5 per cent p.a. We forecast 7 and 3·2 per cent respectively for the next five years.'

'Due to the reduction in inequalities of income that we expect will occur over the next five years, the socioeconomic groups at which our Puffin shops are aimed will benefit substantially. As can be seen from Exhibit 6.3, national expenditure is expected to rise only from £59·8 p.a. per household to £68·6 in year 5 – less than 15 per cent – but average expenditure of our customers should rise by nearly 20 per cent.'

'The economic circumstances of our nation are so appalling and the threat of social disintegration so real that we must assume huge variations in demand. We can only guess what these may be, but 30 per cent above or below current figures seems a good guide.'

'The entire region that we have traditionally served is in gradual decline. The city centre is almost derelict except for a tangle of overpasses and underpasses. The docks are virtually closed, and only one container berth is operating. None of the new satellite towns have attracted important new employers. In spite of this our turnover has increased, because all our competitors have moved out. We believe that these trends will now be reversed.'

Social trends

It is not always easy to distinguish between social and economic trends. Are population statistics social or economic? It is clear that attitudes, habits and patterns of behaviour are social, so we should include under this heading the trends of all such things as working hours,

Exhibit 6.3   Puffin's forecasts of consumer expenditure

(a)   National figures for year 0

Socioeconomic group	% of nation	Expenditure per household in each group (£ p.a.)	Expenditure per 100 households in all groups (£ p.a.)
AB	14	113·2	1,585
C_1	22	86·3	1,899
C_2	29	50·1	1,453
DE	35	29·7	1,040
	100	Average per household = 59·8	

(b)   Figures for Puffin shops for year 0

Socioeconomic group	% of our customers	Expenditure per customer in each group (£ p.a.)	Expenditure per 100 customers in all groups (£ p.a.)
AB	4	112·8	451
C_1	16	88·4	1,414
C_2	35	52·8	1,848
DE	45	31·8	1,431
	100	Average per customer = 51·4	

(c)   Predicted national figures for year 5

Socioeconomic group	% of nation	Expenditure per household in each group (£ p.a.)	Growth of expenditure from year 0 (%)	Expenditure per 100 households in all groups (£ p.a.)
AB	15	123·4	9	1,851
C_1	23	97·5	13	2,243
C_2	30	57·6	15	1,728
DE	32	32·4	9	1,037
	100		Average per household = 68·6	

(d)   Predicted figures for Puffin shops for year 5

Socioeconomic group	% of our customers*	Expenditure per customer in each group (£ p.a.)**	Expenditure per 100 customers in all groups (£ p.a.)
AB	6	122·9	737
C_1	19	99·9	1,891
C_2	35	60·7	2,124
DE	40	34·7	1,388
	100	Average per customer = 61·4	

*Figures assume continuation of past trend resulting from our policy of trading up towards the centre of the socioeconomic group.
**Growth in expenditure in each group is as for national growth figures in (c).

education, housing, trade unions, retirement, leisure and sport, holidays, religion, taste, ethics, and so on.

Changes in society can affect companies in several different ways. That social change can affect a company's market is entirely obvious; the decline in sales of 'quack' medicines is at least partly due to improved levels of education, for example, and an increased volume of pornography runs parallel with changing attitudes towards sex. Such trends are universally recognised by marketing men and managers.

However, society's attitude to companies has an almost equally important and powerful effect on the whole area that I called ethos in Chapter 2, that is, how a company behaves in society. It is not enough for the planning team to describe how the company should behave in today's social atmosphere; it also has to attempt to visualise how that atmosphere will change over the selected planning horizon. Will society continue to pile more and more social obligations upon companies both large and small, or only on the large? What new obligations may be imposed? Will international companies be stripped of their foreign assets in more and more nations of the world? Will consumerism and environmentalism continue indefinitely to gain in strength, or will their demands moderate?

A third important area affected by social change is the company's workforce itself, including shopfloor workers, office workers, advisers and managers, that is, everyone employed. During the 1960s and 1970s there has been a major decline in the Victorian work ethic. Will this continue, reverse or change? What about 'sense of responsibility', pride and the 'will to manage'? Are these also in decline; and if so, where may this lead? How are managers going to motivate employees whose standard of living is rising so far above the 'subsistence' level that they have long ceased to 'need' anything? Also, if unemployment is going to stay at historically high levels, as many economists predict, will the solution be to reduce working hours and retirement ages?

I give below some actual examples from medium-sized companies of the threats and opportunities that they see in social trends:

'The population of the United Kingdom is expected to remain almost static at 55·5 million, but there will be an increase in those over 75 and in school-leavers about to start work. There will be fewer middle-aged and children. The number of school children will decline, and a surplus of teachers may occur. Some of these will be exactly the people whom we shall need to recruit for our new proposed diversification.'

'The whole field of personal care will expand rapidly – in particular health, slimming, exercise, physical appearance, sport and games (but not team games, which we think will decline except for professionals). In the absence of a definition no figures can be given, but 10 per cent p.a. gives the flavour of our optimism. Anti-smoking, anti-drinking, anti-drug and even anti-sugar lobbies will appear in great strength, and we should be able to link these pro-health and anti-illness trends into a very strong double harness. Furthermore, these preventative measures all require serious, trained and confidential supervision of just the sort that we can supply and in which we have such long experience.'

'We have good reason to know the power of a television consumer programme; none of us need reminding of the Robin affair four years ago, when sales fell by 80 per cent in three weeks. We see this possibility's occurring again with almost any of our products, with serious effects, unless we take some measures either to prevent it before it happens or to reduce the impact on our overall profits.'

'The number of mechanical components in our product is declining as the designers replace more and more of them with electronic units – the switchgear and overloads are the latest in this trend – and the product is becoming easier to assemble. There is an opinion in the company that growing boredom on the assembly line is the cause of the increasing discontent in the factory, which shows itself in increased labour turnover. Another view is that we now have too many supervisors for these simpler processes and that our employees resent this 'overmanagement'. Whatever it is, the problem is going to grow with the trend towards electronics, and no strategy that ignores it will be viable.'

'We feel that, in view of the number of elderly people in the population now, a special range of furniture and personal equipment for the over 65s could be developed – a sort of "Grannycare". However, since pensioners are seldom affluent, either it would have to be cheap, or it would have to attract a subsidy from the government or charitable organisations.'

'According to the returns that we make to the Department of Employment the number of managers, directors and supervisors that we employ has risen from 120 to 211 in the past five years. During this time the number of other employees has risen from 840 to 1,050. This means that one supervisor looked after seven employees five years ago but looks after only five now. Why this increase in management should have occurred we do not know, as our products, processes and procedures have changed hardly at all. We cannot believe that this trend is a healthy one, and it certainly does not seem at ease in a society where education, general awareness and personal initiative are supposed to be improving. We feel that it should be reversed.'

'Government interference and social hostility will increase. We must find some way to exploit our market leadership without incurring excessive burdens of social responsibility, that is, those which none of us believe to be best provided by companies and which, we argue, should be met by organisations specially set up, or already specialising in these areas such as charities and government institutions.'

Technological trends

Few companies are unaffected by the endless march of scientific progress. It may be thought, for example, that a firm in the antique business can ignore technology, but, of course the transmission, classification, handling and storage of data are just as important to this type of business as to any other; supermarkets need to take advantage of the latest methods of food storage, pricing, stock control, checkout and security; banks too will ignore the immense electronic data-processing revolution that is now in prospect at their peril. Indeed, no business, however small will escape the coming wave of micro-electronics; for whereas the 1960s saw giant companies beginning to use giant computers, the 1980s will see a revolution at the other end of the scale, that is, small companies using small computers.

Technological trends include not only the glamorous new invention that revolutionises our lives, and which represents a tiny fraction of the real world of technology, but also the gradual painstaking improvements in methods, in materials, in design, in application, in diffusion into new industries and in efficiency. This raises an important point: except in a few industries the rate of technological change is so slow that only the company that is completely asleep will be unaware of all the changes that will affect it in the next few years. The problem is seldom one of identification; the problem is to know when the change will occur, how serious it may be and what response to make to its coming.

It is partly for this reason, I believe, that the advanced techniques of technological forecasting put forward in the 1960s and 1970s have been so little used. Some of these – morphological analysis, diffusion analysis, models and so on – have been the subject of many fine books and articles, but the number of companies in the world of *any* size that are using them is absolutely tiny.

Some of the simpler techniques – trend analysis and delphi, for example – are used quite widely, but this is mainly because they are so simple. (Trend analysis is a generic term covering the study of trends. Thus, if the forecaster is concerned with, say, the power–weight ratio of marine diesel engines, he examines the past trend and tries knowledgeably to project it into the future. Delphi is a systematic method for sounding the opinion of several experts on, for example, when they think a certain technological event may occur.)

Economists have their economic models and their input–output analyses; sociologists have their lifestyle analyses (and they use delphi too); technologists also use their own systematic methods of forecasting. In my view none of these are as reliable as any of their supporters believe them to be. This leads to a sequence of conclusions that are of major importance to the external analysis stage of corporate planning:

(1) Most companies (that is, virtually all companies except very large ones and ones in which technological, economic, political or social change plays an absolutely crucial role) should limit their external or environmental analyses to those matters which *closely* concern them and about which, therefore, the company's own executives know far more than outside specialists.

(2) In making these forecasts what matters is not the use of advanced forecasting techniques but the method of obtaining a genuine consensus among those people in the company, at every level and in every section, who may throw light on the subject.

(3) Very large companies, companies with one or more external trends overhanging them to an unusual degree and companies that believe that they must forecast a trend that lies outside their field of knowledge should all go to the experts. Whether they use advanced forecasting techniques is their business.

What I am saying here is that most companies do *not* need to forecast far beyond their own area of knowledge and do *not* need to employ advanced techniques. If you do have to go outside your field of knowledge, go to the experts, who may or may not use advanced techniques. However, be warned:

(4) Distrust all forecasts! Show the probable range of errors or the bands of confidence, and insist that any experts consulted do so too. The strategy eventually chosen needs to stand up not to the forecast but to the errors in it.

Let me put this another way. Just as the internal analysis is best conducted by members of the company's own senior staff, not by outsiders, using their own common sense, not some complicated analytical device, so, I believe, is the external analysis. Most companies know their business better than any outside expert, and most of the trends and events that are likely to have a strategic impact on any given company can be predicted just as well by the use of normal methods as by the use of very sophisticated ones. This is intended as a crude general statement, and each company should be able to identify its own exceptions to this rule. However, it is somewhat contrary to the advice often proffered by professional corporate planners, who in general tend to rely far too heavily on outside experts and specialists. This is not a specialist exercise; it is corporate planning. However, I must also warn against the danger of perpetuating company myths and self-delusions, and to guard against accepting a too-easy view of the company's future business environment it is often desirable to seek the views of outsiders. In general their views should be sought not as the main source of information about the company's future but as confirmation that the executives' own views are not defective.

What matters beyond anything in *my* system of corporate planning is identifying the half-dozen really important things that are going to happen to the company in the next decade or so. If we are looking for strategic elephants we shall not normally need to use sophisticated detection equipment. What we shall need to be careful about is agreeing among ourselves that this is an elephant and that is not, that there are four of them and not three or five, and that the four are this one, this, this and this – a consensus about the future.

Typical statements on technology include the following:

'We can see no technological trend on the horizon that we consider to be of strategic importance.'

'The group consists of twenty-four subsidiary companies in light mechanical engineering. Each company produces its own specialist range of products, extending from domestic doorlocks and domestic light switches to vehicle-window winding mechanisms and small hydraulic systems. Each company sees its own technological trends, but there is one that seems to threaten all our companies. This is the rapid substitution of electronics for mechanics; in several of our products we have recently incorporated some new electronic part for a mechanical one. However, this trend is far wider than our own business; office calculators, wrist watches, telephone exchanges are totally electronic today – no moving parts, no maintenance, no noise, few breakdowns, low use of energy. All these advantages will grow more and more in importance as the years go by. Although we cannot see any particular or immediate threat to any of our particular products, we feel profoundly uneasy. In theory this trend could leave us without a business at all.'

'We have all expressed grave concern in recent years that some new method of building construction may render our product irrelevant. In theory it is indeed possible to build a building without our product, but in spite of a dozen attempts to do so over the past three decades none have succeeded. Nothing that looks like succeeding is even on the horizon. It would, we believe, take a decade to reduce our turnover by 10 per cent, even if some new system did appear. No, the threat comes from our known competitors, not from the unknown.'

'The threat is quite clear: our product can be made from any of three or four plastics in which we have no experience whatever. The 1973 oil crisis, by lifting the price of feedstock, merely postponed the eventual domination of plastic materials in our industry. We guess the timescale to be five years for the first real impact (this assumes that oil prices remain constant in real terms) and ten years for a severe effect on our product, say a 25 per cent reduction in sales.'

'We are far too small to keep up with the American effort in research and development in this field.'

Ranking

A number of methods of ranking may be used, but the one that I believe to be most useful involves classifying each threat and each opportunity in two dimensions. First we attempt to say how severe an impact on the company any given event will have if it does occur, and then we attempt to state how likely the event is to occur.

Now, if an event is deemed to have a high impact and if the chances of its occurring are deemed to be high, this event will plainly be of major strategic significance; a strategy that did not take it into account would be utterly worthless. At the other end of the scale an event that is thought likely to have a low impact and that in any case is unlikely to occur can quite possibly be deleted from further strategic debates. Also, an event with high impact and low or medium probability will have to be given serious consideration by the planning team, but it may be entirely reasonable to exclude it from the main strategy so long as a contingency plan is devised in case it ever does occur.

I show a simplified example of this double-ranking method in Exhibit 6.4. It is perfectly possible, although not quite so useful, to use single-ranking systems, such as the ones described in the previous chapter (see Exhibit 5.2), based solely on the level of strategic importance ascribed by the team to each event.

Exhibit 6.4 A simplified example of ranking threats and opportunities by impact and by probability of occurrence

Event	Impact on company	Probability of occurrence
Major technological breakthrough that renders our product obsolete within 10 years	High	Low
Economic growth continues at 5% p.a.	Medium	High
Economic growth falters and stops within 5 years	Medium	Medium
Legislation to free our product from credit restrictions	Low	Low

It is clear that the ranking operation is an important one here; it is an even more valuable and informative exercise for threats and opportunities than it is for strengths and weaknesses. The really big problem with the external analysis is that in theory almost every event in the future of the world is going to affect your company, but of these countless billions of occurrences only a handful are of strategic importance. We must retain a sense of proportion when conducting our search for these crucial ones; and if we think we have identified one, we should be prepared to spend much time and money in examining it, its possible impact and the probability of its happening. We should search for possible 'lead indicators' for it – trends or events whose occurrence may herald the event itself and which we should therefore watch carefully and continuously.

Summary

Attempting to draw up a strategy for a company without first carefully and systematically surveying the future environment is unthinkable. However, a survey such as this is no light undertaking. If the company has never before made such a systematic study as the one described in this chapter, it will require a great deal of time and resources. Mercifully, most companies will have made parts of such a study and may only have to fill in the gaps revealed by the use of my checklists.

No checklist is foolproof; examining competitive, political, economic, social and technological trends is merely a useful framework in which threats and opportunities of strategic importance may be found. Dividing the checklist into local, national and world trends may be useful in the case of competitors, political, economic and social trends, although this is less relevant for technological trends.

I recommend the use of the same procedure as for the internal appraisal: identify the trends that look really significant; examine these in detail; distil this inquiry to a few key sentences or headings agreed by everyone who ought to agree them; and then rank them. Identify, examine, distil, rank.

Together, this external appraisal, the internal appraisal, the target and the forecast provide the planning team with all the data that they need to make the strategic decisions. In my opinion any such decision taken in the absence of any significant part of any of these major areas of discovery is doomed to failure. All the facts, opinions, figures and beliefs must be present, and strategic decisions must be taken in the light of all these taken together as one coherent picture of the company in its entire future environment. Anything less is just useless.

CHAPTER 7

Alternative Strategies

By this stage in the corporate planning process the planning team has obtained a clear consensus in all the main areas of strategic information. It has agreed upon targets, forecasts and gaps, it has identified the company's major strengths and weaknesses, and it has listed all the threats and opportunities lying ahead of the company.

The purpose of all this heart-searching is to construct a sort of sieve by means of which one particular set of strategies may be selected as being more appropriate than any other set of strategies. Precisely how this sieve works I shall discuss in the next chapter, but it is obvious that there is little point in developing an elaborate screening mechanism of this sort unless the number of alternative strategies to be considered is very large. A vital stage in this planning process, then, comes at this point, where the planning team makes a list of all the alternative strategies of which it can think. The more there are, and the more imaginative and wide ranging they are, the better.

Listing alternative strategies

Executives are often heard to exclaim 'We have no alternative in this situation but to . . .', 'There's nothing that we can do', 'We are too small to do anything about . . .', or 'The only thing that we can do now is . . .'. These remarks may sometimes be justified in short range planning, with which most executives are normally mainly concerned, because shortage of time and rapid rates of change do sometimes leave a company with no alternative; but by definition this cannot be true in long range planning, the purpose of which is precisely to look far enough ahead to allow many alternatives to be considered. The further ahead a company looks, the more numerous the alternatives become; theoretically, it is possible to look so far ahead that the alternatives become literally infinite. In long range planning, then, there is *never* 'no alternative' or 'only one thing that we can do'. The problem is diametrically opposite this; there are so many alternatives that it is necessary to spend six months building a sieve to reduce them to one.

In any company that is even half alive a plethora of ideas for the future of the company will have existed at all levels in the management hierarchy long before this exercise begins and before some have even heard of corporate planning. During the planning process itself innumerable new ideas will be sparked off by the very act of identifying strengths, threats, targets, and so forth. It is the duty of the planning team, especially the planning assistant, to collect all these ideas and list them. In some cases it will have no difficulty whatever in doing this, for some senior executives in some companies hold their strategic opinions so fervently that they become something of an irritation to their colleagues, who may have to resort to such evasive tactics as not sitting next to them at lunch in order to avoid having to listen to the same old arguments yet again!

Other views are more discreetly and perhaps more rationally held. Some are put forward half in jest, some with great solemnity. Some are displayed on the back of an envelope, others in formal reports bulging with detailed appendices. All these should be collected and listed throughout the whole exercise.

By this stage, therefore, the team will already be in possession of an impressive list of ideas. Now is the time to try to place these items into categories: market strategies, product strategies, finance strategies, and so on. Even more important, however, now is the time deliberately to add to the list – to enrich it and widen its range. There are many ways in which this may be done, and I shall describe five of them below: the 'What business?' question, brainstorming, opinion surveys, logical methods and imitation.

'What business are we in?'   Many textbooks on corporate planning recommend that each company ask itself 'What business are we in?' We can imagine a company manufacturing pencils asking itself this question and answering 'We are in the business of manufacturing writing materials' – a reply, the textbooks suggest, that opens up a wider and more exciting range of product ideas than the company may otherwise have considered. Before asking this question the company may have been thinking only in terms of pencils: bigger ones, smaller ones, longer ones, shorter ones, harder ones, softer ones, round ones and square ones. After the question all sorts of new ideas will suggest themselves: not just pencils but also pens, nibs, chalk, felt pens, charcoal, artists' paints, typewriters and so on.

It must be stated that, although this question does often provoke new lines of thought – and the 'What business?' question should always be asked, therefore – it does not necessarily provoke the right thoughts.

Just because a pencil manufacturer defines his business in wider terms, it does not necessarily follow that it would be right for him to begin to manufacture pens or typewriters; some enthusiasts for this question seem to imply that it would be right.

My criticism goes a little wider. In the 1960s it was fashionable for companies to diversify, and in those days any mental aid that pointed managers in this direction was accepted as beneficial. The question 'What business are we in?' is specifically designed to provoke a definition that is wider and more general than existing product lines; thus, a wallpaper company sees itself in the business of interior decoration, a pump manufacturer sees itself in 'fluids engineering', and a rat poison producer sees itself in 'pest control'. This is all good stuff, but I am going to suggest later that, for a large number of companies in the 1980s, diversification is quite the worst strategy that they could choose. If so, every one of the above ideas could be disastrously wrong.

I should add this: every company is in a unique strategic situation – no other company in the world has quite the same permutation of targets, strengths, threats, and so on – so *any* aid to planning that carries within it any bias towards some universally applicable strategy – diversify, add value, increase market share, or whatever – is unhelpful.

My position on this question, then, is this: all companies should ask themselves 'What business are we in?' – it is a useful and important question – but it is not *the* question; it is only one question out of several dozen that planners should ask themselves about their company. Also, it does not give *the* answer; it gives a few extra possible ideas that may not otherwise be considered. There are other techniques that do the same thing – brainstorming, for example.

Brainstorming. During the past decade or two a number of creative-thinking techniques have appeared, some of which are used by some companies (early enthusiasm for such techniques has waned considerably). For generating new ideas for strategies this technique may be used as follows. Gather into one room a number of employees from any levels in the hierarchy and any specialisms; the more mixed the group is, the better. Then ask them to suggest answers to the question 'How could we alter the structure of the company over the next five years?', having first explained to them the basic rule of brainstorming, namely, that no criticism of any one's ideas is allowed.

The first few answers will be rather dull: 'We should introduce new products', 'We should increase training', and so on. However, after a few minutes someone may suggest something quite new; later, another idea will appear, then more, then two ideas will coalesce into another, and so on. Provided that everyone is allowed to speak freely such sessions do sometimes yield new and useful ideas that would not otherwise be considered. Sessions need not be longer than 30 minutes; 2 hours is much too long.

In one company (a bank) no less than 378 suggestions were made by eighty employees split into four sessions with twenty people in each (rather too many, perhaps, for full participation). To be truthful, only a few of these ideas were truly strategic in concept. However, the fact that half a dozen major themes kept recurring in all four sessions did point to a consensus about possible new products and markets for the company, the existence of which was not previously known to the planning team. This suggested that company-wide acceptance and enthusiasm would be more likely to exist for diversification into these popular areas than for other strategies.

Opinion Surveys.   These consist of systematically enlisting the ideas of all those people inside and outside the company whose opinion on the future of the company is valued by the planning team. The two most usual sources to tap are employees and consultants. I know of several companies that successfully invited their employees to contribute ideas. In one case the company received no less than eighty-two suggestions; again, not all of them were strategic, and some consisted of just a word or two. None of them was used. However, the exercise itself is a valuable exercise in employee participation, provided, of course, that it is made clear at the start that the company may not be able to use any of the ideas. In another case the company invited employees to submit their ideas only in considerable detail. In this case thirty-two ideas were received, one of which (at the time of writing) looks highly promising.

More reliable and much more costly is asking consultants to submit ideas. Normally, the request is limited to consultants specialising in one particular field, for example, 'opportunities for the sale of glass fibre technology in the nations of Eastern Europe' – this sort of thing. Sometimes a company will invite a panel of scientists or a group of academics to contribute ideas, or it will commission surveys, and so on.

Logical methods.   Quite a valuable technique is to take a list of alternative strategies that has already been prepared and to perform logical operations on each item. Suppose that the list already includes 'Increase our share of the market'; add the negation of this, namely, 'Decrease our share'. If the list contains the idea 'Sell know-how to developing nations', add the negation, namely, 'Buy know-how from advanced nations'.

Also, try 'doubling and halving'. Suppose that the company operates four factories. What about two twice the size, or eight half the size? Suppose that there are forty products in a range of products. What about cutting it to twenty, doubling it to eighty, or even quadrupling it?

Normally, when thinking from a marketing viewpoint we should contemplate adding or subtracting only one or two products in a range of forty, but here, where we are thinking strategically, we can allow ourselves much greater latitude. We can think of halving the weight of the product or fitting a motor with ten times the power. Anything is possible given plenty of time, which is exactly what we are giving ourselves in long range planning. Such latitude does not apply only to products, of course. We can think of halving the labour force, decimating it or ceasing production altogether. We can think of new materials from new suppliers, and so on. Some examples appear in the next section.

Finally, there is one more method of enriching a list of strategies that I must briefly describe.

Imitation. All the textbooks draw attention to the need for innovation. Of course, being first in the field is an excellent strategy, but it is not without its disadvantages. Risk is one; cost is another; the fragility of patents and the danger of imitation are others. For all these reasons being the first with a new product is not for everyone. However, I am not talking about being first with a product; I am talking about being first with a strategy. Being the first company to introduce self-service in a food store, the first company to put workers on the board, the first company to sell and lease back its own property – all these, it seems to me, were excellent examples of innovative strategies. If a company identifies a strategy of equal brilliance, there is an exciting prospect for it.

However, most companies do not have the necessary mixture of luck and flair; most companies, on inspecting their list of alternative strategies, have to admit that it is really rather dull. For these companies I suggest that they look around systematically and methodically at their smarter competitors or at companies that are in some way similar and see what they are doing. Whatever it is that seems to bring them such enviable success may well be a useful addition to the company's own list.

A plethora of strategies

Whether any or all of these techniques are used, the number of strategies that is open to any company is truly formidable, and the planning team will find its list running away with it. Good. The more the better at this stage.

Consider a company manufacturing dining-room furniture; let us call it Harrier & Sons. It employs 100 people, its turnover last year (year 0) was £2m., and profits were 10 per cent of turnover (£200,000).

The management believes that the market for dining-room furniture at home (Harrier does not export at all) will rise at 5 per cent p.a. Now just consider all the alternative strategies that Harrier can contemplate in order to hit the profit target that it has set itself for year 5, namely, £255,000 or 5 per cent p.a. growth from year 0.

Size strategies

(1) Stay the same size physically; that is, Harrier can allow turnover to rise at 5 per cent p.a. (the rate at which it expects the market to rise) and ensure that all productivities also rise at 5 per cent p.a. Thus, if employee productivity rises by 5 per cent p.a., the company will still employ 100 people in year 5; if productivity per square foot rises by 5 per cent p.a., it will need the same sized factory; if storage efficiencies rise by 5 per cent p.a., the warehouse need not be enlarged; and so on.

(2) Become smaller in size. Harrier can aim at a 5 per cent p.a. increase in sales but a 6 per cent p.a. increase in all productivities. By year 5 the number of employees will be down to ninety-five, some warehouse space be available for letting out to someone else, and so on.

(3) Become much smaller. Instead of increasing sales by 5 per cent p.a. Harrier can allow turnover to remain constant or even decline; but if it increases selling prices and improves productivities, profits can easily hit the target. If turnover falls by 5 per cent p.a. and employee productivity rises by 5 per cent p.a., turnover will be down to £1·55m. by year 5 and employees down to sixty-one; so the margin on sales may quite possibly rise to the necessary 16·5 per cent to achieve the profit target in year 5.

(4) Grow slowly in size. If sales rise at any rate that exceeds the productivity improvements, the number of employees, the size of the factory, and so on will increase.

(5) Grow rapidly. Harrier could throw all its effort into increasing sales at say, 10 per cent p.a., or even 15 per cent. It may achieve its profit target even if it does nothing at all to improve productivities; sales can reach £4m. by year 5, requiring 200 employees. So long as margins do not fall below 6·4 per cent, the profit target will be achieved.

(6) Grow explosively! Harrier can choose to flood the market with cut-price furniture. Instead of a turnover of around £2·5m. and margins of 10 per cent it can aim for a massive £10m. at 2·5 per cent. Five hundred employees!

(7) Even more exciting as far as size is concerned, why not follow an aggressive acquisition strategy? Turnover can rise to over £40m. if Harrier acquires one company a year, even if each company

acquired is only one-third of the current size of Harrier. Two thousand employees!

(8) Still more megalomaniacal, why not reorganise the entire industry? The furniture industry is (in all nations) considerably fragmented, and Harrier may well be able to persuade its government that the industry needs to be restructured. In such a reorganisation Harrier will, of course, come out on top of a major new grouping of companies with a turnover of £100m. Five thousand employees!

These examples relate only to size. Similar multifarious options exist in all other strategic areas.

Product strategies. Let us continue to use Harrier as our example and consider the several product-range strategies that it can adopt:

(1) Do nothing. Leave the product range exactly as it is for some years.

(2) Reduce the range slightly, moderately or severely. Harrier makes twenty different suites of furniture, and it can choose to cut this to eighteen, fifteen, ten or even three. In making these cuts it can concentrate chiefly on reducing the up-market expensive lines or the down-market ones, or it can balance the cuts equally across the range.

(3) Add to the existing range. Harrier can aim to add two new suites by year 5, or ten new ones or twenty. These can all be at the top end of the market, the bottom end, balanced or merely inter-leaved with the existing range.

(4) Add products just outside the existing range. Down-market, Harrier can offer second-hand dining-room furniture; up-market, it can offer reproduction furniture, or perhaps even genuine antiques!

(5) Move a little further out into the manufacture of kitchen or bedroom furniture, or perhaps even further into upholstery or soft furnishings.

(6) Move still further out into 'white goods' – refrigerators, dish-washers, and so on (which, we can assume, Harrier will factor only) – or perhaps even further in a slightly different direction, namely, into products made of wood for the house – wall panels, doors, decorative wood floors, even roof timbers.

(7) Move a long way out into anything made of wood (whether for the house or not) or anything for the house (whether made of wood or not) – even wooden houses.

(8) Anything!

(9) Add a service to the product, such as hire-purchase, maintenance or polishing.

Market strategies.   The same rampant variety can be seen here:

(1) Do nothing. Harrier can just go on selling into its current segments of the home market.
(2) Either increase the share of the existing market or decrease it, by either a little or a lot. These alternatives have all been covered under size strategies above.
(3) Move into a new segment of the same market, or tilt the existing balance of the sales mix without entering a new segment at all. Harrier can enter the luxury end of the market by selling a special new product through leading stores in big cities; or since its traditional place is in the middle of the market, it can move down-market with a very inexpensive new range.
(4) Expand into new geographical areas of the home market, or tilt the existing geographical mix.
(5) Export. Here there are a dozen sub-alternatives: export to Europe, to Africa, to developed Western economies only, to developing nations only, to both or to all; export a lot or only a little; or manufacture abroad.
(6) Open new outlets. Instead of selling through furniture retailers, Harrier can open its own retail shops.

Other strategies.   With only a few exceptions all the market strategies listed above can be combined with any of the product strategies and with any of the size strategies. The permutations are already enormous, and I have not even mentioned production strategies, personnel strategies, financial strategies, organisation strategies, and so on. Let me mention a tiny number of these.

Consider production strategies. Let us assume that Harrier at present sells only the products that it makes in its own factory. It can decide to increase production beyond its own sales requirements for sale by competitors; or to go the other way, it can cease production of some or all of its lines and have them made by a competitor. It can sub-contract some of the work on some of the products or their components. It can adopt the strategy of completely modernising its existing factory, move to a new site or start manufacture abroad.

As to personnel strategies, Harrier can move towards lower pay and lower skills or more skills and higher pay. It can introduce profit-sharing. It can become a workers' co-operative. It can seek to reduce the number of employees or to increase them.

As financial strategies it can increase gearing or decrease it, seek to raise dividends more rapidly than earnings or less rapidly, issue new equity or more debentures, go public, go private, go into liquidation or enfranchise any non-voting shares.

As organisation strategies, Harrier can seek to centralise or decentralise, adopt a matrix form of organisation, reduce the density of supervision on the shopfloor, increase the number of departments or split the organisation by geographical area instead of by product group.

Also, there can be acquisition strategies, and licensing strategies, know-how strategies, added-value strategies, and so on almost to infinity. We have not even thought about cutting prices to damage a competitor, moving the registered offices to a tax haven and other slightly dubious measures; nor, less dubious, have we considered strategies to bring in foreign shareholders or form joint companies (Shell, Unilever, Estel and Agfa all have radically different financial and organisational structures that span international boundaries). Indeed, we have not considered any strategies involving a foreign link-up.

There is one other vital type of strategy not yet mentioned, namely, risk-reducing strategies. Most textbooks mention risk, but few say how to deal with it when there is too much of it! If a company's profits are exposed to violent fluctuations, for example, it is possible to reduce the riskiness of the company by (1) seeking a countercyclical product or market, (2) adjusting prices to even out demand, (3) seeking to reduce the financial leverage of the company, (4) manufacturing less of the product, (5) increasing the amount of buying in or subcontracting, or (6) entering long term contracts with customers. Again, there is a very large number of alternatives. Also, there are strategies for reducing the riskiness of a purchasing or sourcing situation – multiple sourcing, materials substitution, paying the supplier a premium price for special service, penalty clauses in his contract, vertical integration backwards, long term contracts, and so on – and for reducing customer risks, production risks, and so on. So, if your Fo forecast shows a very wide spread between the optimistic and pessimistic edges, identify what it is that gives so much uncertainty to your future and, having made a note that your corporate plan must include a risk-reducing strategy to deal with this problem, list now, at this stage, all such strategies that are relevant.

I have felt it to be necessary to place so much emphasis on the number and variety of strategies that are available to any company because, in general, the list from which most companies select their final set of strategies is rather brief and unimaginative. In the Argenti system of corporate planning the planning is done not by some high-powered expert but by busy executives. Many of these are not used to having time to make long imaginative lists of alternatives. Most of them spend most of their time dealing with immediate problems and crises in which there really is often 'only one alternative'. If this habit is not avoided in long range planning, much of the value of their lifting their eyes to more distant horizons will be lost.

Apart from all these major positive reasons for introducing a little imagination into usually rather sterile planning procedures there is this negative one: how embarrassing it would be if, *after* you had selected your strategy, someone casually asked 'Did you think of doing so and so?' and on inspection his idea turned out to be plainly better than anything that you had had in your list!

Strategies for today

There are thousands upon thousands of possible strategies, but for any given company in any given situation there is only one. Precisely how a company can, using our target–strengths–weaknesses–etc. sieve, whittle down all these alternatives to the right one will be described in the next chapter. Each company is unique, and no two companies will ever adopt exactly the same set of strategies. However, there are some broad families of strategies that at any given moment in history seem to be appropriate for a large number of companies.

In the remainder of this chapter I shall describe some of the strategies that, it seems to me, will be appropriate to quite a large number of medium-sized companies in the developed nations of the world over the next two decades, that is, strategies for just the sort of company for which this book is mainly written. In putting these forward I am fully aware of the fallibility of statements about the future course of the world over such a long horizon, and I hope the reader is too.

Specialising strategies

I have mentioned (page 147) how the 1960s and early 1970s were characterised by a fashion for diversification. With many companies growing rapidly in an atmosphere of economic optimism it was not surprising that managers felt inspired to move into new and exciting fields of business.

At the time of writing, however, it looks as though the 1980s will follow the late 1970s in remaining rather flat and difficult economically. Added to this is a widespread feeling, fairly well substantiated by recent literature, that those companies which diversified in the 1960s did not do as well as they then appeared to be doing. (This conclusion applies also to companies that engaged in extensive acquisitions – another of the fashionable strategies of the 1960s.)

Moreover, the intensity of competition among the world's businesses is continually growing and will continue to do so, we may assume, unless a new strenuous strain of protectionism emerges, and in order to survive in any field of business every company is going to have to be really good at its job. Managers are beginning to ask themselves whether they can successfully run a business in two fields at once or whether it would be better, that is, more profitable *and* less risky, to concentrate all their attention in the one specialised field that they know best.

It will be interesting to see how the 1980s turn out in this respect. I am quite sure that for some companies a policy of diversification will be correct. However, for the majority it will be incorrect; the majority will specialise.

Stay-small strategies

So onerous are the burdens now being placed on companies by governments, such international bodies as the European Economic Community, trade unions, pressure groups and the media that the incentive for finding some way of evading these responsibilities is now very great. The only companies that can evade them successfully are small ones.

Time after time in recent years managers of small companies have told me that growth is decidedly not one of their objectives and that on the contrary they wish their company to remain small. Some go so far as to set nil growth targets for profits (in real terms), relying upon high dividends to meet the required return on shareholders' funds. However, this is rare. Much more common is the search for rising real profits but constant levels of physical size and constant, or even declining, numbers of employees. Some managers do seek increased physical growth but are determined not to expand any further on their existing sites. Many place a limit of approximately 400 employees as the maximum permitted on any one site and in any one profit centre. Some managers seeking diversification specify the area of interest as 'any area related to our own skills, provided that a company does not have to be big to be successful in it'. In other words, however attractive a business area may appear to be, they will not enter it if it requires more than, say, 400 employees on one site in order to be economically viable.

Managers of medium and larger-sized companies are busily searching for some way to reap the rewards of being big while avoiding the growing disadvantages. There is one pattern of organisation structure, which I call the federal company, that seems to me to meet many of these requirements.

This consists of a very small parent or group board consisting solely of executive and non-executive directors all of whom have group duties but none of whom have any duties in any of the subsidiary companies. They are responsible for three things: (1) overall group strategy, (2) setting targets and budgets for each subsidiary and monitoring their performance, and (3) selection of key personnel. A number of key specialists or specialist departments may be located at head office or anywhere that is geographically convenient.

The subsidiaries or profit centres are both far more numerous and far more autonomous than is common today. Each has its own board of directors, its own shareholders (who may be the employees themselves as in the Mondragon Co-operative in Spain) and its own specialised area of business.

Head office and profit centres live in symbiosis. The profit centres benefit from the name lent to them from membership of the group (a name that they will cease to be able to use if they do not meet the standards set by the group) and from the group's advice, buying power or whatever other advantages are conferred by size in their particular industry.

Meanwhile, the group benefits from the spread of interests represented by the numerous profit centres and from the fees that it charges for management and other services performed. A considerable number of organisations already exist that conform to this specification. Franchising is one form that is growing rapidly in popularity.

I believe that many large companies with their monolithic hierarchies will gradually move towards this form of organisation, or something similar, over the next two decades (see Exhibit 7.1) and that accretions of small companies will build up to form a very similar structure. Thus, it can be formed from the breakdown of a large company or built up from a number of small ones.

Whether or not this particular form is appropriate for the 1980s, I am quite sure that any company that does not have an organisation structure strategy, coupled to a size strategy of some sort, will have a corporate plan that is seriously defective.

Management style strategies

As people become more wealthy and better educated they are progressively less inclined to tolerate being bossed around by managers who in their eyes are little better than themselves. It is therefore almost inconceivable for a corporate plan in the 1980s to ignore this trend.

I believe that all corporate plans will contain a major element of decentralisation, delegation of responsibility and devolution of power down the line. Management densities will decline rapidly (that is, the number of employees per manager or per supervisor will increase), and the 'span of control' of each manager will increase (that is, the number of managers in the middle and lower echelons will decrease). However, the number of general managers, profit centre managers or entrepreneurial managers will increase; and the number of specialist advisers, either employed by and within the company or, more likely, retained by it but independent of it, also will increase.

Exhibit 7.1 How federal companies may form over the next few decades

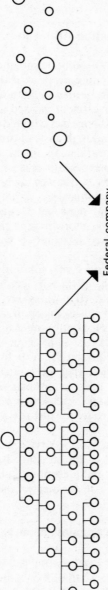

Method 1

From the disintegration of very large monolithic hierarchical organisations employing, say, 6,000 people, of whom 1,000 are management

Method 2

From the accretion of a large number of small companies typically employing 200 people, of whom 10 are management

Federal company

In which there is (1) a very small corporate management staff with (2) a group of specialists and a large number of profit centres, none of which employs more than 400 people. Each has its own board and few other managers, and most of them are co-operatives. Total: 6,000 employees, of whom, say, 400 are group and company management

It will be noted from Exhibit 7.1 that the federal company shows these features very strongly. (I must add, however, that a company facing serious financial difficulties usually needs a strong autocrat to rescue it, and decentralisation is totally inappropriate in this case.)

Automation strategies

During the second half of the 1970s most companies in most developed nations have seen inflation running away with their cash flows; any cash flow that they had has been needed to finance stocks and work in progress to the exclusion of investment in fixed assets. As a result of this many companies now find themselves with old-fashioned plant and equipment, low productivity and high costs of production.

It seems to me that, until world demand picks up, many companies should concentrate their capital expenditures less on increased capacity and more on improved productivity, for we may be sure that wages will rise faster than other costs in most nations, although we cannot be so sure that business demand will increase. Modernisation of capital equipment seems to me all the more urgent since a revolution in production methods due to microelectronics is widely predicted to be upon us.

I should add that this microprocessor revolution may result in a more impressive labour-saving in offices than in factories, and this comes just when many of the developed nations are entering the 'post-industrial' or service-orientated phase of economic development. Thus, although banks, insurance and other office-intensive companies will see a major expansion in business, the number of employees that they will need will decline very rapidly indeed over the next two decades, thus creating a major challenge to their personnel policies.

A further sharp spur to the need to automate is that employees in developed nations are becoming increasingly reluctant to work on boring, noisy, dirty or repetitive jobs – just the sort of work that can be given to a robot.

Although not every company in the developed world will need to embrace automation strategies of the sort that I am describing, most will need to do so vigorously, and a corporate plan without an automation strategy will look very odd for most of them.

Strategies against imports

As suggested above (page 129), the developing nations present a major threat to established companies. In theory they should provide a major opportunity also, since in their headlong rise to prosperity in the next two decades they will need many of the goods and services that only companies in developed nations can provide at present. Unfortunately, they seldom have the necessary currencies, often impose severe tariffs and frequently make decisions on political or personal grounds rather than economic ones. Nevertheless, it is possible for a company, by carefully identifying the exact needs of a developing nation, to obtain that vital first order which may well become the envy of its competitors all over the world.

The threat from imports from developing nations into home markets must be treated seriously. The havoc wreaked by Japan on European radios, televisions, textiles, shoes, ships, motorcycles, cars and other industries in the 1970s is only a foretaste of what the Taiwanese, the Nigerians, the Mexicans, the Koreans or the Malaysians – to name a few – may do in the next two decades and India and China in the decades after that!

One response is to specialise. It is just possible that a developed nation company, by really concentrating on its traditional business and doing it superbly, can do it better than these newcomers in spite of their modern plant and low wages. Indeed, it is fear of these new competitors that partly lies behind the trend towards specialisation noted above (page 155).

A second response is to add value – add something to the existing product that these competitors will find especially difficult to emulate. Two particular techniques may be mentioned. One is to upgrade the technological content of the product; add some electronic wizardry, perhaps, or a new function, or make it from some new material. The product will cost more, but it will be distinguished from that of the new competitors by this more advanced feature. Naturally, micro-processors, which at the time of writing are only just on the horizon, may provide a ready means of upgrading products and services. The other technique is to provide with the product a service that relies on some skill, knowledge or ability that is not available to these new competitors – a detailed appreciation of Western culture, perhaps, or something that makes use of the extensive infrastructures that developed nations enjoy but are rare in developing nations.

The threat from these new competitors is so serious, I believe, that a corporate plan that does not include some response to it must be defective.

Summary

All through the corporate planning process, and long before it begins too, the executives in the company will all have their own ideas for the future of the company. Some may always have held the view that, for example, it should expand in Europe; others believe that it should diversify, and yet others that salvation lies only in being acquired by a major competitor.

Many executives spend their working lives making rapid decisive choices between two or three alternatives. The whole purpose of corporate planning, however, is to look so far ahead that choice becomes almost infinite. Anything is possible. It provides a glorious and almost unique opportunity for the top executives to inspect the crossroad that lies beyond the crossroad at which they are now. Let the choice before them be well and truly mind-boggling; if their minds do not boggle, use such techniques as brainstorming to widen the choice until they do boggle. Then use the sieve as described in the next chapter.

I believe it to be true that every company is unique. No two companies are in such a similar strategic situation and have such similar strengths and weaknesses that the same set of strategies should be chosen for both. Company A should be diversifying and expanding, company B should be diversifying and contracting, company C should be specialising and expanding, and so on through all the infinite permutations that I have described. Only by using the sieve can any given company decide which out of all these strategies is the right combination for it. Yet, at any given moment in history there may well be a few broad strategic choices that are right for a great number of companies.

Thus, it may have been right for many companies to diversify in the ebullient 1970s. It may have been right for many companies in the 1960s not to issue new equity shares and not to invest in new capital equipment but to use bank loans to finance increased working-capital requirements; a vast number of companies certainly did so. In just the same way it may be that there are one or two strategies, or even a certain combination of strategies, that will be appropriate for many medium-sized companies in the developed world in the 1980s and 1990s.

If there is such a combination, it may look like this. The ideal firm will be small (only a few hundred employees) or a loose assembly of small companies in a federal group, or a big company that has split itself up into several small almost-autonomous profit centres. It will be highly specialised; that is, each company will produce only a small range of absolutely superb or unique products or services. Each profit centre will be one of the leaders in its field; indeed, there will be only a few other companies in the world doing the same thing. Its product will be high in added value; that is, *very* great skill or knowledge, special equipment or care, or *something* will be needed to produce it. Its market will be the entire world.

The company (or each company in the group) will be at least partly owned by many of its employees. Its management density will be extremely low – spans of control will be twenty subordinates compared with five or seven today – and managers will act mainly as advisors and only seldom as bosses. Most dull jobs will be automated. The company may possibly not aim to grow physically and may not even aim for profits to rise faster than inflation; it may instead pay high dividends (much of which may go to the owner–employees).

Whether this is an appropriate set of strategies for any given company, however, can be determined only by considering the particular company's particular and unique situation. In other words we must learn to use the sieve described in the next chapter.

CHAPTER 8

Selection and Evaluation

By this stage in the process the team has had approximately fifteen meetings over a period of six to nine months (see Exhibits 1.2 and 1.3). All items of strategic importance have now been agreed and listed: the target and forecast, the strengths and weaknesses, the threats and opportunities, and the list of possible strategies.

In the first section of this chapter I shall describe, with the aid of an extremely simple example, how a suitable strategy emerges from all these strategic facts, figures, opinions and hunches. Then, I shall describe a much more complex and realistic example to illustrate the process again. Finally, I shall describe the steps that are necessary to evaluate whether the strategy that emerges is really the right one.

How a strategy emerges

Imagine a company called Eider Engineering. It employs 600 people on one site in a large industrial town. Last year turnover totalled £15m., and it made a profit of £2·5m. Its Tsat target is £4m. by year 5 – approximately 10 per cent p.a. growth.

It manufactures two different products. The main product, listed by the managers as an outstanding strength, is a patented scaffolding system known almost throughout the world. Almost all the catalogues of building and construction industry suppliers list the Eider system along with three or four others. Turnover of this product last year was £12·3m., and profits from it were £2·3m. Due to the efforts of a managing director many years ago this product is very well known in several African nations. The other product, listed as a minor strength, is an overhead conveyor system used in assembly plants – cars, domestic appliances, and so on – for moving parts and subassemblies round the factory. All the patents on this product have lapsed, and the designers who developed it have long since left the company. In spite of its obsolescence it still sells well; its turnover last year was a useful £2·7m., and its profits were £0·2m.

A major threat applies to both products but for slightly different reasons. Over the past two decades there has been a great number of mergers in the car industry and in many of the assembly industries as well, especially domestic appliances. Now, this means that there are fewer potential customers for the conveyor system, and they are all now very big companies. So, if they do place an order, it is a large one for a firm the size of Eider; most of the £2·7m. turnover last year came from just three orders. The same phenomenon is affecting the scaffolding, but this is not because of mergers; this is due to the growing influence of government and international agencies in the developing nations. Increasingly, Eider is being invited to supply scaffolding systems not just for building a warehouse in a port but also for building an entire new port.

As the finance director points out, it needs only a few months' delay in payment on one of these enormous projects for Eider's cash flow to be dangerously stretched. The company's bank overdraft is already high, and this is on top of several long term loans.

Nevertheless, the developing nations, in Africa especially, are plainly a most important opportunity, especially as Eider's managers believe that building and construction activity in the developed nations will remain very flat for almost a decade.

Among the many ideas considered by Eider's planning team only three are worthy of mention here. One became known grandiosely as the 'Africa Policy'. This envisaged a major sales drive in several developing nations in Africa with the aim of becoming, within five years or so, the leading scaffolding supplier and a major supplier of conveyors for the assembly factories that, Eider's managers believed, would spring up like mushrooms in Africa all through the next three or four decades. A second strategy was to reduce the riskiness of the company by acquiring a company in a new but similar field of business. This 'Third Leg' could easily be formed by acquiring a company that they knew quite well in the same town as Eider, which manufactured factory ventilation systems. Finally, there was the 'One Leg' strategy, which suggested that Eider sell off the conveyor product and concentrate its limited resources on expanding in scaffolding.

Now, the items described so far can be summarised very briefly as follows:

Strengths:	Excellent scaffolding system
	Conveyor system
	Quite well known in Africa
Weaknesses:	Rather high gearing

Threats: Obsolescence of conveyors
                    Huge size of orders
                    Poor growth in developed nations
Opportunities: Developing nations, especially in Africa

I think that it is fair to say that until quite late in their planning process the Africa Policy was the favourite among Eider's managers. The Third Leg was strongly criticised as being subject to the same threats as those which currently worried the managers: poor growth in the building and construction of factories in developed nations, and the growing size of orders in the developing nations. As for the One Leg strategy, this was considered unnecessarily drastic.

However, I must now introduce a set of weaknesses into the argument. These were listed early on as weaknesses by the planning team, but their importance was only gradually recognised. Eventually, they became one of the key elements in the choice of strategy. These weaknesses can be summarised as:

Weaknesses: Cramped factory
                    Old-fashioned equipment
                    Poor human relations in conveyor works

As Eider's managers began to make rough calculations of the factory space required to meet a profit target of £4m., especially bearing in mind the erratic size of orders, it became totally clear that the existing site could not possibly accommodate both activities. Furthermore, although human relations were good on the scaffolding side, in the conveyor works they were, and had always been, appalling.

The 'strategic scorecard'

As can be seen in Exhibit 8.1, these newly appreciated weaknesses swung opinion away from the Africa Policy towards the One Leg idea. Exhibit 8.1 shows how Eider's managers marked their strategic scorecard. If a strategy was thought to take advantage of a strength or opportunity, it was given a tick. It also scored a tick if it obviated or ameliorated a weakness or a threat. It scored a cross if the opposite was true, and a zero or a blank if it was irrelevant. The result was a decisive victory for the One Leg strategy.

If we ignore the weaknesses relating to the factory – and Eider's management very nearly did ignore them, as I have explained above – the Africa Policy scores +3 (five ticks minus two crosses), the Third Leg – 2 and the One Leg +6. Although the One Leg does still beat the Africa Policy, it is nothing like as decisive as the 9 to 1 victory if the

Exhibit 8.1 Strategic scorecard for Eider Engineering

		Strategies	
Strategic factors	*Africa Policy*	*Third Leg*	*One Leg*
Strengths:			
The scaffold product	✓	×	✓
The conveyor product	✓	×	×
Known in Africa	✓	×	✓
Weaknesses:			
Rather high gearing	×	×	✓
Small factory	×	×	✓
Old-fashioned equipment	×	×	✓
Human relations in conveyor works	0	×	✓
Threats:			
Obsolescence of conveyor	0	✓	✓
Large size of orders	×	×	✓
Poor growth in developed nations	✓	✓	✓
Opportunities:			
Developing nations, especially Africa	✓	✓	✓
Score +1 for a tick and −1 for a cross	+1	−5	+9

factory weaknesses are included. This (oversimple!) calculation merely underlines the necessity to spend a good deal of management time on agreeing what are the strategic strengths and weaknesses.

Try scoring using any points system you like. Give the scaffolding system 10 points for being an outstanding strength, give 2 points only for the weaker conveyor product, and so on. Does this complication make any difference to the choice? I doubt it. In view of the arbitrary nature of these figures I am less than enamoured of this complex approach in most cases.

Some corporate planners try to score from 0 to 10 on strategic scorecards of this sort, but I find it difficult enough just to put ticks and crosses without attempting to value these relationships. In any case I see these scorecards as little more than *aides memoires,* which are mainly useful as a check that each strategic factor has been considered and that none have been omitted. The really important mental processes take place in discussion, not in marking the scorecards. Furthermore, strategic conclusions seem to be reached gradually and cumulatively over almost the entire process, lasting perhaps nine to fifteen months, not suddenly at one scorecard meeting at the very end of the data-gathering stages.

(However, consider one company that I know that adopted a particular strategy that it felt to be rather ingenious. Just as a check the planning team scored the strategy against the strengths, weaknesses, and so on and found to its amazement that the strategy failed to deal with one particular very important threat, namely, one particularly aggressive competitor. In fact it took several weeks for the team to come up with a strategy that did deal with this threat and scored well with all the other items, and this strategy bore little resemblance to the earlier one. The value of the scorecard is unquestionable, I believe, but as a check rather than as a creative tool.)

Although there may be other strategies as good as Eider's eventual choice, the chosen strategy is an amalgam of the One Leg and the Africa Policy. Its main steps are seen as follows. (1) Move the conveyor business, including its labour force, to a new site on the other side of the town. (2) Inject all possible resources into modernising the now enlarged scaffolding works and obtaining and coping with large new orders in Africa. (3) Meanwhile, decide what to do with the conveyor side of the business. Sell it and inject the proceeds into scaffolding? Set up a joint company with another conveyor company? Set up several joint companies in Africa with African nationals?

Although many details remain to be worked out, the central core of the strategy for Eider is clear. It can be summarised in just two words: scaffolding and Africa. Everything else that Eider's managers must do in the next few years will be merely subservient actions designed to bring these two features to the forefront of the company. The modernising of the factory, the raising of any new equity, the training of African nationals to sell scaffolding, the detailed design of any new parts of the scaffolding system, the search for a rented site for the conveyor works – all these activities are to be coherently geared together to produce a company that in five years' time will be making a profit of £4m., essentially from selling scaffolding systems all over the world but most intensively in Africa. The company may or may not also be involved with conveyors by year 5. If a satisfactory route can be found, yes; otherwise, no.

The strategy described above is an amalgamation of the Africa Policy and the One Leg idea. It seems to happen quite often that the strategy eventually selected by a planning team bears close resemblance to one or more of the ideas that have been hovering around the collective corporate consciousness for some time. The planning process that I am describing seems to bring these ideas down to earth, where they can be captured and inspected. At the same time it seems to force a company's top managers to face up to problems that have worried them (or opportunities that have dazzled them) for years.

I shall describe the emergence of a strategy again below. All that I have wanted to do in this section has been to demonstrate in the simplest possible way how the strategic factors, as I collectively call them – the targets, the strengths and weaknesses, and so on, which have been so laboriously identified in the earlier parts of the planning process – all come together in the minds of the planning team to form a consensus concerning the long term strategic situation of the company. Our future lies *this* way, not that way; by *this* means, not that. Scaffolding and Africa, not conveyors or ventilation.

There normally is, I believe, a number of interlinked strategies, usually not more than two or three, that form the absolute essence – the kernel, the core – of the corporate plan for the long term destiny of any company. I believe this to be true regardless of a company's size or complexity. Small simple companies can define their destiny in terms of just two or three major interlinked decisions; so can huge complex ones. It is the main purpose of my system of corporate planning to reveal this core. Once it has been identified, everything else that needs to be decided follows readily.

I should add that Eider's planning team must put its chosen strategy through the evaluation process described later in this chapter. One of the many questions that it must ask about this strategy is how much of the company's turnover and profits it will be prudent to allow to be generated in Africa, bearing in mind that even with Eider's experience of that continent it is a high risk area. Presumably, the maximum stake in Africa must be no more than that amount of business which, if sequestered without compensation, would still leave Eider with a viable business elsewhere.

The case of Fulmar & Co.

I intend to use this company partly to illustrate again how a central core of strategies emerges from the data-gathering discussions and partly to describe how a planning team may draw up a formal statement of its conclusions for inspection by its colleagues, the board, or other interested parties.

In my system the written corporate plan will consist of ten to fifteen pages of typescript together with another ten to fifteen pages of calculations in an appendix. Page one of the plan consists of a brief summary sheet as shown for Fulmar & Co. in Exhibit 8.2 in the Appendix. We can see at once that Fulmar has set itself a very ambitious target, and from page two (Exhibit 8.3) we can see the detailed thinking behind this. Page three (Exhibit 8.4) shows the forecasts and page four (Exhibit 8.5) the gaps.

Already we get the impression that Fulmar's managers want to see a much better performance than they have achieved in the past few years and even on their worst assumptions it looks as though the company should exceed Tmin on present strategies. With ordinary luck, they think, it should exceed Tmin by £1m. However, an extra £3m. profit has to be found from new strategies if Tsat for year 5 is to be hit. It looks extremely ambitious, especially in view of the performance over the past few years. It is worth commenting here that the layout of these planning documents demands that only a brief simple summary need be made in each section, and this makes it very difficult to hide embarrassing facts or dubious reasoning behind elaborate calculations or verbose jargon.

In Exhibit 8.6 the first strength listed is the product. This consists of a range of prefabricated wooden agricultural buildings that are suitable for sheep shelters, calving pens, storage for fodder or agricultural machinery and suchlike in outlying and remote areas, where rugged construction against rain, snow, gales, frost, drought and all extremes of weather is needed. The product was first invented by Mr Fulmar twenty-five years earlier, and its tremendous indestructibility is due to the use of a glass fibre resin to bond together the wooden members, the wood itself having been treated against bad weather conditions.

The company went public ten years ago when Mr Fulmar also brought in a team of professional managers at board level. For a few years the company continued to grow; but as can be seen from the forecast (Exhibit 8.4), it has plateaued for the past five years, partly due to growing competition (now somewhat reduced again; see forecast) but partly also due to Mr Fulmar's poor health.

Exhibits 8.6 to 8.9 tell a fairly consistent story; Fulmar is living on its past. It has a first-rate product that sells well, but the management has taken almost no steps at all to modernise the product or the factory nor to enter some fairly obvious new markets. Cash is piling up in the bank. He cannot say for sure, but it may be that Mr Fulmar himself has caused the blockage because of his poor health – he is still chief executive as well as chairman – and he has now agreed to step down as chief executive. Indeed, he proposed this himself after it gradually became clear to him, during the discussions of the planning team, that it may be he himself who is holding up the advance of the company.

I should like to pause in the story here to draw attention to two important aspects of the Fulmar case that are of very general application.

Notice first how the strengths and weaknesses tell a brief, succinct but revealing story: 'Fulmar is living on its past'. In the case of almost every company it is possible to boil down the entire internal (and external) appraisal to a few brief sentences. If this cannot be done, it may indicate that these analyses are incomplete or defective.

Notice secondly how the list of strengths and weakness balances; this can be most readily observed from the 'cruciform chart' in Exhibit 8.2.

The strengths and weaknesses are approximately equal in number and weight – just what we should expect from a company that is neither hugely successful nor unsuccessful. Check this for your company; if it has been extremely successful, strengths will surely be more numerous or weightier than weaknesses, and vice versa for unsuccessful companies.

Also, notice the disposition in the cruciform chart of the threats and opportunities. There really are not too many threats, although there are several massive opportunities – excellent. Also, notice that in Fulmar's case the threats and opportunities are together convincingly numerous. Some companies seem quite unable to examine the outside world, and they produce so few threats and opportunities and so many strengths and weaknesses that it is only possible to assume a severe case of introspection.

Do you have many strengths and opportunities? This would be most encouraging. However, can you exploit these opportunities using these strengths without first putting some weaknesses right or reducing the risk from some threats? In other words stand back from the completed cruciform chart, and examine its balance.

Now let us return to Fulmar.

Outline of Fulmar's strategies

At the start of the planning exercise most of the members of Fulmar's team believed that their company's most significant weakness was the lack of new product ideas. The fact that no development department had ever existed was openly criticised. Some of the executives were certain that the strategy that would save the company was to design and launch one or more major new products; indeed, a number of ideas had been discussed from time to time, although nothing practical had ever been done. It came as a considerable surprise, therefore, when it emerged from their discussions that lack of new products was not their most urgent weakness.

As the process continued, one weakness after another was found in the production area. Many of these on their own were not strategic in nature. Poor stock control, high stocks, poor production-planning, old equipment, no method study, no incentive schemes, overmanning, low materials efficiencies – none of these alone was of great proportions, but taken together they added up to an area of very considerable waste and inefficiency. Eventually, the planning team called in a firm of production-engineering consultants, who reported that savings of £1m. could be made even without any capital expenditure and that an outlay of £3m. of capital could purchase a further saving of £2m. a year from higher productivity, reduction of scrap, and so on. It was this discovery that led to the adoption of strategy S1, namely, 'Put the production department right within two years'. This alone would place the profits in the target area.

It was also something of a surprise when the 'new product' idea gradually gave way to the 'new market' idea – see the short list of strategies considered by Fulmar's team in Exhibit 8.10. The factors at work in this movement of opinion were as follows: (1) The company had no development department and no new product development experience either, so any new home-grown product would be long delayed and risky. (2) The new product would have to be produced, but it would be another two years before the factory was reorganised for the existing product, let alone ready for a new one. (3) In any case the existing product was still highly successful and, now that they had had a good look at it, was seen to have a great deal of potential. In favour of a 'new market with same product' strategy were several of the strengths – the product itself, the company's unique depot system, its knowledge of exporting and selecting suitable agencies and merchants, and so on – and the glaring opportunities in Asia and North America, which represented two huge untapped markets. The planning team decided that strategy S2 would be 'Get into the Asian or North American markets' with the existing product. Naturally, this was not to be at the expense of existing markets, where, it was hoped, market shares could be maintained and even expanded. The latter was not a new strategy; this was something that Fulmar's salesmen were already doing in these areas and that had been included in the Fo forecasts.

One of the management's great anxieties, and quite rightly so, was not to try to do everything at once. How marvellous it would be to put the production side right, enter new markets, launch new products and take over a couple of competitors! However, managers are only human and cannot do everything at once. A corporate plan that places excessive demands on management is doomed to disaster in just the same way as one that stretches a company's finances too far. This is one major reason why a 'new products' strategy was placed further down the list of priorities.

A further action that was patently needed was the selection of a successor to Mr Fulmar as chairman, chief executive or both; and should that successor be promoted from within the company, several consequential changes would be called for. Furthermore, as so often happens, Fulmar's executives realised that, if they were now going to place more accent on long term planning, the top management levels in the company would need to be strengthened or modified in some way to reflect this change in style and emphasis. So, another strategy, dubbed S3, dealing with management changes was adopted.

Strategy S4 dealt with finance. Calculations showed that in addition to the cost of S1 (approximately £3m. over two years) the penetration of the new market areas in S2 would demand well over £4m. in the next three years for purchasing and stocking new depots, and so on. (These calculations, not shown here, would be included along with several others in the appendices to Fulmar's corporate plan.) Additional finance would be needed.

Two further strategies remained to be thrashed out later, and these will be briefly discussed below. However, first let me summarise the effect on profits so far by means of Exhibit 8.11. The Fo forecast for year 5, it will be remembered, is £5·5m. Add to this the profits attributable to S1, which, as can be seen from Exhibit 8.11, are rather on the cautious side compared with the consultants' report, because, Fulmar's executives feel, this report did not take sufficient account of the practical difficulties of such a major modernisation. Now add the profits attributable to S2 – again a very cautious estimate considering the enormous size of the markets involved; but, Fulmar's executives feel, the difficulties of breaking into new markets, especially the highly competitive one in America, must not be underestimated. As can be seen, the gaps are closed immediately and decisively right up to year 5, when the Tsat is £8·5m.

Whether it really will be so easy is a matter of opinion (I shall discuss a method of evaluating strategies below), but it is worth noting three things: (1) Fulmar's main problem is that it has not been taking advantage of its undoubted strengths. It has been asleep. If it is now going to wake up, it should surprise no one if it does rather well for a few years. (2) Both strategies are within its known competence; S1 merely looks to an improvement in its own factory. It is true that it involves a major improvement, but it does not call for an adventure into new unknown technologies. Similarly, S2 rests solidly on the company's undoubted know-how in selecting agents and merchants in foreign lands and servicing them from depots. It has done this repeatedly in dozens of nations all over the world in the past two decades. (3) Furthermore, the improvements in productivity arising from S1 will release approximately the same number of employees as will be required to man the increased throughput arising from the natural increase in existing markets plus the incursion into the new markets in S2. There should be no redundancies. There should be no problems with pay either, for a new bonus scheme will be linked to improved methods and productivity.

At this point Fulmar's executives, being agreed that they have satisfactorily completed a major stage in their corporate plan, have decided two things: (1) The company should go ahead with S1, S2, S3 and S4 subject only to sufficient further calculations to convince everyone that these strategies are practicable – to evaluation of the strategies, as I call it. Instructions should then be given to go ahead with modernising, opening new depots, and so on. (2) After a pause to complete (1) above, the planning team should start on the next major phase of the corporate plan, which, as far as can be seen at present, will consist of two main strategies: S5 and S6.

It looks as though an S5 strategy will be needed to deal with the problem of Mr Fulmar's shares. This is not considered to be urgent, but it is going to be important. However, in addition a considerable number of other legal–financial matters are going to need attention, quite apart from Mr Fulmar's shares. What about the employees and managers owning some shares, for example? What about a bid for Petrel – the small competitor mentioned in 'opportunities' whose price–earnings (P/E) ratio is now 8 compared with Fulmar's 4? It should not be long before Fulmar's is also 8 or above. Also, if Fulmar really does do much better, what about dividends? They cannot be allowed to continue at the present levels for long, and yet there are government constraints on raising dividends. There are other questions also – quite a bundle of interconnected financial conundrums to bring together in a S5 strategy in a year or two.

Meanwhile, S6 will concern new products. Does Fulmar need any new products, or does it need merely to update and modernise its existing products? What about fireproofing? What about a new bonding resin? Is a development department needed? Should Fulmar license a new product? Should the company manufacture it itself? Should it take over Petrel?

The executives have decided that these two strategies (S5 and S6) can wait for a year or so. The important task now is to get ahead with the major new strategies (S1 and S2) together with the secondary ones (S3 and S4).

Fulmar's planning team should now complete the last section of page one (Exhibit 8.2) and compose a summary of its selected strategic decisions on page ten (see Exhibit 8.12). (As a matter of fact they should do neither of these until after evaluating the strategies properly, but I wish to postpone discussing this until the next section below.) Notice, by the way, the use of named project-managers for each important part of the strategies.

The strategic decision can be briefly described in the summary given on page one (Exhibit 8.2 in the Appendix) as follows:

Strategies selected

S1, a major modernisation of production
S2, break into Asian and North American markets
S3, top management changes
S4, obtaining finance
Later S5 and S6 will be required

As a very crude generalisation most corporate plans seem to contain four components very much as Fulmar's does. There is almost always a major strategy relating to products and markets (Fulmar's S2), and there is nearly always another strategy of equal pre-eminence (Fulmar's S1). In Fulmar's case this has to do with production, but it may well be concerned with any other non-product or market area: closing down a part of the company, relocation of the entire company, a merger, a major change in the purchasing posture of the company, or whatever.

Also, there are nearly always two secondary strategies (Fulmar's S3 and S4). I call them secondary because usually they can only be spelt out after the primary or pre-eminent strategies are known. Fulmar, for example, could not have spelt out either its financial or its management needs before S1 and S2 were known. Like Fulmar, most secondary strategies are concerned with these two major resources, namely, finance and management. Occasionally, some other resource has to be specified in one of these secondary strategies: production facilities, advertising, manpower, warehousing, research, computing skills, or whatever. It naturally depends on what sort of company the plan is for, but normally these can safely be left to departmental heads.

In other words the average corporate plan consists of: (1) one or two primary strategies, one of which will almost certainly be a product or market strategy; (2) two secondary strategies, almost always concerned with finance and management; and (3) occasionally some other secondary strategy, but more often everything else that needs to be planned will be handed over for planning and executive action to the departmental executives and not included in the corporate plan itself. Let us remember two things. First, the corporate planning team consists of very senior executives who do not want to spend any more of their precious time in long range planning than they need to. Secondly, as most companies enjoy the services of marketing men, production specialists, buying directors, and so on, it would be doubly wasteful for the planning team to go on planning down to the last nut and bolt.

All these departmental plans can in any case be clearly identified once the overall structure of the company for year 5 is known. Departmental plans fall out of the corporate plans with smooth efficiency: manpower plans, production plans, research and development plans, marketing plans, management succession plans, computer plans, training plans – all for five years ahead if necessary.

I should add some comments about management strategies. These often seem to contain four main elements. One relates to a reorganisation or reallocation of top management time. The planning team comes to recognise that part of the job of top executives is to consider the long term future of the company, and the members of the team very often formalise their recognition of the importance of this aspect of their jobs by permanently reallocating their own duties to allow more time for it. Usually, they delegate a little more of their day-to-day executive duties, but sometimes they go so far as to form a sort of group board where they all have corporate executive duties but no departmental duties. They become corporate managers.

The second element is the increasing use of non-executive directors on boards. This seems to me entirely consistent with the above remarks, and no further comment seems necessary.

A third element is the attempt to build flexibility into the company as a deliberate feature of its organisation structure. This is more easily said than done. I know of no secret formula, although the profit centre approach seems to have some beneficial effects. However, if more responsibility for decisions is delegated downwards, which is what the profit centre philosophy demands, it is necessary to install efficient control systems as well. Efficient control and monitoring systems are needed for all the new forms of delegated management, not only for profit centres. They are needed, for example, in the project team concept, mentioned above in the Fulmar case. They are needed in venture groups, task forces and strategic business areas, all of which fit very neatly into the implementation stages of corporate planning of the type that I have been describing.

The final element is changes in management style. I have mentioned several times that corporate planning is almost certain not to get off the ground if the company is run autocratically. On the other hand it will enhance and strengthen a team of top managers led by a *primus inter pares* chief executive. The whole planning exercise as I have described it will ensure that a participative approach to problems will be adopted throughout the top several levels in the hierarchy. Everyone will come to understand how the company works and why it has chosen this route rather than that. Once this style of management has been established or reinforced, it is surely appropriate for the management strategy of the corporate plan to endorse and encourage it.

Evaluating the strategies

The procedure that I call evaluating a strategy is very similar to project appraisal, but it is more general and on a larger scale.

As a result of using the sieve of strategic factors the planning team will have whittled down the number of possible alternative strategies from several hundred to a small knot of two, three or four broad strategic ideas. At that stage the team cannot possibly know whether these ideas are practical or not. The company's future seems to lie in this direction, not that; by this means, not that. Statements like 'We believe that it would be better to sell existing products into new markets than to sell new products into existing markets' are almost philosophical in their generality.

To determine whether any of these broad concepts are likely to be real practical possibilities the team has to subject each of them to the following tests:

(1) Describe the actual real-life steps that have to be taken to put this idea in practice. Are these realistic?
(2) Show that the company has the necessary resources – especially management, financial and experiential – to bring this idea to practical fruition.
(3) Show how this strategy helps the company to achieve its Tsat target.
(4) What may go wrong? Which of these events will, if they occur, bring the company's profits dangerously near Tmin? What contingency plans are needed?
(5) Are any strengths, weaknesses, threats, opportunities or ethical features of the company not fully taken into account by this strategy?

In order to answer these penetrating questions, the team members have to get their feet firmly on the ground and discuss practical details with their colleagues in middle management and below. I doubt that a set of strategies for any company can be adequately evaluated in less than two or three months.

In the case of Fulmar, for example, one awkward practical problem was how to keep the factory going at full capacity while at the same time making major alterations to the layout. Another was the discovery that the delivery of new up-to-date timber-treatment equipment would take fifteen months. Another surprise was that, although the factory modernisation was unlikely to stretch the production management too far, the setting up of depots in the United States was going to require the recruitment of nearly a dozen extra middle managers. Frankly, however, all these were details. Nothing of any major significance emerged from the team's detailed evaluation to invalidate the selected strategies.

Furthermore, as Exhibit 8.11 has foreshadowed, detailed calculations of costs, revenues, interest on loans, and so on did nothing to reduce confidence that the S1 and S2 strategies would indeed achieve Tsat for every year up to, and even beyond, year 5. A large number of Fp forecasts were made using a company model similar to the one described in Exhibit 4.6. Some forecasts assumed realistic rates of economic growth, realistic margins, realistic rates of new market penetration and realistic rates of inflation. In other runs on the model unrealistic assumptions were made to test the robustness of the company to a severe economic slowdown, a resurgence of inflation, an exchange rate crisis, a rise in timber prices, a fall in timber prices, and so on. Naturally, the planning team was interested in what effect any of these might have not only on profits but also on many other aspects of the company as well – overdrafts, to mention one obvious example.

To answer the question 'What may go wrong?' the same model was used to examine possible failures of parts of S1 or S2. One discovery made was that, if in S2 Fulmar attempted to open up new market areas too rapidly, it might be possible to repeat a serious mistake in a second area before observing its consequences in the first area, and two areas failing together would have severe effects on cash flow. The results of several Fp forecasts are shown in Exhibit 8.13. As can be seen, most of them lie acceptably close to Tsat, but one or two of them, including the two-area failure, look rather serious.

I must emphasise the importance of Exhibit 8.13. This represents the evaluation section of a corporate plan; in this case it is page eleven of Fulmar's corporate plan. This is the section where the members of the planning team have to show that they have got their feet firmly on the ground, that their plans are not pie in the sky or castles in the air and that this really is a practical route to a new level of profits in five years' time. I can only give an outline here, and undoubtedly more calculations should be shown (either on page eleven or as an appendix) than I show.

As can be seen, page eleven answers all the five evaluation questions listed above (page 175). If the evaluation does reveal a defect or danger point in the chosen strategies – and it would indeed be a remarkable strategy that had no defect – the planning team should put forward either a proposal to redesign the strategy (such as to rephase cash flows, to quote a common example) or a contingency plan to deal with the defect should it appear.

Occasionally, all the curves of the forecasts turn out to lie below Tsat, and the model indicates cash building up in the bank; this suggests that the strategies concerned are not sufficiently ambitious. Vice versa, of course, indicates overambition.

Finally, question 5 above asks whether the strategies leave any loose ends. As can be seen from Exhibit 8.13, Fulmar's team found some of these, and the team has noted here on page eleven that strategies S5 and S6 are to be developed to deal with them. The final pages in Fulmar's corporate plan (pages twelve and thirteen) would contain a list of major actions to be taken and the items to be monitored. Both of these will be discussed in the next chapter.

Summary

During the whole of the period of six to nine months preceding this point in the process (see Exhibit 1.2 for a timetable of the whole process) various strategic ideas will have appeared and been noted, and been rejected or acclaimed. Occasionally, the entire team will have latched on to one seemingly superb suggestion that looks as though it will solve all the company's problems at a stroke. Then, someone points to a flaw, then another, and the vision shatters into pieces.

However, one thing will certainly have been happening during this time: countless ideas will have been rejected as either not truly strategic or not relevant to the company's situation, which, as I have emphasised, is unique. No other company displays the same strengths and weaknesses, selects the same targets or is faced with the same threats and opportunities, and it follows that there is one unique strategy or set of strategies that is right for each company. All the others are wrong. One out of millions! In most cases the inappropriate ones fall out of the race quite early in the process, and by the point reached at the beginning of this chapter there will probably be only a few left.

That is why, in spite of valiant efforts to think up a creative and imaginative list of strategies all through the process, when it comes to this stage the space on the corporate plan form marked 'strategies considered' contains so few proposals. They may be few, but at least most of them are relevant.

In order to reduce these still further, down to a central core of two or three strategies that are very often interlinked in some way, some corporate planners recommend that the planning team actually use a form of scorecard in which marks are allocated to each strategic idea according to its relevance to each strategic factor. Although I do not reject this technique, I believe it to be more useful as a checklist by which to verify that a chosen strategy does deal with these factors satisfactorily.

In my experience the final strategy or set of strategies emerges from discussion among the members of the team over a considerable period of time rather than from one meeting set aside for the purpose. My experience further suggests that one or more of the major features of most new strategies are in fact rather old ideas that have been around the company for many years but now reappear, somewhat modified or amalgamated with parts of other old or new ideas.

I also have the distinct impression – and this is an encouraging discovery – that companies often find that their strengths have been previously underestimated and their weaknesses and threats over-estimated, so that, when the strategy is finally chosen, it is a surprisingly powerful package. The company seems to unlock funds of ability that were always there but are now guided accurately into more appropriate channels. Instead of being dissipated and weakened by lack of direction they are concentrated and invigorated by the clarity of the purpose and goals now set before them.

A set of strategies emerges, then. However, before it can be adopted, it must be thoroughly tested to ascertain its defects. Does the company have the resources to carry it out in practice? Will it overstretch the management or the finances? Will it achieve the target? What can go wrong? If it did, what would happen? Could a failure produce a situation so catastrophic that not even Tmin would be attained?

Eventually, everyone will be satisfied that the choice is the right one for the company in its present position and that the company is still robust against adversity, even when the strategies are in their most vulnerable stage. Then, the next step is to draw up an action plan and a budget and to begin the procedure of monitoring.

CHAPTER 9

Action Plans, Budgets and Monitoring

The planning team now has only three major tasks left to complete. It must take the selected strategies, which up to now exist in outline only, and fill them out in sufficient detail to be able to give clear instructions to the company's executives so that they can put the strategies into action.

It must also issue a 'five-year budget' that shows everyone how the performance of the whole company – the existing parts of the company together with any new additions called for by the strategies – matches up to the corporate targets, how the resources are to be allocated, how the total cash requirements are to be met, and so on.

Finally, the team must decide how it should monitor its plans and how frequently this should be done.

All this takes a very long time; it is sometimes well over a year before some companies are finally satisfied that they have got it right at last and a corporate plan is approved. What happens, it is sometimes asked, if a major strategic decision has to be taken before the plan is complete? The answer is quite simple: take the decision (assuming that it really cannot be postponed) in exactly the same way as such decisions were taken before the company began corporate planning.

Targets for subsidiaries

Many companies today consist of groups or holding companies that operate through a number of subsidiaries or profit centres. In this section I want to consider how a group planning team should give its instructions to subsidiaries or profit centres. In the next section I shall discuss giving instructions to functions, geographic divisions or product divisions, that is, not profit centres but cost centres.

I must make it clear that *the* central theme in a group's strategy will normally consist of decisions relating to the role of each profit centre in the whole. A group corporate plan is largely about the future dispositions of its various profit centres; for example:

'We see profit centre A growing and expanding much faster than profit centre B, and we shall divert resources from B and C into A; profit centre C will be sold.'

'We believe that the group as a whole is vulnerable to too many risks. We feel it to be essential to reduce our exposure to political changes in Asia. Therefore, subsidiary E will be closed down, and subsidiaries A, B and D will be expanded. We shall search for a sister company for subsidiary C.'

Normally, each subsidiary company in a group has its own board of directors and is expected to form a planning team and to prepare its own corporate plan. The only difference between this plan and the group's is that its freedom of choice of strategies is constrained by any conditions imposed upon it by the group. If these are numerous and definitive the subsidiary may feel that it is not worth bothering with a plan; the degrees of freedom are too few. This may be a perfectly legitimate way for a group to run its affairs. I believe that it is rapidly becoming less appropriate, as my remarks on page 156 and Exhibit 7.1 indicate, but for some it will continue to be valid, especially for groups facing severe difficulties.

Let us assume, however, that the group team wishes to aim for the optimum group corporate plan, which is where enough has been specified to show each subsidiary what its role is yet not so much that the subsidiary's freedom in playing that role is constrained. How should the group plan be designed in order to achieve this ideal?

The minimum instruction that any group can give to a profit centre is a specified target for return on capital employed (ROCE). If a group declares 'All subsidiaries must achieve 25 per cent return on capital employed', this represents the very least that any group can say to its profit centres. The great advantage is that, provided the target is pitched somewhere above the cost of capital and provided the subsidiary hits the target, the subsidiary's management can be left alone by the group. What is not generally realised, however, is that a ROCE target on its own is not sufficient. This is partly because it says nothing about growth – Exhibit 9.1 shows how a subsidiary can achieve the 25 per cent target in a number of ways, some of them quite absurd – and partly because it does not specify what the subsidiary's role in the whole should be.

No, I am convinced that a ROCE target on its own is not enough and that the group plan must add two more statements. One must

Exhibit 9.1 One of the problems of using ROCE

A subsidiary company, currently showing a ROCE of 15 per cent is given a ROCE target for year 5 of 25 per cent. Some of the different ways in which it can achieve this target are shown.

	Year 0	Year 5			
		(1)	*(2)*	*(3)*	*(4)*
Profits (£m.)	2·1	2·1	3·5	1·1	9·0
Capital employed (£m.)	14·0	8·4	14·0	4·4	36·0
ROCE (%)	15·0	25·0	25·0	25·0	25·0

specify something about growth of profits, cash flows or risk, to exclude some of the ridiculous results shown in Exhibit 9.1, and the other must say something about changes in the nature of each subsidiary's business.

Let us take the statement about growth first. We may be sure that the group planners want all profit centres to make a ROCE that exceeds the cost of capital. Some companies believe that setting a ROCE target well above the cost of capital encourages a subsidiary to grow faster than one with a target only just above the cost of capital. In fact the opposite may on occasions be true, because it is harder to find new projects at high returns than at low. So, the low target company may find millions of pounds' worth of projects at 26 per cent return, while the high target company can find only one small project at 40 per cent.

I believe that there is only one way for a company to make sure that the results that it wishes to see will be encouraged by the targets that it sets, and this is to work it out. Rather than set the targets and hope that the result will be achieved it should decide the desired result and then calculate what the target figures would be if that result were achieved.

Suppose that a group has three subsidiaries – A, B and C – and that it wants C to grow faster than B and B faster than A. What ROCE targets should it set? I don't know; but if we write down the result that the group wants to see, we can work backwards and find out. In Exhibit 9.2(a) I show the figures for year 0. In Exhibit 9.2(b) I show that the group plans wants the group profits to rise by 15 per cent p.a.; at the same time company A's profits are to rise by 10 per cent p.a., B's by 15 per cent p.a. and C's by 30 per cent p.a. This is the strategic decision.

Now let us work backwards. If the group's profits are going to grow from £4·3m. to £8·6m., the retained profits plus loans will add £15m. to the capital employed, making £34·5m. by year 5. (I am simplifying, of course, but I am only interested here in the train of thought. The detailed calculations can be made by any accountant or by using the

Exhibit 9.2 Calculating ROCE targets

(a) Profits, capital employed and ROCE for a group and its three subsidiary companies in year 0

	Group	Company A	Company B	Company C
Profits (£m.)	4·3	2·1	1·7	0·5
Capital employed (£m.)	19·5	10·5	7·3	1·7
ROCE (%)	22·0	20·0	23·3	29·4

(b) Same for year 5

	Group	Company A	Company B	Company C
Profits (£m.)	8·6	3·4	3·4	1·8
Capital employed (£m.)	34·5	14·1	13·6	6·7
ROCE (%)	25·0	24·1	25·0	26·8

model shown in Exhibit 4.6.) This means that the £8·6m. profit is going to have to be achieved from £34·5m. capital, and this means the ROCE target for the group comes out at 25 per cent. Now, the group team will have to allocate how much of this extra £15m. each subsidiary needs to hit its targets, so the capital employed for each can be calculated, then the ROCE. Notice from Exhibit 9.2 that the ROCE of the rapidly growing subsidiary goes down while those of the others go up in this case.

Let me spell out the conclusion again, for I believe that it is not generally known. On its own a ROCE target merely specifies how efficiently capital is to be used; it says nothing at all about the *volume* of capital to be used. Two targets must always be used: ROCE and profits, ROCE and growth, ROCE and capital employed, ROCE and cash flow, or *something* (but make sure that they are mathematically compatible!).

In addition, I believe, the role of each subsidiary within the whole should be specified as well as their profitabilities: 'Subsidiary A is to be the group's leader in high technology', 'Subsidiary B must move rapidly up-market', 'Subsidiary C will reduce its exposure to profit fluctuation by entering into long term contracts', or whatever the group corporate plan indicates.

I am suggesting that there is a happy medium, then, between saying absolutely nothing or merely stating a ROCE return (which are both, I believe, abdication of head office responsibilities) and the other extreme, namely, strangulation by target-setting! Remember, every target that a company sets its subordinates (this is true of people as well as profit centres) is one more hand tied behind their backs. Set a subsidiary targets for ROCE, growth *and* sales margin, and at once that subsidiary's degrees of freedom are cut by a massive factor, for all its possible pricing strategies save the one that hits the particular margin target are eliminated at a stroke.

I must repeat one more warning (first made on page 63) concerning ROCE target-setting. It is absolutely essential, although sometimes quite incredibly difficult, to get the accounting bases right. The definitions of return, capital, turnover, and so on – all the important terms – have to be standard throughout the group; the revaluation of assets must be based on the same year; work-in-progress and stocks must be valued on the same basis. Transfer prices have to be correct, whatever this is taken to mean. Loan capital and head office charges must be properly allocated. Multinational activities must be harmonised for exchange rates.

The subsidiary companies of some large groups own their own subsidiaries in turn. Very well; have a hierarchy of corporate plans. Eventually, we get to a company that is broken down not into further profit centres but into cost centres. These cannot have corporate plans, but they still need a set of targets to show them their role in the whole.

Targets for cost centres

Giving strategic instructions to such cost centres as functional departments, geographic divisions, product teams, and so forth is conceptually quite straightforward. Before describing it I shall return to one important aspect of the membership of the planning team.

It is abundantly clear that, if the small top-level team that I have recommended should do the corporate planning (see page 18) attempts to give instructions to cost centres (or profit centres) without first consulting closely with the executives in charge of them, very serious errors due to the team's ignorance of practical details may be made. The problem is this: if the corporate planning team is small and composed of only the two or three top men, it is in danger of reaching impractical conclusions and of giving impractical instructions. So, would it not be better to widen the team to include the second (and even third) level of executives?

I can only say that it is rare to do so. There are two dangers in widening the membership of the team. One is time; it takes longer to make a decision with ten men than with three. The other is departmental loyalties; some companies are cursed with a major department that is managed by an inadequate executive or that in the corporate plan is almost certain to be closed down, curtailed or disposed of, and the team's deliberations are likely to be disrupted by the presence of this department's representative.

Another reason why corporate planning teams are often limited to so few people is the fear among the top men that their subordinates are not going to be able to take a corporate view of the company's problems – a view only sometimes justified, I believe.

How can this very small top-level team ensure that its feet are firmly on the ground? The answer is by frequently talking to, consulting with, reporting to, explaining to and discussing with the second and third-level executives. In most companies this is no problem at all; it is second nature. In some it may be a problem, and to make sure that it does not cripple the corporate planning process a series of meetings should be arranged at which the team formally reports progress to a wider circle of managers and hears their views.

Let me return to giving instructions to cost centres. If the team has been in proper communication with the second-level executives, these 'instructions' will come as no surprise to the recipients, because they will have played a major role in drawing them up. Indeed, surely no planning team could adopt a strategy that demanded, say, the launch of three new major products in the next five years without consulting the product development department? So, these instructions will be little more than formal confirmation of a decision already known.

Nevertheless, they are important. It is particularly important to try to quantify. Naturally, this is easy enough when it comes to such very important matters as factory output, sales, fuel efficiency or labour productivity, but it may not be so simple for aims such as 'making this company a more interesting and rewarding place in which to work'. Now, either such statements are written into corporate plans for public relations reasons, or they are supposed to mean something. If the latter, a considerable effort is needed from the planning team that promulgates such aims and from the executives who are going to carry them out to give some concrete meaning to them.

Some of these statements are of the utmost importance. The example quoted, for instance, if it means anything, implies that a company-wide campaign to eliminate boring jobs in the factory and the office is about to be undertaken, coupled with a campaign to reward the employees more comprehensively – not merely with material rewards, of course, but also with improved promotion, job satisfaction, respect from the senior executives, and so on. The onus is on the planning team that makes this sort of statement to say what it means. The onus is probably on it also to show how meaningful targets can be set and monitored. In this case an annual opinion survey among the employees, especially among employees leaving the company, may provide this means.

Also, such instructions as 'Upgrade the technological content of the company's products' or 'Improve after-sales service' must be clearly defined and targets set. Of course, a very common type of target is the completion date of some specific action called for in the plan. Wherever it is thought necessary, the bracket target method should be used; that is, a Tsat and a Tmin should be set for any important element in the plan.

Giving instruction to departments, then, is very like giving instructions to subsidiaries. In every case there is a bare necessary minimum that has to be laid down to ensure that the terms of the corporate plan are met, and there are the same serious disadvantages in overspecifying what the departmental managers must do and how they must do it. Just as with profit centres two numerical targets (ROCE and profit, for example) have to be set, so in the case of cost centres one or two numerical targets have to be set – usually measures of efficiency (such as tonnes per man-hour, scrap ratios and units per day) and measures of completion (such as 'by year 3'). Also, just as some more qualitative statements have to be made concerning changes in the structure of the profit centres, so similar statements may have to be made for cost centres. In other words there are some non-quantifiable and non-targetable instructions that have to be given; for example, 'middle management must realise how important the consumer pressure groups and environmental lobbies are today for a chemical company such as us'.

One further problem should be noted. Some of the decisions in the corporate plan will call for entirely new activities not intimately related to existing operations. These projects, which will normally be placed under the responsibility of a project manager, can be targeted and monitored quite easily. They are both concrete and separate. However, other major plans refer to improvements or changes to be made to the existing business. Here there is usually little difficulty in setting targets but great difficulty in keeping track of the results. An example is labour productivity. The company plan may call for an improvement of 50 per cent in labour productivity over a five-year period, but an endless number of factors can enter the scene over such a period: changes in working hours, incentive schemes, new products, and so on. Thus, although it may be possible to set a target, it may not be possible over long time periods to monitor results.

Budgets

There are very few conceptual difficulties here either, but notice how the five-year budget 'emerges' from the end of the corporate planning process. In evaluating the final strategies the team had to make a number of Fp forecasts (see page 175). To do so it had to pin the strategic ideas firmly down and to put some concrete figures on to them. This was where such vague aspirations as 'We shall attack the

American market' were brought down to hard facts: volumes, prices, costs, competitors, legislation, exchange rates, and so on endlessly. Several trips to the United States, much desk research, the opinion of experts, the views of the project managers – all these have gone into the evaluations.

Recall that a number of calculations on a number of differing assumptions have been made (see Exhibit 8.13). Now, one of these, perhaps in this case run 8 in Exhibit 8.13, will reflect the middle, most probable or most reasonable set of assumptions. What a marvellous base for a five-year budget!

Consider. The calculations have been made for five years in order to show that this strategy is capable of hitting Tsat for year 5. The calculations include volumes, prices, costs, the effect of all the new strategies – everything! They give a complete numerical picture – five annual pictures – of the entire company under 'normal' or most probable conditions in the next five years. This is just what the traditional five-year budget is, except that ours is much less detailed and, of course, has been prepared by an entirely different procedure. The traditional five-year budget is produced by projecting the one-year budget another four years into the future – an extraordinarily dangerous thing to do, as already explained (page 8). Here, however, the figures are the result of a coherent overall plan for the company as a whole. Thus, the five-year budget falls out of the end of the corporate plan.

In general the budget will reflect changes of two sorts. Some of these refer to changes within the existing structure of the company; the others are new projects added on to the existing structure. Together, the profits should achieve or exceed Tsat on the most probable set of assumptions. In Exhibit 9.3 I show an outline budget for Magpie Ltd, in which both types of change can be seen.

Thus, in the main body of the operating budget the profits arising from the existing business are shown. A feature of these is that the plan does not see its existing business improving very spectacularly; profits rise by only 5 per cent p.a., and most of this is due to growth of volume. Sales margins actually deteriorate.

It is also clear how the two new projects are expected to contribute to profits. One of these is the manufacture of a new product at a new factory in Southtown, and the other is the launch of an exporting operation in Northport. For the sake of simplicity I show the operating budget only; a five-year cash-flow budget, a capital expenditure budget and a five-year balance sheet are also necessary, but all these fall out of the same evaluation as the operating budget, and all these data (and management ratios as well) will come pouring out of the company model (such as the one shown in Exhibit 4.6).

The outline budget may or may not be in sufficient detail for the

Exhibit 9.3   Summary of five-year operating budget for Magpie Ltd, based on the evaluation forecast considered most likely to occur

	Year 0	1	2	3	4	5	Explanation
Existing business (£m.)							
Sales turnover	100·8	107·1	114·4	122·0	129·9	138·0	Market size up 2%; market share up from 10% to 12·5%
less Discounts	1·8	2·0	2·2	2·4	2·5	2·8	Discounts planned to increase slowly
Net sales	99·0	105·1	112·2	119·6	127·4	135·2	
less Direct costs:							
Components	28·8	30·6	32·7	34·8	37·1	39·4	No major changes
Wages	17·9	19·0	20·0	21·3	22·4	23·0	Slight reduction per unit sold
Fuel	18·6	20·2	22·0	23·9	25·9	28·1	Slow increase per unit
less Overheads:							
Production	4·8	5·1	5·4	5·7	6·1	6·5	No major changes per unit
Sales	4·0	4·2	4·5	4·8	5·1	5·4	No major changes per unit
All others	5·5	5·8	6·2	6·6	7·0	7·4	No major changes per unit
Trading profit	19·4	20·2	21·4	22·5	23·8	25·4	
less Interest	1·1	1·4	1·6	1·9	2·2	2·1	Substantial bank loans needed
Profit	18·3	18·8	19·8	20·6	21·6	23·3	
Southtown project (£m.)							
Profit	—	0·3	2·1	3·7	4·6	5·5	As planned
Export operation (£m.)							
Profit	—	—	1·2	2·2	2·6	2·9	As planned
Total profits (£m.)	18·3	19·1	23·1	26·5	28·8	31·7	(Note gaps in years 4 and 5)
Tsat profits	18·3	20·0	23·0	26·5	30·5	35·0	15% p.a. growth

executives in charge of the various parts of the company; if not, their accounts departments will have to be asked to fill out the necessary detail. If the production-manager wishes to know what 'production' on Exhibit 9.3 includes, for example, his account department will have to split it up into labour, materials, rent or whatever.

Finally, this 'most likely' run on the model, which is converted into the five-year budget, should appear as an appendix of the company's corporate plan. In some cases a version of the same figures with inflation included for each year (using the most likely rates of inflation) should also be attached. (Remember that one of the assumptions already examined in the evaluation stage is the effect of high and low rates of inflation on the company's cash-flow situation. So, it may not be thought to be necessary to include a with-inflation budget as well as the non-inflation one in the actual corporate plan documents. Some companies do; some do not. Some include inflation in the first year of the five-year run only, so that progress can be monitored against actual during the first year, and put the remaining years in the first year's currency values – a compromise that seems very sensible to me.)

I have explained that the five-year budget that emerges from the final stages of a corporate plan is generated by a mental process that is quite different from that which gives rise to the traditional accountant's budget. Some companies no longer call it a budget. When they talk about their budget, they refer to the one-year budget (and control) only;

the five-year sequence is called the five-year plan, business plan or strategic plan.

Monitoring confidence

We now turn to the last task for the team, namely, monitoring. I have to make it clear at once that what the team should monitor is not the progress of the company towards its targets, important though this is, but the team's own confidence in its plan. It is a quite different concept.

Let us consider the position reached. The team has produced a plan intended to bring about a number of major changes in the structure of the company over the next few years – changes that will alter the whole destiny of the company. We all know how long a year is and how much can happen in such a span of time, but we often forget how vast are the cumulative changes that can take place in five years. Although most of the corporate plans that will be born of the process described in this book will be sufficiently robust to last unchanged for many years, not all of them will be, and a number of minor changes will certainly have to be made annually. Occasionally, the whole plan will collapse in ruins in the face of some momentous unexpected event or the culmination of some long term trend.

How does the team know when to change its original plan? It will change it when it loses confidence in the original. It will lose confidence either (1) when the company's results do not match the targets (that is, there is a severe shortfall in performance), (2) when the actions being taken do not match the actions called for in the plan (that is, there is a major failure in executive action), or (3) when a massive unforeseen trend or event occurs. Thus, confidence depends on company performance, executive action and the occurrence of events. A major upset in any of these on its own can cause a collapse of confidence, but so can minor but persistent discrepancies in several of or all these three areas over several years.

Notice that, when most people use the word 'monitor', they really mean 'check results' or 'compare actual performance with plans'. However, this is only one of the elements in monitoring confidence; indeed, it is probably the least significant.

In Chapter 1 I described how short and long range planning are radically different in a number of respects (page 8). Here is another difference. In short range planning the results of an executive action follow quite quickly from that action. It is therefore possible in short range planning to modify a plan almost continuously as the results become known. So, checking results is the most appropriate way to test the continued validity of plans. In long range planning it may be years

Exhibit 9.4 The problem of checking results

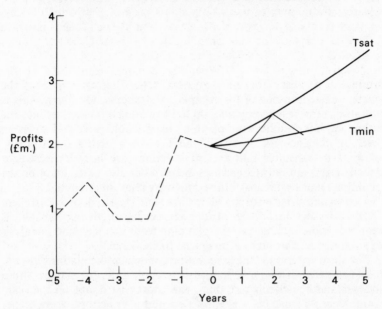

before the results come through! So, although undoubtedly an eye is kept on results, they may mean nothing for some years.

I attempt to show this in Exhibit 9.4, where the Tsat and Tmin of a company are plotted together with its actual results in years 1, 2 and 3. Because the profits of this company have fluctuated so much in the past (most companies' have), we cannot tell whether its executives should be worried or not, and it is already three years into the plan. The problem here is simple; the principal of feed-back is perfectly adequate in short term planning and control, but here we need feed-forward. We can achieve this by reforecasting the profits now expected from existing strategies to year 5 – and the planning team will certainly do this annually when it revises the plans, as described below – thus completing a feed-forward loop: forecast–plan–reforecast–replan. Even so, although this is better, it still does not provide a very reliable alarm system, because, as we know, forecasts are themselves unreliable.

So, let us turn to the second group of indicators to monitor, namely, executive actions. In most plans there are a number of key actions. In the case of a company that decides to build a new factory, for example, there are a few milestones that stand out way above all the thousands of actions that have to be taken to complete such a project as this: the date on which planning permission is obtained, the day on which the first brick is laid, the day on which the main furnace (or whatever) is delivered, the start-up date, and so on. This is true for every plan. Clearly, if a number of these key actions are not completed on time or if one crucial action goes badly astray, confidence in the company's ability to carry out the plan on schedule or even to complete it all is weakened.

However, this is not all. When the planning team drew up the strategies, it presumably did so in the belief that each limb of the strategy rested on one of the company's strengths. Of course, this is not always the case; companies do have to launch themselves into the unknown, but even here the planning team would have had a certain level of management ability in mind when selecting the strategy. Now, if it transpires that executive actions are late, ineffective or deficient, this not only jeopardises the plan but also casts doubt on the planning team's estimate of the company's relevant strengths.

This second criterion of confidence in a plan, then, is double-barrelled. If executive action falls short, confidence in completing the plan is reduced, and confidence in the planning team's fundamental analysis of strengths and weaknesses may also be weakened.

The third criterion is the assumptions on which the plan is based. If it was assumed that no new competitors would enter the market within five years and suddenly one does, this must cast doubt on the plan. Confidence will also be weakened if economic growth rates are higher than expected, there is new legislation, a supplier goes bankrupt, or whatever. Thousands of things may happen that it was thought would not or do not happen that it was thought would. Most of these will be peripheral in effect. Eventually, however, enough drips will have worn away the core of the strategy, and the team's confidence will finally evaporate; or perhaps some sudden unexpected event will put an early end to the plan.

What happens then? I shall discuss revision below. I must first describe a monitoring procedure. All that is needed, I believe, is for the team to meet again at regular but infrequent intervals to review every aspect of its plan: targets, forecasts, strengths, budgets, and so on. However, this need not be done more frequently than every three months. Do it more frequently, and there may be a tendency to react to every tiny variation: sales volume last week, a minor breakdown in the factory this week. Do it less frequently, and there may be unnecessary delay in taking a corrective action. Once again, do not forget the value of an outside or independent viewpoint; consider setting up a routine meeting every six months or so with your merchant bank, stockbroker or accountants for a critical unbiased review of your performance.

One final remark. Oddly enough, monitoring should probably begin *before* the first corporate plan is completed. Monitoring means a team's testing its confidence in its plans. However, the corporate planning process may take many months; a whole year may pass between the setting of the corporate target and putting the final touches to the five-year budgets. So, it sometimes makes sense for the team to sit down and test its confidence in all the targets, forecasts, gaps, and so on before it reaches the end of the process.

Revising the corporate plan

Imagine a planning team at a routine three-monthly monitoring meeting. They have before them the corporate planning document described in the previous chapter and illustrated in Exhibits 8.2 to 8.13. They start with the target and ask 'Do we still believe these target figures to be correct?' The answer may be 'no' for two reasons.

First, shareholder expectations may have changed, in which case the figures that were thought to represent a 'satisfactory' performance (or an unacceptably bad one or an embarrassingly good one) for this company may no longer do so. The team should revise or update these targets.

The other reason is inflation. Remember that the target may have been set many months earlier. Since then the cost-of-living index may have risen by 10 per cent, 5 per cent or whatever. So, *all* last year's figures will have to be increased by 10 or 5 per cent to bring them to the current year's values. Every year all the figures must be rolled forwards one year: targets, forecasts, cash flows, and so on. This is exceedingly irritating and confusing, but it has to be done. Frequently, executives are heard arguing about the latest target for year 5: 'I thought that we were aiming for £2·8m. profits'; 'Yes, but that was in last year's money; it's £3·1m. now. In any case they've rolled it forwards to year 6, so it's £3·5m. now.' Great care has to be taken to make these changes with the utmost clarity.

However, is there not a third reason for altering a target, namely, the actual performance of the company? Suppose in year 0, when profits are £1m., a company sets itself a target of £2m. by year 5, and suppose that by year 2 profits are already £2·2m. Surely the target for year 5 should be raised? Conversely, if the profits in year 2 are £0·1m., surely the year 5 target should be reduced? Theoretically, no, because the plain fact remains that to go from £1m. to £2m. in five years *is* satisfactory! However, of course, most planning teams would say 'water under the bridge' and reset the targets from a new 'Where are we now?' analysis (described at length in Chapter 3).

As can be seen already, in these monitoring sessions the team should move carefully and systematically right through the corporate planning process. In its discussion on targets the team must consider indicators, where we are now, the Tmin and Tsat targets and the requirements of stakeholders, all exactly as set out in Chapter 3. Instead of taking weeks over it, as they may have done the first time, they usually need take only a few minutes.

The forecasts will take longer, partly because they may have to be revised for inflation but more likely because the team has lost confidence in the original Fp forecasts. One or other part of the company will not be performing as expected, and new forecasts will have to be prepared. Furthermore, each year the Fp forecasts must be rolled forwards another year, and this will certainly call for a number of calculations; new data will have to be collected from subsidiary companies, new opinions, and so on.

Next to be considered are the gaps. This is where a new sense of confidence, or lack of it, will be thrown up clearly. The gaps are the difference between targets and forecasts; and if for any reason the targets have to be revised upwards and the forecasts downwards, a larger or earlier gap may appear. I show the original gaps and the revised, inflated and rolled-forward gaps for a typical company in Exhibit 9.5.

Exhibit 9.5   Original and revised gaps for Bird & Sons

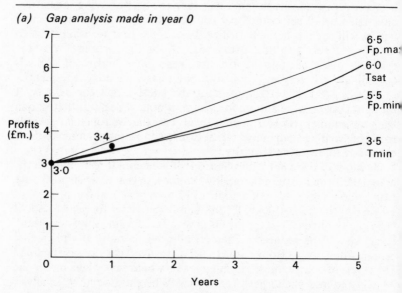

(a)   Gap analysis made in year 0

Note: Profits are expected to be £3·0m. Bird hopes to double profits by year 5 and certainly to exceed £3·5m. Its strategy will take profits well above Tsat if all goes well; and even if it does not, they will not descend to near Tmin. All the figures are in real terms (that is, at year 0 values), and the strategy sees profits of approximately £3·4m. in real terms in year 1. (Tsat is based on 15 per cent p.a. growth and Tmin on 3 per cent p.a.)

(b)   *Gap analysis made one year later, in year 1*

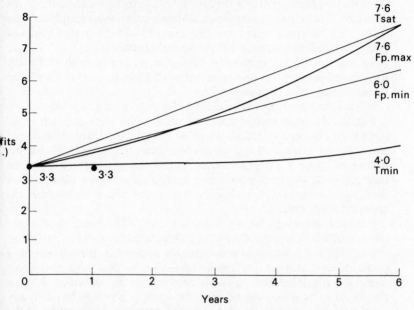

Note: Profits in year 0 have been confirmed at £3·0m., but profits this year are expected to be only £3·3m., and inflation during the year has been 10 per cent. Bird can either escalate all figures by 10 per cent or deflate this £3·3m. out-turn by 10 per cent to last year's (that is, year 0's) values. In the exhibit the company has chosen the former. So, all the figures above have been (1) escalated by 10 per cent (including year 0's profit, which has now become £3·3m.) and (2) revised where necessary and rolled forwards another year. For example, Tsat has become £7·6m. (from £6·0m. plus 10 per cent for inflation plus 15 per cent for another year), and Tmin has become £4·0m. (from £3·5m. plus 10 per cent for inflation plus 3 per cent for another year).

Notice that Bird is not now expecting its strategy to take profits above Tsat in year 6, although they will be safely above Tmin. Obviously, if the profits in year 2 do not bounce up to, say, £4·5m., Bird will have to reconsider its entire strategic situation.

The team should then look through the strengths, weaknesses, threats and opportunities analysis. Since the original planning exercise, events may well have confirmed or undermined some of the strengths. Certainly, any of the weaknesses that are to be corrected in the corporate plan may now be responding to treatment, and this may allow an adjustment to a part of a strategy. For example, a company with a very low share price (less than half of its break-up value) was advised by its merchant bank that it would take two years to improve its stock market rating significantly. In fact, quite by chance attention was drawn to the company in the financial press, and a significant rise in its share price occurred within months. This allowed the part of the plan that depended on share price to be brought forwards.

Threats and opportunities also may change. The team should study its original list and test its continued confidence in it. Has some new threat or opportunity appeared?

What about alternative strategies? Has anyone any new ideas?

Finally, the team should ask itself what this review adds up to. Is some minor change in emphasis needed in the plan or not? Should the whole thing be scrapped and the entire exercise begun again? Is there a feeling of anxiety emerging such that, although nothing need be changed now, the next monitoring session should take place sooner than three months? Should it be let go for six, unless some unexpected event occurs?

I should warn against one common error. The team should not attempt to alter a section of the plan piecemeal in response to particular events. Thus, if a major new competitor appears in the market, it is preferable not to take any particular action to deal with that event alone. It is much better to call a monitoring meeting and to go through the whole exercise, noting not only this new competitor but also any other new data and figures of strategic importance. Then, when *all* the data are before the team, the new strategic situation of the company can be seen *in its totality*. It is only from its *total strategic situation* that a company's strategic plan can emerge.

Once a company starts reacting to pieces of information piecemeal, the whole concept of corporate planning collapses. It may be that the only new item of strategic significance is this competitor, in which case action specific to this threat may be suitable, but suppose that there is some other revelation – a massive accumulation of cash in the company's bank accounts, for example. It is just possible that some imaginative new twist to the company's strategies may be able to deal with both of these at once.

Summary

Once the planning team has evaluated its chosen strategies, it has three tasks left.

First, the team has to turn its rather broad conceptual decrees into some very down-to-earth practical instructions to the executives in charge of the various parts of the company. In fact, since these executives either will be members of the planning team itself or will have been very closely consulted all through the planning process –

especially at the evaluation stage, where a great deal of detail is often required – these 'instructions' will come as no surprise.

Great care has to be taken, however, to avoid the two extremes. At one end groups or holding companies give no instructions at all to their subsidiaries or merely give them a ROCE target. This allows the subsidiaries to do anything that they like, and it represents an abdication of responsibility by the group. At the other end companies give their subsidiaries so many targets that they can display no initiative whatever. I believe that a happy medium consists of (1) a ROCE target, (2) a growth target (or a target for profits, cash flow or something), and (3) a verbal statement showing what broad changes are required in the role of each profit centre within the whole.

Similar remarks can apply to cost centres. One or two definitive targets for the chief strategic areas of the cost centre (output per man in production departments, for example, or sales per annum in sales departments) and, where relevant, a verbal statement describing any major qualitative decisions are what is required.

The planning team's second task is to issue five-year budgets. These are not prepared by the highly dubious traditional method, which involves projecting forwards from one year to five years. These budgets fall out of the evaluation process, in which a considerable number of five-year forecasts are made, each on a different combination of assumptions in order to test the stability of the strategies in the face of huge errors in the long range forecasts. Now, one of these combinations will most closely resemble the conditions that the executives think are most likely to occur in real life. The figures in this particular case make an excellent outline budget. From this everyone can see what financial resources are available, where it is planned they should be allocated, how much cash is generated from the sales envisaged, and so on – these are just the same advantages that all five-year budgets share, but in this case the method of calculation lends the budget additional validity.

Finally, the team must monitor its plan at three-monthly intervals, starting immediately or even before the plan is promulgated. The word 'monitoring' in this context means monitoring the team's own confidence in its plan. Since the plan depends on the targets, forecasts, strengths, weaknesses, and so on – all the strategic factors described in this book – all these have to be reviewed every three months. Unless a major change has to be made to the strategies – and this is rare in practice – such meetings need not take more than a few hours.

Every year, however, the targets and forecasts have to be recalculated for inflation and to be rolled forwards one further year.

So long as the team is confident that its original plan is still valid, no action other than updating and rolling forwards all the figures need to be taken. Certainly, no change need be made in the strategies.

However, the time will eventually come when confidence finally evaporates and a new strategy has to be devised. As in the original corporate planning exercise a proper corporate plan can only be devised if the entire strategic situation of the company – its *strategic totality* – is considered.

It is therefore recommended that, before a major revision is made, all the new strategic data be collected together, just as described in the chapters of this book, and that the revision be made not in a piecemeal manner based on individual items of information but in an integrated manner based on their totality.

Once the corporate planning process has been started, it does not end at the completion of the first plan but should be continued in an endless cycle for the rest of the life of the company. As the process continues, the top executives will become progressively more attuned to long term thinking and progressively more skilful in mastering its difficulties. They will habitually look ahead several years. Soon the second level of executives will be drawn further into the process and will find it second nature to join in the top-level management discussions. A cohesion, a coherence, a congruence of aims and ambitions will form among them, and morale and confidence in the company's future will soar. Soon, this will be reflected in the company's performance.

The Corporate Planning Process at a Glance

A. *Starting the corporate planning process (takes up to 3 months)*
(1) Form the planning team. This may include the chairman, the finance-director, one or two other top executives or non-executive directors, and the chief executive as team-leader.
(2) Appoint and then train a corporate planner to act as executive secretary to the team and as technical adviser on planning techniques.
(3) Hold a company seminar. Its main aims are (a) to describe what corporate planning is to the second (and third) level of executives and (b) to sound out their views on the company's strategic situation.
(4) Arrange the team's first meeting. The aims of this are (a) to discuss the findings of the company seminar and (b) to plan the work pro- gramme of the team and the corporate planner. Commission any reports that may have a long lead time.

B. *Setting objectives (takes up to 3 months)*
(1) Determine the corporate objectives, ethos and corporate targets. Pay special attention to stating which indicators are to be used and where the company is now (year 0) and to setting both Tsat and Tmin. (Takes 1–2 meetings.)
(2) Draw up the Fo forecasts. Be careful to show the optimistic and pessimistic limits of confidence, that is, Fo.max and Fo.min. Calculate the gaps. (Takes 2–3 meetings.) The corporate planner should start building the model.

C. *Drawing up the strategic factors (takes up to 6 months)*
(1) Identify all the strategic strengths and weaknesses. Then examine them carefully, writing a report on each. Then distil them to a single page. Then rank them by importance. (Takes 2–3 meetings.)
(2) Identify all strategic threats and opportunities. Then examine them carefully, writing a report on each. Then distil them to a single page or two. Then rank them by impact and probability. (Takes 5–10 meetings.)
(3) Hold a second company seminar. The aims of this are (a) to report the team's findings to the original participants, (b) to hear their views on these findings and (c) to hear their suggested alternative strategies.
(4) List alternative strategies. Eliminate, say, 90 per cent, leaving a short list of those which are most likely to be relevant to the company's total strategic situation. (Takes 1 meeting.)

D.   Selection and evaluation (takes up to 3 months)
(1) Select the best set of strategies. (Takes 1–3 meetings.)
(2) Evaluate this set of strategies by making a number of Fp forecasts, by using the strategic scorecard and by extensive research, discussion and calculation using the model. (Takes 2–4 meetings.)
(3) Prepare the corporate plan (see Exhibits 8.2–8.13) for formal approval by board.

E.   Action plans and budgets (takes a few weeks)
(1) Draw up action plans for profit centres or major cost centres. These must include one or two numerical targets plus a description of the role of each part in the corporate whole. (Takes 2–3 meetings.)
(2) Decide how the monitoring process is to be tackled: what is to be monitored, how often, and by whom. Start monitoring. (Takes 1 meeting.)

F.   Monitoring (continuous)
(1) Monitor continuously to determine the team's confidence in the current corporate plan. (Takes 1 meeting every 3 months.)

The Corporate Planning Process for Groups at a Glance

The detailed steps are very similar to those shown on pages 197–8, but the sequence is not so simple. For a group it will follow the pattern described below:

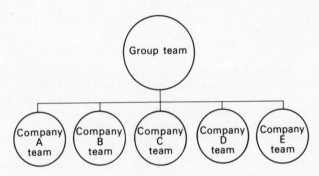

A. *Starting the process*
(1) Form a group corporate planning team.
(2) Appoint and train a corporate planner.
(3) Hold a company seminar, making sure that everyone who may become a member of a subsidiary company team is invited.
(4) Form planning teams in each subsidiary. Unless these subsidiaries are very large, no corporate planner may be needed.
(5) Group team and all the subsidiary teams have their first meetings.

B. *Group objectives, ethos and targets*
(1) Determine *group* objectives, ethos and targets. Subsidiaries omit this step.
(2) Subsidiaries prepare and submit to group their Fo forecasts. These may, if suitable, simply be the five-year budgets that most subsidiaries will already have prepared.
(3) Group team totals up these forecasts to derive group Fo.
(4) Calculate the gaps for the group.

C. *Drawing up the strategic factors*
(1) Group and subsidiary teams identify strengths and weaknesses.

(2) Group and subsidiary teams identify threats and opportunities. In both of these exercises, of course, the group team searches only for group factors, the subsidiary A team searches only for factors that are relevant to subsidiary A, and so on.

(3) Hold the second company seminar just as before, but this has two main aims: (a) to exchange views on all the main conclusions so far reached by all the teams; and (b) to discuss alternative strategies for all the teams. (May take 2 days.)

(4) Group team lists alternatives for the group. Subsidiary teams each list alternatives for the respective subsidiaries.

D. and E.   Selection, evaluation, and target-setting for subsidiaries

(1) Group selects overall group strategy in which targets and role of each subsidiary is a vital part.

(2) Group evaluates this strategy in close liaison with all the subsidiaries.

(3) Group prepares its corporate plan for formal approval.

(4) Group draws up action plans and budgets to show targets for each subsidiary together with a description of the subsidiaries' role in the whole.

D. and E.   Selection, evaluation, action plans and budgets for subsidiaries

(1) Subsidiaries now know their targets. They have already made their forecasts (B2 above), so they can now calculate their gaps.

(2) Subsidiaries have already examined all the other strategic factors, so they can now select and evaluate their strategies.

(3) Subsidiaries prepare their corporate plans for formal approval by the group.

(4) Subsidiaries draw up action plans and five-year budgets to show each department what is expected of it as part of the whole.

(5) All teams consider how to monitor.

F.   Monitoring

(1) All teams monitor.

Some Common Mistakes

Starting

The chief executive.   The chief executive must play the leading role in initiating corporate planning into his company. He should be the planning team leader. If this is not the case, either: (1) the whole exercise will fizzle out; or (2) it will continue vigorously, with the team making detailed plans for things that really do not matter a hoot.

The other top executives.   On the other hand the exercise must not be carried out solely by the chief executive and his planner; this is just a trick to allow an autocrat to continue his autocracy behind a screen of participative respectability. If the other team members do not participate, the plans will be defective in some important respect.

The corporate planner.   He is often appointed at the very highest level in the company, and everyone expects him to do all the planning (brilliantly, of course); or he is a technician who produces masses of detailed plans based on advanced mathematical calculations that no one understands. In both cases bitter disappointment is the (well-deserved) reward. It is better to appoint someone too low in seniority; at least the top executives will then realise that it is up to them. It is better still to appoint someone just below their own seniority to act as executive secretary and technical adviser to the team.

Objectives and Targets

Corporate objectives.   It is a common mistake to believe these must be terribly complex, abstruse and philosophical. In ninety-nine cases out of a hundred the team can simply say 'return on shareholders' capital' for objectives – not something elaborate such as 'provide the goods and services that we believe society needs'.

Ethos.   Some companies do have problems here, but most do not. Again, this is not something terribly philosophical for most companies;

most companies are fully aware of their responsibilities towards employees, customers, suppliers, and so on. There is no need to write a book.

Targets.   Again, the most common error is overcomplexity. A target is what you *want*. So, select an indicator, and choose a verifiable figure to aim at five years ahead. The more targets you set, the more mistaken you will be; every figure that you set as a target precludes a couple of dozen strategies. For most companies the target can be expressed as growth of earnings per share (EpS) and profits. Use return on share-holder's capital (ROSC), and return on capital employed (ROCE) too if you are sure that you understand it. Never grab a whole bundle of ratios out of the air. Never use 'maximise', 'survival' or any accounting or management ratios as corporate targets. ROCE must be used (carefully!) for subsidiaries. Always use a bracket, preferably Tsat and Tmin.

Forecasting

Methods of forecasting.   Do not use simple projection (Foo). Do not use elaborate techniques that you do not fully understand. Because this is *long range* forecasting, what you want to know is not masses of detail but what the errors are likely to be for the few things that really matter. So, use bracket forecasts showing Fo.max and Fo.min.

Errors.   Most of the errors are irradicable because the future is unforecastable, but most long-range forecasts are redolent with human error too. All forecasts that start at year 0 are wrong; they must be rooted at least five years in the past. Strip out inflation. State assumptions. Make numerous cross-checks.

Internal and External Appraisals

Internal.   The most common mistake is not, as some people believe it may be, allowing departmental loyalties to bias the analysis; it is generating such a smokescreen of detail that the really important strengths or weaknesses are underestimated. The four-stage technique (identify, examine, distil and rank), coupled with the syndicate sessions in the company seminar, usually blow these smokescreens away. An outsider's opinion will often do the same.

External.   There are two common mistakes here. The first is that the executives just do not want to look at the outside world. This is frequently seen at the first seminar, where the strengths and weaknesses come tumbling out in profusion but where, when the syndicates emerge from their discussions on external factors, the reports that they make to the plenary session are barren. The planning team has to watch this carefully; it seems especially prevalent in engineering firms.

The other mistake is failure to evaluate the threats correctly. Opinion swings from 'It won't affect us at all' to 'It spells instant disaster'. Again, my rather elaborate (deliberately so, of course) four-stage procedure (identify, examine, distil and rank) may help here. So will an outsider's view.

Strategies

Alternatives. A very common failing is the lack of imaginative, wide-ranging, entrepreneurial and alternative strategies. Although I hope that my system, including as it does a special section where such ideas are invited, will help to reduce this failing, I rather fear that a managed company is by its nature less innovative than an entrepreneurial one. Flair and planning would make ideal bedfellows, but they are seldom even seen together.

Evaluation. All the Fp forecasts will be wildly optimistic. It is essential to test the chosen strategy in all manner of pessimistic conditions. Ask some really damning 'What if . . .' questions to see how well the company as a whole will stand up to adversity if it adopts the chosen strategy. Thoroughly test its practicality from the point of view of the company's finances, management and skills.

Action Plans, Budgets and Monitoring

Action plans. Once again the enemy is excessive detail. Most companies employ perfectly competent marketing managers, production planners and financial specialists, who are fully capable of turning a general strategic statement into a tight well-knit marketing plan, production plan or whatever. The planning team does not have to do this – certainly not if it has been keeping everyone properly informed during its deliberations.

Monitoring. Most people still restrict monitoring to checking results. I have explained (page 188) why this is inadequate and that what needs to be monitored is the team's overall confidence in its current corporate plan.

General

Urgency. Unless the company faces severe difficulties, there is no need for urgent strategic decisions; but if it does face severe difficulties, it should not do corporate planning at all. Even so, many firms rush the process. Not only do they therefore sometimes miss important factors, but, even worse, they do not allow the important factors that they do identify to sink in. Considerable mental and emotional adjustment is often called for from some or all the top executives. This is why I believe the planning process should take about a year, even though it is physically possible to complete it in two months. In any case my system depends heavily on the team's doing the planning, not a planner, and the team members are normally able to spare only half a day every two or three weeks or so.

Concepts. Finally let me repeat that corporate planning is not budgeting, not co-ordinating, not long range planning and not just strategic planning. All these mistakes are common. Corporate planning is a systematic method of forming a consensus about the long term future of a company. In nearly every case this boils down to a very few simple statements describing a very few major strategic decisions that will affect the destiny of the company as a whole for a considerable period of time.

Appendix: Further Exhibits

Exhibit 8.2 Corporate plan for Fulmar & Co.: page one

Summary

Target	Forecast	Gap
Profits to rise from £4·2m. to £8·5m. by year 5 (Tsat) and to exceed £4·8m. (Tmin)	Profits will probably rise to £5·5m. and will almost certainly exceed £4·8m.	Even on present strategies we should exceed Tmin, but we need an extra £3·4m. for Tsat

Strengths

Excellent well-established product
Fulmar well known and respected
    among agricultural merchants
Unique depot system
Exports equal 80% of turnover
Low gearing

Weaknesses

No new products or even ideas
Production, stock control,
    methods, etc. all poor
Mr Fulmar in poor health; no
    children
P/E ratio = 4

Threats

Competitors
New materials
Fire legislation
Mr Fulmar's shares

Opportunities

World markets: enormous potential
Industrial buildings
DIY
Added value
Environmental and scenic

Strategies considered

Simple expansion in existing
    markets
New products: DIY, industrial, etc.
Acquisition of Petrel Ltd

Improve
    production
Move into new
    markets
Changes in shares

Management
Finance

Strategies selected
(See text)

Exhibit 8.3   Corporate plan for Fulmar & Co.: page two

Targets

The company's profits (before interest and tax) for the year just ended were £4·2m. Loan interest totalled £0·6m. and tax £1·8m., leaving earnings at £1·8m. On the 5 million shares issued this represents an EpS of 36p. Our P/E ratio is 4·1 (average for our sector is 7), and the price per share is currently 148p, making the total capitalisation £7·4m. Mr Fulmar's 2 million shares are worth £2·96m.

Over the past few years profits have not grown in real terms, and dividends have actually fallen. We feel that it would be disgraceful if we repeated such a poor performance over the next five years, and we must seek to grow, even if at only 3 per cent p.a. or so. We therefore set our Tmin at £4·8m. If we achieve this, our P/E will probably remain around 4, and all other financial indicators — market value, price per share, and so on — will move *pro rata* with profits.

We should like to catch up some of the ground that has been lost over the past few years and have selected the very ambitious growth target of 15 per cent p.a. Our Tsat for year 5 is therefore a profit of £8·5m. (at which EpS should be 73p). If we achieve this performance, which is likely to be well above the performance of the sector as a whole, our P/E ratio should start to move up within two years and by year 5 should exceed 10, making a share price of over 700p and a market capitalisation of £35m. by year 5. Mr Fulmar's holding will then be worth £14m.

Note: Detailed financial calculations, not shown here, should be included as an appendix to Fulmar's corporate plan. These should show ROCE, shareholder funds, and so on.

Exhibit 8.4 Corporate plan for Fulmar & Co.: page three

Forecasts

The company's performance over the past five years has been, on today's values, as follows:

	Year −5	−4	−3	−2	−1	0
Turnover (£m.)	40·1	43·2	40·3	41·1	42·7	44·6
Profits (£m.)	4·1	3·9	3·8	4·0	4·3	4·2
Margin on sales (%)	10·2	9·0	9·4	9·7	10·0	9·4

The market is now expanding quite rapidly worldwide after its collapse three years ago and will continue to grow at between 2·5 and 5 per cent p.a. We believe that margins will improve certainly to 10 per cent and probably to 10·5 per cent by year 5, due to two major competitors withdrawing from the market in the last two years.

If the market grows at 2·5 per cent and margins rise to only 10 per cent, turnover and profits will rise to £50·5m. and £5m. respectively. On the more optimistic assumption of 5 per cent p.a. growth and 10·5 per cent margins turnover and profits will be £57m. and £6m.

Taking a middle figure as the most likely, turnover will be £53·7m. and profits £5·5m.

Note: A more detailed forecast should appear in an appendix, not shown here.

Exhibit 8.5   Corporate plan for Fulmar & Co.: page four

Gaps

No further action is needed to achieve Tmin. Even on quite pessimistic assumptions we should exceed Tmin (£4·8m. profits by year 5). With quite ordinary luck we should exceed it by £1m.

To achieve our ambitious Tsat, however, we need to generate an extra £4m. over and above our current profits and an extra £3m. over and above what we expect to achieve by year 5 on current strategies. Furthermore, this must be achieved by a new strategy that, if it fails, will not jeopardise the Tmin of £4·8m. by year 5.

As can be seen below, the gaps become quite significant two years from now.

	Year 0	1	2	3	4	5
Worst gap						
Tsat (15% p.a. growth)	4·2	4·8	5·6	6·4	7·3	8·5
Fo. min (market grows at 2·5% p.a.; margins 10%)	4·2	4·6	4·7	4·8	4·9	5·0
Worst gap	0·0	0·2	0·9	1·6	2·4	3·5
Least gap						
Tsat (15% p.a. growth)	4·2	4·8	5·6	6·4	7·3	8·5
Fo. max (market grows at 5% p.a.; margins 10% for year 1 then 10·5%)	4·2	4·7	5·2	5·4	5·7	6·0
Least gap	0·0	0·1	0·4	1·0	1·6	2·5

Exhibit 8.6   Corporate plan for Fulmar & Co.: page five

Strengths

The product	The product was introduced twenty-five years ago and was instantly accepted by the agricultural and forestry industries as a most useful concept. It now has several competitors.
The Company	We are well known in many developed agricultural areas of the world, and our name is respected by merchants. We have always taken great care to keep our delivery promises, ensure constant quality, put defects right at once, and so on.
The Depots	Because our product is heavy and bulky, merchants do not keep the full range on their own premises. Our depots are unique, and we now have several in each major national market. No competitors have this important selling aid.
Exports	Well over 80 per cent of our turnover goes abroad to Europe, Africa and South America. (We do little business in North America or Asia.)
Gearing	We have not invested heavily for several years and have a cash balance at the bank. If we needed it, we could borrow at least £6m. almost immediately before reaching any sort of limit.

Exhibit 8.7 Corporate plan for Fulmar & Co.: page six

Weaknesses

New Products — No new products are being developed. There are no ideas for new products; and even if there were, there is no development department to turn them to practical use

Production — The planning team invited a well-known firm of production engineering consultants to report. Production planning, stock control, quality control, methods, layout, bonus schemes, equipment — everything, they say, is twenty years out of date. They state that £3m. of investment would in time yield an extra £3m. p.a. savings

Mr Fulmar — Mr Fulmar is now 62 and in poor health. He wishes to reduce both his time and his financial commitments over the next few years. He has no heir.

P/E Ratio — Our P/E ratio is 4, which is well below our sector average of 7 as a result of our poor past performance. It makes the possibility of a bid highly likely, but Mr Fulmar states that he will reject any bid from anyone while our P/E is so low.

Exhibit 8.8 Corporate plan for Fulmar & Co.: page seven

Threats

Competitors	We know of only five competitors, three of which are small. The other two both produce a very good product, but neither presents a threat over and above normal competition in the modern world. (Two competitors have recently withdrawn.)
New Materials	Our bonding system is twenty-five years old. We know of no new developments here, but these must happen eventually.
Fire Legislation	Our buildings are made of wood, and the bonding does present a minor fire hazard. So long as our products are used only in agricultural areas and not for human occupation, this threat should not materialise.
Mr Fulmar's Shares	Neither Mr Fulmar nor anyone else knows what to do about his shares.

Exhibit 8.9 Corporate plan for Fulmar & Co.: page eight

Opportunities

World Markets	So far as we can estimate, we have 30 per cent of the markets that we serve. The markets that we do not serve (North America and Asia) are probably equal to the ones that we do. The total market is probably £300m. p.a. and growing at 3–5 per cent p.a.
Industrial Buildings	A market survey suggests that robust wooden shelters do have a place in industry as stores for such items as bulk raw materials, unprocessed parts awaiting painting, and so on.
DIY	The DIY market is expanding rapidly, and a much scaled-down version of our buildings could be designed for the householder, gardener or smallholder to erect for himself from a kit.
Added Value	We could build into our shelters such items as cattle-feeding or milking equipment, overhead hoists, electrics or forestry equipment. We could improve appearance, fit decorative doors, and so on.
Environmental	There are an increasing number of environmental or scenic activities today requiring sturdy attractive rustic premises: for example, picnic shelters in forests and caravan sites, and shops and ticket offices at stately homes. One of our small competitors, Petrel, has developed an attractive range in this market.

Exhibit 8.10 Corporate plan for Fulmar & Co.: page nine

Strategies Considered

The planning team originally looked at over eighty strategic ideas submitted to it, but the list rapidly came down to the following:

(1) Expand in existing markets.
(2) Move into new markets, namely, either (a) areas of the world in which we do not operate or (b) non-agricultural areas.
(3) Develop new products in DIY, in industrial buildings, in scenic or environmental or tourist markets.
(4) Acquire Petrel or similar competitor.
(5) Improve the production side of the business.
(6) Change Mr Fulmar's shareholding.
(7) Decide on management succession.
(8) Finance: equity, gearing, P/E ratio.

Exhibit 8.11 Summary of Fulmar & Co.'s Fp forecast (£m.)

	Year 0	1	2	3	4	5
Fo forecast	4·2	4·6	5·0	5·2	5·3	5·5
S1 profits	0·0	0·3	0·9	1·5	1·8	2·0
S2 profits	0·0	0·0	0·3	0·7	0·9	1·2
Total profits (Fp forecast)	4·2	4·9	6·2	7·4	8·0	8·7
Target (Tsat)	4·2	4·8	5·6	6·4	7·3	8·5
Remaining gap	0·0	—	—	—	—	—

Exhibit 8.12 Corporate plan for Fulmar & Co.: page ten

Strategies Selected

Of the eight strategies considered (see Exhibit 8.10), the planning team decided to concentrate on only two major areas. We were surprised by the inefficiency of the production side and believe that putting this right is by far the most profitable single action that the company can take. This strategy (S1) calls for a major modernisation over a two-year period and will cost £3m. Almost the entire factory will be renewed or replaced. A project team under Mr Drake is to be formed.

We assume that the company will contine to expand in its existing markets, but we do not feel that any special effort should be made to increase our shares here, which at 30 per cent are already sufficient to give us the role of market leader. However, we believe that we should enter some of the major national markets in Asia and North America at once and with some vigour. This, we estimate, will cost £4m. over three or four years. A project team under Mrs Teal is to be formed. We call this strategy S2.

We do not believe that any new products should be considered at present, nor that a bid should be made for Petrel and its new product range. Strategies to cover new products will be considered later (temporary number 'S6'). Also, we do not believe that Mr Fulmar's share deal, an equity issue or a new dividend policy is needed yet — perhaps not until our P/E ratio rises to the sector average. When it is devised, we hope that this strategy ('S5') will link many of these features together in one package: a bid for Petrel, a new issue, Mr Fulmar's shares, employee shares, and so on.

A strategy is needed now, however, to cope with the financial demands of S1 and S2, which, if they go according to plan, will demand £7m. in the next three years. Very little of this will be available from cash flows; and if something goes wrong with S1 or S2, we may need a peak of £9m. from external sources. The finance director is discussing a suitable financial strategy (S4) with our advisers.

Finally, Mr Fulmar wishes to reduce his level of participation in the management of the company. Strategy S3 involves management succession and top management reorganisation over the next two years.

The planning team hopes to start work on S5 and S6 next January.

Exhibit 8.13 Corporate plan for Fulmar & Co.: page eleven

Evaluations

(1) The planning team, together with the relevant project teams, has drawn up a step-by-step programme of action needed to give effect to S1, S2 and S4. (The team has left S3 to Mr Fulmar for execution.) In the case of S1 the production engineering consultants have also played an important part. (Details should be included in an appendix.) We can see no unrealistic assumptions here.

(2) As to the resources that we have to bring these strategies to a successful conclusion, we list the following:

    (a) S1 involves no new technology, only new equipment; it does involve a very long complex programme of factory modernisation, but the consultants are well known and have handled many such projects before. S2 is completely within our own competence and experience. S3 is much more difficult, since it involves selecting a new chief executive (among others); but again consultants are helping, and time is not pressing. S4 merely calls for new finance; the finance director has undertaken a similar operation before, and here again expert opinion is available.

    (b) Finance is available to meet all but the most outrageous outcomes.

    (c) The total demands on management time arising from actions to give effect to the four strategies, in addition to attending to the usual day-to-day affairs of the company, are worrying us, but S3 includes a reorganisation of top management with precisely this problem in mind.

(3) Calculations using the model suggest that the most likely outcome for profit is as follows:

	Year 0	1	2	3	4	5
Profits from Fo + S1 + S2 (£m.) .	4·2	4·9	6·2	7·4	8·0	8·7
Tsat profits (£m.)	4·2	4·8	5·6	6·4	7·3	8·5
Gaps (£m.)	0·0	0·0	0·0	0·0	0·0	0·0

These are the figures shown in run 8 (see below), in which all the assumptions made were as reasonable and as neutral (that is, neither optimistic nor pessimistic) as possible.

(4) We made twenty-eight runs using the model under varying assumptions. Only the five most interesting are shown below. (The others may appear as an appendix.)

    The situation that we think is most probable and would be most damaging is a prolonged strike towards the end of the S1 factory-modernisation programme (run 11). We doubt that this would be due to redundancies, as S2 will need all the men ever likely to be displaced by S1; it is more likely to arise through clumsiness in introducing the incentive schemes. To obviate this we suggest that a joint participation team be set up now to introduce the employees to this idea as soon as possible. If there were a three-month strike, the effects would be very serious. We have no contingency plan for the eventuality of a strike.

As can be seen, a two-area failure in S2 would also be serious (run 3), not so much because of lower profits as because, as the model shows, the overdraft would rise to £9m. due to heavy stocks in depots and in transit. The project leader for S2 says that this two-area failure can be avoided by rephasing the programme.

Results of runs on model

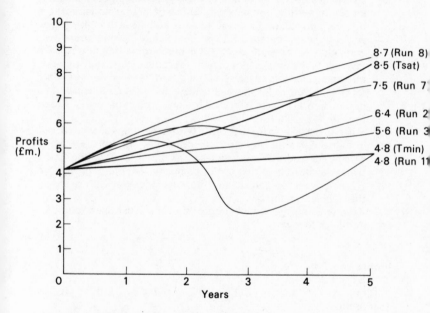

Assumptions in these runs:

run 8 – all assumptions 'neutral';

run 3 – as run 8, but sales in two areas fall 50 per cent below target during S2;

run 7 – as run 8, but there is six months' delay in completing S1;

run 11 – as run 8, but a complete strike of three months occurs in month 15 of S1;

run 24 – as run 8, but growth in any market is nil until year 3 and then 5 per cent p.a.

(5) The team is satisfied that S1, S2, S3 and S4 will deal with most of Fulmar's long-term problems for several years ahead and that they will make use of all strengths and opportunities and obviate all weaknesses and threats except the following: no new products, Mr Fulmar's

shares and (less important, we believe) new materials and fire legislation. New strategies, at present known as S5 and S6, will be considered in a year's time to deal with these. At that time our P/E ratio may already be moving upwards, changing from a weakness to a strength.

Bibliography

I would like to suggest that all the members of a company's planning team should read this book, so that they all have a clear idea of the process itself and its pitfalls. However, at least one member should also read or have ready for reference a more advanced book. The corporate planner himself, in addition to attending a course on corporate planning, should certainly be familiar with one or more of these more advanced volumes:

Ansoff, H. I., *From Strategic Planning to Strategic Management* (New York: Wiley, 1975), 257 pp.

Argenti, J., *Systematic Corporate Planning* (London: Nelson, 1974), 316 pp.

Hussey, D. E., *Corporate Planning: Theory and Practice* (Oxford: Pergamon Press, 1975), 399 pp.

Taylor, B. and Sparkes, J. R., *Corporate Strategy and Planning* (London: Heinemann, 1977), 402 pp.

There are today a number of societies devoted to this subject all over the world. Perhaps the best known is The Society for Long Range Planning, 15 Belgrave Square, London. This Society publishes booklists, a learned journal and a newsletter, holds seminars and discussions, and so on.

Index